汉英上海方言字典

[美] 戴维斯 薛思培 著
钱乃荣 编

上海译文出版社

导 读

这本字典详细记录了19世纪末上海方言的字形和语音，是基督教系统记录上海方言语音最完整的字书。作者是基督教上海方言协会的两位负责人。薛思培(J.A. Silsby)在1897年出版了《上海话和官话字音对照表》，戴维斯(D.H. Davis)曾担任基督教上海教会中文研究所所长，在薛思培之后编写了《上海方言练习》一书。

本书总共收录7779个上海话汉字(包括重复的在内)，并标注读音，读音之后配以简短的释义。本书中收录的许多字在上海话的口语中从未使用过，怎么会有准确的读音记载呢？很可能是作者根据这些字的中古音读音，按照上海方言的音系规律推论出的读音，或者是记录了当年书塾里讲究文读且相当通用的发音。

这些汉字来自威廉(William)和翟理斯(Giles)所编的词典。其发音按照罗马字拼音联合体系给出。汉字按部首顺序排列，汉字后第一个数字是该字在威廉所编字典中的页码，第二个数字是该字在翟理斯所编字典中的字编号，由字母G表示。因此，为方便读者查询，笔者未对书中汉字进行繁简转换。

本书强调文读音与口语音的差异。文读音更接近杭州官话的语音。

所收录的汉字中大部分只有一个发音，少数汉字有两到三个不同的读音，其中文读音排在前面，未做标记，紧接着是口语音，前面用英文字母 c 标示。需要注意的是，在阅读该字典时，不能简单地认为无标记的音都是文读音。事实上，在现在的上海话中，很少有字存在文白读音的差异，大多数字的发音没有明显的区别。在该字典中，以“全”字为例，记载了 *dzien*、*zen*、*dzen* 3 个音(依次)，并非意味着“全”没有白话音。同样地，在“晚”字下列出了 *ean*、*wan*、c. *man*、*en* 4 个音，其中 c 后两个音属于白话音；而在“昨”字中收录了 6 个音：*dzauh*、c. *dzok*、*dzo*、*zau*、*zauh*、*zo*。除第一个音外，其余均为白话音，其中前两个声母仍保持为 *dz*，尚未转变为 *z*。这些白话音至今仍在上海市郊口语中使用，只是前两个声母已经变为 *z*。比如，以从母字“钱”为例，记录有 *dzien*、c. *dian* 两个音，*dian* 为口语音。又如，以从母字“情”为例，标注了两个音：*dzing*、*zing*，均无标记，表示普通说话音；而在“前”字下，只有一个声母已变读音 *zien*，没有标记。然而，根据 1853 年艾约瑟氏所著《上海方言口语语法》中的数据显示，“前”字中读未变音 *dz* 的有两个字，读已变音 z 的有 20 个字，表明 *dz* 向 *z* 的转变历时近 60 年逐渐完成。因此，一个字是读作 *dz* 还是 *z* 不能作为区分文白读音的标准，声母 *dz* 向 *z* 的变化只是语音词汇扩散的过程。

本书使用的上海方言拼音字母是由基督教上海方言协会的戴维斯和薛思培制定的音系。这一音系与卜舫济的《上海方言教程》中所用音标相同。这本字典中的罗马字注音字母大致对应于国际音标的读音，是在 19 世纪末 20 世纪初上海方言口音中设计得较为完美的一套拼音系统。

本书的音系表详细列出了音系表中的41个声母、39个韵母和8个声调，精确地反映了上海话语音的实际情况，通过简洁的标注方式，清晰地呈现了声母、韵母和声调的结构特点。因此，这一拼音系统为理解和学习上海方言提供了重要的参考依据。

声母:41个

p[p]百杯　p‘[p‘]拍坯　b[b]白赔　’m[ʔm]每螟　m[m]末煤　f[f]法粉　’v[ʔv]勿　v[v]罚忿

t[t]丁堆　t‘[t‘]脱推　d[d]叠停　’n[ʔn]乃懦　n[n]纳内　’l[ʔl]拎捞　l[l]垃铃

ts[ts]执节　ts‘[ts‘]切叉　dz[dz]集茶　s[s]息衰　z[z]席裁

k[k]鸽加　k‘[k‘]磕揩　g[g]搿茄　’ng[ʔŋ]眼颜　ng[ŋ]兀呆　h[h]黑海　‘[ɦ]学害

ky[tɕ]吉鸡　ch[tɕ]怯气　j[dʑ]及旗　’ny[ʔȵ]拈揿　ny[ȵ]热年　hy[ɕ]歇响

kw[kw]规骨　kw‘[kw‘]块阔　gw[gw]葵睽　hw[hw]欢忽

i[i]一因　y[j]叶刑　’w[ʔw]威碗　w[w]活完

韵母:39个

ɑ[ɑ]挨筛　ɑng[ã]樱生　ɑk[ɑk]白栅

ɑn[æ̃]晏三　ah[æʔ]押杀

e[e]哀衰　en[ẽ]暗擅　eh[eʔ]末磕

ɪ[i]衣西　ien[iẽ]先烟　ing[ɪŋ]林心　ih[ɪʔ]必雪

ɑu[ɔː]凹烧　ɑung[ɔ̃]盎霜　ɑuh[ɔʔ]恶朔

o[o]马沙　ong[oŋ]翁松　ok[ok]屋束

oe[ø]岁随　oen[ø̃]安酸　oeh[øʔ]曷率

eu[ɤː]偶讴　ung[ʌŋ]恩深　uh[ʌʔ]德色

ui[y]雨须　uin[yn]云熏

u[ʮ]主书　oo[u]乌枯

iɑu[iɔː]桥小　ieu[iɤː]流忧

iɑ[iɑ]谢雅　iɑng[iã]样厢　iɑk[iɑk]削约

iau[iɔ]夭小　ieu[iɤ]忧修

m[m̩]呒姆　ng[ŋ̍]鱼吴　'r[ʔr]耳　r[r]而儿

ts[tsɿ]纸资　tsh[t'sɿ]此痴　s[sɿ]思施　dz[dzɿ]池迟　z[zɿ]时是

上面最后一行中如用舌尖元音概念，韵母都是一个[ɿ]，在这样的情况下，书中遇到这类音节时不标韵母。

由于在书中使用hy表示[ɕ]，而用 y 作为声母表示[j]，因此成功地简化了只包含一个字的两个韵母[iu]和[iɔ̃]（靴 hyoo，旺 yaung）。

声调：8 个

在音节声母左上角标记小圈表示上声，右上角标记则表示去声，而以[h]或[k]结尾的音节为入声，未标记符号的则为平声。

上平声：刀叽犀　　　　下平声：桃排徐

上上声：祷堺死　　下上声：道罢荠

上去声：倒败壻　　下去声：导败谢

上入声：沰八息　　下入声：度拔席

国际音标在 1899 年诞生，而这本字典中的罗马字注音与国际音标的读音大致对应，符合上海话的实际语音情况。它准确标示了上海话中的鼻音、边音、v 声母和 r 音，有上层阴调和下层阳调的区别。在韵母部分，这套系统将 8 对阴声韵、阳声韵和促声韵在字母标音排列上进行了对应。这套系统类似粤语，将[kw]一类的声母单独列出，一方面在实际发音中[w]比[u]更接近读音，另一方面也简化了韵母表中的韵母数量。

笔者在 2014 年出版的一部著作《1847—1950 年的上海话——西方传教士上海方言著作研究》中，以现代通行形式，以音系韵母为主线，重新整理了这本字典的大部分内容，创建了一份便于查询的 1900 年左右的同音字表，可供参考查询。

钱乃荣

2024 年 8 月 25 日于上海土山湾听雨阁

Contents

PREFACE

The *Wu*（吳）dialects, to which group the Shanghai Vernacular belongs, are the language of those Chinese who occupy the southern part of Kiangsu, all of Chehkiang, and a portion of the adjacent provinces of Anhui and Kiangsi. Mr. Von Möllendorf estimates their number at forty-four millions, while the Shanghai-Soochow dialect is used by ten millions, and can be understood fairly well by the more intelligent all over the *Wu* district. As distinct from that of Soochow the Shanghai Vernacular must be the language of at least five millions and it has been extensively used by foreign missionaries and merchants for more than half a century.

The *Wu* dialects are of special importance in linguistic research. The best philologists seem to agree that they form the basis of the Japanese *go-on*（吳音）, and Corean and Japanese transcriptions of sounds, made contemporaneously with the dictionaries, indicate that the *Wu* dialects are nearer to the "Old Chinese" that prevailed in North China in the time of the classics than any other of the dialects of China. These dialects are more ancient than the Mandarin, which, according to Mr. E.H. Parker, is a "corruption of Old Chinese," chiefly caused by the immense admixture of Tartar and Tibetan blood during the period 300—900 A.D. Nearly all the characters used to represent the Shanghai syllables are found in Mandarin and classical dictionaries. The idiom does not greatly differ from the Mandarin, but the Shanghai dialect is greatly superior in the number of its syllables, having 720 as compared with 420 in Pekingese.

Why Giles should ignore the Shanghai Vernacular in his dictionary, while giving the pronunciation of dialects much less important, it is difficult to explain. The absence of the Shanghai pronunciation in Giles' dictionary and the unsatisfactory and unreliable pronunciation given in Williams', will make the present work, we trust, a welcome addition to the equipment of a Shanghai student. It will assist him in ascertaining the true sound of the characters as pronounced by the people of Shanghai, and will enable him to guard against the careless and faulty pronunciation of incompetent teachers, while furnishing a handy pocket dictionary which can be taken along on trips into the country.

In this little volume there will be found 7779 characters (including duplicates) with pronunciation according to the Shanghai union system of Romanization, the classical pronunciation being first given and then the colloquial (following the letter *c*) when that differs from the classical. The first numeral refers to the page in Williams' dictionary, the second to the number of the character in the dictionary of Giles (indicated by the letter G.). These numerals furnish a convenient index to the larger dictionaries, where most of the characters are further defined and illustrated. The brief definitions which follow will generally be found sufficient for practical use. The numeral after the definition gives the number of the character from the beginning: this will be found convenient for reference.

While this dictionary is primarily designed for the use of students of the Shanghai dialect, it will also be found very helpful to those who make use of the kindred dialects of Soochow and Ningpo. No doubt mistakes will be found and definitions will sometimes be unsatisfactory, but in this we beg the indulgence of our friends and ask for their assistance in making needful corrections. Our chief Chinese assistant has been Mr. Li 'Ung ts'ung (李恒春), to whom much credit is due for his diligence and carefulness, both in preparing this work for the press and in revising and correcting the proofs.

D.H. Davis

J.A. Silsby

Shanghai, August, 1900.

PRONUNCIATION OF SHANGHAI SYLLABLES AS REPRESENTED BY THE UNION SYSTEM OF ROMANIZATION

The true pronunciation of Chinese sounds can only be learned from a Chinese teacher. A large majority of the sounds have no true equivalent in English; hence the student should bear in mind that any *Romanization used does not represent English sounds, but Chinese sounds*. This fact can not be too strongly emphasized. The committee which formulated the present Union System of Romanization did not have in mind the representation of Chinese sounds by their nearest English equivalents so much as it had in view the production of a complete, simple and systematic table whereby all the Chinese sounds should be represented by Roman letters or combinations thereof—and this without the use of diacritical marks. It should be borne in mind by the student that this system does not divide a word into all its phonetic elements; but rather does it follow a plan well-known to Chinese scholars; viz., that of dividing each syllable represented by a Chinese character into two elements—one initial and one final.

THE INITIALS

The Initials are divided into a "Higher," a "Middle" or "Aspirated," and a "Lower" Series.

1. The HIGHER SERIES comprises sounds represented by *p*,

'm, *'v*, *t*, *ts*, *s*, *'l*, *'n*, *'ny*, *'ng*, *k*, *ky*, *kw*, *pure vowel sounds*, *i* and *'w*.

2. The MIDDLE OR ASPIRATED SERIES comprises sounds represented by *p'*, *f*, *t'*, *ts'*, *k'*, *ch*, *k'w*, *h*, *hy* and *hw*.

3. The LOWER SERIES comprises sounds represented by *b*, *m*, *v*, *d*, *dz*, *z*, *l*, *n*, *ny*, *ng*, *g*, *j*, *gw*, '(*or low vowel sounds*, *slightly aspirated*), *y* and *w*.

N.B. Let it be remembered that the difference between the Higher and Lower Series of initial sounds is *not so much a difference in consonantal quality as a difference in pitch*; but there is a real consonantal difference.

The following description of sounds may be found helpful, but the true sound in most cases must be learned from a Chinese teacher. After each description there is given a Chinese character representing, or containing, the sound described,

p—pronounced much the same as in English, but a little harder and without any aspiration. 百

p'—aspirated; somewhat as an American or Irishman would pronounce *p* in *pin*, but with a still more decided aspiration. 拍

b—not quite so hard as in English. 白

'm—higher and more explosive than *m*. 每

m—as in English. 煤

'v—a sound slightly harder and less aspirated than the English *f*. 勿

f—as in English. 法

v—nearly as in English, but often approaching *w*, with which it is often confused. 罚

t—harder and with less aspiration than in English. 丁

t‘—with more aspiration. 聽

d—softer than in English. 停

ts—harder and less aspirated than in English. 節

ts‘—with more aspiration. 切

dz—softer than in English. The majority of Shanghai natives fail to distinguish between this sound and that represented by *z*. 集

s—as in English. 息

z—softer and more sibilant than in English. 席

’l—higher and more explosive than *l*. 拎

l—as in English. 鈴

’n—higher and more explosive than *n*. 乃

n—as in English. 内

’ny—higher and quicker than *ny*. 拈

ny—much the same as *n* in *new*, but with a more decided *y* sound following the *n*. 年

’ng—higher and quicker than *ng*. 顔 as in 一顔

ng—harder than *ng* in *song*. 顔

k—harder and with less aspiration than in English. 加

k‘—with more aspiration. 揩

g—as in *go*, but softer. 茄

ky—a peculiar sound which can not be represented by any English combination. Perhaps *tky* might better represent it. 雞

ch—softer and with more aspiration than *ch* in *church*. 氣

j—a little harder than *j* in *jug*. 旗

kw—as *qu* in *quart*. 規

kw'—the same sound aspirated and softer. 塊

gw—softer than *gu* in *Guelph*. 葵

Vowel initials are pronounced higher and purer than in English.

h—as in *hat*, Confused with *f* sounds by many natives. 海

'—before an initial vowel indicates that the word belongs to the lower series and that the vowel is slightly aspirated. This aspiration is little more than a huskiness in the throat attendant upon the lower pitch of the voice. It should not be confused with *h*. 害

i—lighter than the *y* sound,—as in *view*. Only as an initial is the *y* sound given to *i*. In other positions *i* represents a vowel sound. 因

hy—somewhat like *sh* in *should*, but less sibilant. It is more like *ti* in *initial*. 興

y—as in *young*. 刑

'w— higher, lighter and quicker than *w*. 碗

hw—as *wh* in *where*. 歡

w—as in *way*. 完

DOK-YONG Z-MOO

In this class there is no clear and distinct vowel sound. The final sound in the syllables formerly written *tsz*, *ts'z*, *dzz*, *szz* and *zz* might be regarded as a vowel sound akin to that in the final syllable of *able*—prolonged, but without any *l* sound, as pronounced by some foreigners. Edkins, Mateer, Baller and others represent this sound by *ï*, and would spell—*tsï*, *ts'ï*, *dzï*, *sï* and *zï*. Others insist that there is no true vowel sound in the syllables represented, and that there is only a prolonged sounding of *s* or *z*. In this book these syllables are written *ts*, *t's*, *dz*, *s*, and *z*; i.e., without the final *z*, the use of which seems to be unnecessary, if not misleading. The syllables represented by *m*, *r* and *ny*, have a slight vowel sound before the consonant, this sound being much the same as that represented by ï in the list mentioned: *m* represents much the same sound as *m* in *chasm*—prolonged: and *ny* is much the same as *ng* in *song*: *r* is an indescribable sound between that of the English *r* and *l*—or rather a blending of them. We give below a Chinese character representing the syllables described as *Dok-yong z-moo*.

m—無	*ts*—紙	*t's*—此	*s*—思	*'r*—耳
ng—魚	*dz*—池	*z*—時	*r*—而	

THE FINALS

The Finals are divided into three classes; viz,—

1. VOWEL ENDINGS, comprising sounds represented by *a*, *e*, *i*, *au*, *o*, *oo*, *oe*, *eu*, *u*, *ui*, *ia*, *iau*, and *ieu*; also the *wên-li ie*.

2. NASAL ENDINGS, comprising sounds represented by *ang*, *an*, *en*, *ien*, *ing*, *aung*, *ong*, *oen*, *ung*, *uin*, and *iang*.

3. ABRUPT VOWEL ENDINGS, comprising sounds represented by *ak*, *ah*, *eh*, *ih*, *auh*, *ok*, *oeh*, *uh*, and *iak*.

The *ng* sounds are less distinct than the English *ng* in *song*.

Final *n* is sounded in the combination *uin*, and then approaches an *ng* sound, but in other combinations does little more than lengthen out and impart a nasal quality to the preceding vowel.

Final *k* and *h* are not pronounced: they indicate that the preceding vowel is pronounced in a short, abrupt manner. Single vowels followed by *k* retain their long sound,—followed by *h* are shortened.

The vowels are sounded as follows:—

a, *ang*, *ak*—*a* as in *father*. 挨櫻白

an, *ah*—*a* as in *mat*. 晏押

e, *en*—*e* as in *prey*. 哀暗

eh—*e* as in *met*. 末

i, *ien*—*i* as in *caprice*. 衣先. In the combination *ien*, *ie* may be regarded as a diphthong, the *e* being lightly sounded, its quality being nearly that of *e* in *prey*.

ing, *ih*—*i* as in *pit*. 林必

au, *aung*, *auh*—*au* as in *fraud*. 凹力惡

o—*o* as in *no*. 馬

ong—*o* as *ou* in *mourn*, or as *oo* in *moon*. The true sound seems to lie between, or rather, it is a combination of the two English sounds in the words given. 翁

ok—*o* as in *mote*. 屋

oo—as in *moon*. 烏

oe, *oen*, *oeh*—*oe* somewhat as in the German Goethe. 崴安曷

eu—somewhat as *i* in *mirth*, *Eu* should be carefully distinguished from *ir* as in *sir*. Foreigners often mistake by adding an *r* to the vowel sound. 傴

ung, *uh*—*u* as in *sun*. 恩德

u—somewhat as *oo* in *foot*, but lengthened out. 主

ui—as *u* in the French *vertu*. 雨

uin—*ui* somewhat like the preceding, but only to be learned from a Chinese teacher. 雲

ia, *iang*, *iak*—short *i* is followed by *a* as in *father*. 謝雨削

ieu—short *i* followed by *eu*. 流

ie—an occasional sound used in reading *wên-li*: short *i* is followed by a sound akin to *e* as in *prey*.

TONE SIGNS

° to the left of a word indicates the tone to be °*zang-sung*.

° to the right indicates the *chui*°*-sung*.

Final *h* or *k* indicates the *zeh-sung*.

All other words are in the *bing-sung*.

TABLE OF THE RADICALS*

1 Stroke

1 一 ih.
One, unity. 乙
Colloquial, 一畫 ih wak.

2 丨 °kwung. To pass through, an upright. 袞
Colloquial, 一竪 ih °zu.

3 丶 °tsu.
A point, a dot. 主
Colloquial, 一點 ih °tien.

4 丿 p'ih.
A stroke to the left. 瞥
Colloquial, 一撇 ih p'ih.

5 乙 ih.
One, a curve. 一
Colloquial, 甲乙个乙 kyah-ih-kuh-ih.

6 亅 joeh.
A barb, a crook. 橛
Colloquial, 一鉤 ih-keu, 一竪有——踢脚 ih-°zu °yeu—t'ih-kyak.

2 Strokes

7 二 r°.
Two. 貳

8 亠 deu.
A cover, a hat. 頭

9 人亻 zung.
A man. 仁
Colloquial, 戤人傍 ge°-nyung-paung, 單戤人 tan-ge°-nyung (2nd form).

10 儿 zung. A man, the legs of a man. 人

11 入 zeh.
To enter. 寶

12 八 pah.
Eight. 捌

13 冂 kyong.
A limit. 扃

14 冖 mih.
To cover, a cover. 覓

* As very few Chinese teachers can give the names of all the radicals, a well known character is added to aid the teacher in giving to each radical its proper pronunciation, and in a number of cases the colloquial designation in also given. When written above, the radical is designated *deu* (head); e.g., 草字頭 *°ts'au-z°-deu*. When at the side, it is designated *paung* (side); e.g., 羊字傍 *yang-z°-paung*. The general designation is *boo*, or *boo-we* 部位; e.g., 口字部 *°k'eu-z°-boo*.

15 冫 ping.
Icicle, ice. 冰
Colloquial, 兩點水 °liang-°tien-°s.

16 几 °kyi.
A bench. 幾

17 凵 °k'en.
A receptacle. 坎

18 刀刂 tau.
A knife, sword. 倒
Colloquial, 側刀 tsuh-tau (2nd form).

19 力 lih.
Strength. 立

20 勹 pau.
To wrap. 包

21 匕 °pi.
A ladle, a spoon. 比

22 匚 faung.
A chest, a case. 方

23 匸 °yi.
To conceal. 奕

24 十 zeh.
Ten. 入

25 卜 pok.
To divine. 北

26 卩㔾 tsih.
A joint, seal. 節

27 厂 hoen°.
A cliff. 漢

28 厶 s.
Selfish, perverse. 私

29 又 yeu°.
Also, again. 宥

3 Strokes

30 口 °k'eu.
A mouth. 釦

31 囗 we.
An inclosure. 囬

32 土士 °t'oo.
Earth. 妥
Colloquial, 踢土傍 t'ih-°t'oo-paung (2nd form).

33 士 °z.
A scholar, a sage. 仕

34 夂 ts.
To follow, a step. 摋

35 夊 se.
Moving slowly. 衰

36 夕 dzih.
Evening. 集

37 大 da°.
Great. 汏

38 女 °nyui.
A woman. 語

39 子 °ts.
A son, child. 梓

40 宀 mien.
A roof. 绵
Colloquial, 帽子頭 mau°-°ts-deu, 寶蓋頭 °pau-ke°-deu.

41 寸 ts'ung°.
An inch. 秤

42 小 °siau.
Small. 蕭

43 尢尣兀 'waung.
Lame, weak. 汪

44 尸 s.
A corpse. 斯

45 屮 ts'eh.
A sprout. 徹

46 山 san.
A mountain, hill. 删

47 巛川 ts'en.
Mountain, streams. 穿

48 工 kong.
Labor, a workman. 公

49 己 °kyi.
Self. 紀

50 巾 kyung.
A napkin. 金

51 干 koen.
A shield, to oppose. 竿

52 幺 iau.
Immature, tender. 夭

53 广 °yien.
A roof, shelter. 醃

54 廴 °yung.
To move on. 引

55 廾 °kong.
Joined hands. 拱

56 弋 yuh.
A dart. 翌

57 弓 dong.
A bow, archery. 宫

58 彐彑 kyi°. A pig's head, pointed. 寄

Colloquial, 横山 wang-san (1st form).

59 彡 san.
Plumage, hair. 衫

Colloquial, 三撇 san-p'ih.

60 彳 ts'uh.
A step. 敇

Colloquial, 雙戤人 saung-ge°-nyung.

4 Strokes

61 心忄⺗ sing.
The heart. 新

Colloquial, 豎心傍 °zu-sing-paung (2nd and 3rd forms).

62 戈 koo.
A spear. 鍋

63 户 °'oo.
A door. 祜

64 手扌 °seu.
The hand. 首

Colloquial, 挑手傍 t'iau-°seu-paung (2nd form).

65 支 ts.
A branch, a prop. 枝

66 攴攵 p'ok.
To tap, to rap. 撲

Colloquial, 反文 °fan-vung (2nd form).

67 文 vung.
Literature. 紋

68 斗 °teu.
A bushel, a peek. 抖

69 斤 kyung.
An axe, a catty. 筋

70 方 faung.
A square. 芳

71 无旡 voo.
Without, not. 無

72 日 zeh.
The sun, a day. 入

73 曰 yoeh.
To speak. 越

74 月 yoeh.
The moon, a month. 軏

75 木 mok.
Wood, a tree. 沐

76 欠 chien°.
To owe, deficient. 謙

77 止 °ts.
To stop. 芷

78 歹 歺 oeh.
Rotten bone. 遏

* Note. This radical is usually pronounced °te, but Kanghi gives oeh as the proper sound.

歹 °te.
Bad, vicious.

79 殳 zu.
To kill. 殊

80 毋 voo.
To deny. 無

81 比 °pi.
To compare. 匕

82 毛 mau.
Hair, wool. 旄

83 氏 °z.
Family name. 是

84 气 chi°.
Breath, vapor. 氣

85 水 氵 氺 °soe.
Water. 税

Colloquial, 三點水 san-°tien-°s (2nd form).

86 火 灬 °hoo.
Fire. 虎

Colloquial, 四點火 s°-°tien-°hoo (2nd form).

87 爪 爫 °tsau.
Claws. 抓

Colloquial, 一撇三點 ih-p'ih-san-°tien (2nd form).

88 父 °voo.
Father. 輔

89 爻 yau.
Crosswise. 肴

90 爿 ziang.
A couch, a frame. 戕

91 片 p'ien°.
A splinter, a slice. 騙

92 牙 ya.
A tooth. 芽

93 牛 牜 nyeu.
An ox, a cow. 鈕

Colloquial, 斜牛傍 zia-nyeu-paung (2nd form).

94 犬 犭 °choen.
A dog. 圈

Colloquial, 反犬傍 fan-°choen-paung (2nd form).

5 Strokes

95 玄 yoen.
Sombre, black. 懸

96 玉 王 王 nyok.
A gem. 馭

Colloquial, 斜玉傍 zia-nyokpaung，斜王傍 zia-waung-paung (2nd form).

97 **瓜** kwo.
A melon，cucumber. 騧

98 **瓦** °'wo.
A title，brick. 邸

99 **甘** ken.
Sweet. 柑

100 **生** sung.
To produce，live. 甥

101 **用** yong°.
To use. 容

102 **田** dien.
A field. 甜

103 **疋** soo.
A foot. 疏
p'ih. Roll of cloth. 匹

Colloquial，疋字部 p'ih-z°-boo.

104 **疒** nyuh.
Disease. 逆

Colloquial，疾字傍 dzih-z°-paung

105 **癶** peh.
Back to back. 撥

106 **白** buh.
White，in vain. 帛

107 **皮** bi.
Skin，bark. 疲

108 **皿** °ming.
A dish，a platter. 閔

109 **目** mok.
The eye. 牧

110 **矛** meu.
A lance，halberd. 謀

111 **矢** °s.
A dart，an arrow. 始

112 **石** zak.
A stone. 碩

113 **示礻礻** ji，z°. A divine omen，reveal. 其，事

Colloquial，禮衣傍 °li-i-paung (3rd form).

114 **禸** °zeu.
A foot-print. 蹂

115 **禾** 'oo.
Grain. 和

Colloquial，禾木傍 'oo-mok-paung.

116 **穴** yoeh.
A cave. 越

Colloquial，穴字頭 yoeh-z°-deu.

117 **立** lih.
To set up. 力

6 Strokes

118 **竹** tsok.
Bamboo. 竺

Colloquial，竹籬頭 tsok-li-deu.

119 **米** °mi.
Rice. 迷

120 **糸糹** mih.
Raw silk. 覓

Colloquial，絞絲傍 °kau-s-paung.

121 **缶** °feu.
Pottery. 否

122 **网罒⺳** °vaung.
A net. 網

Colloquial，四字頭 s°-z°-deu (2nd

from).

123 羊 yang.
A sheep. 陽

124 羽 °yui.
Feathers. 禹

125 老 °lau.
Old, venerable. 銠

126 而 r.
Still, yet. 兒

127 耒 le°.
A plough. 類

128 耳 °r.
The ear. 洱

129 聿 ioeh.
A pen, a pencil. 鬱

130 肉月 zok.
Flesh. 孰

Colloquial, 肉字傍 nyok-z°-paung (2nd form).

131 臣 dzung.
A statesman. 成

132 自 z°.
Self, from. 字

133 至 ts°.
To arrive. 志

134 臼 °jeu.
A mortar. 舅

135 舌 zeh.
The tongue. 十

136 舛 °ts'en.
Opposing. 慘

137 舟 tseu.
A boat. 周

138 艮 kung°.
Perverse. 更

139 色 suh.
Color, vice. 嗇

140 艸艹 °ts'au.
Grass. 草

Colloquial, 草字頭 ts'au-z°-deu and 艹草頭 nyan°-°ts'au-deu (2nd form).

141 虍 hoo.
A tiger. 呼

142 虫 °hwe.
An insect. 卉

Colloquial, 蟲字傍 dzong-z°-paung.

143 血 hyoeh.
Blood. 泬

144 行 yung.
To go, travel, do. 形

145 衣衤 i.
Clothes. 依

146 襾 ia°.
To cover. 亞

西 sl.
West.

7 Strokes

147 見 kyien°.
To see. 劍

148 角 kyak.
A horn, corner. 覺

149 言 yien.
Words, to speak. 弦

150 谷 kok.
A valley. 穀

151 **豆** deu°.
Beans. 竇

152 **豕** °s.
A pig. 始

153 **豸** °dz.
Reptiles. 茌

154 **貝** pe°.
Precious. 背

155 **赤** ts'uh.
Naked, flesh color. 尺

156 **走** °tseu.
To walk, to go. 箒

157 **足 ⻊** tsok.
The foot, enough. 竹

Colloquial, 踢足傍 t'ih-tsok-paung (2nd form).

158 **身** sung.
The body. 申

159 **車** kyui.
A wheeled carriage. 居

160 **辛** sing.
Bitter. 新

161 **辰** zung.
Time. 長

162 **辵 ⻌** ts'iak.
Walking. 鵲

Colloquial, 牽走之 chien-° tseu-ts (2nd form).

163 **邑 阝** ih.
A region, a city. 浥

Colloquial, 右耳� yeu-° nyi-° too (2nd form).

164 **酉** °yeu.
Must, wine. 脜

165 **釆** °bien.
To pluck, sort out. 辨

166 **里** °li, A li. One-third of a mile. 裏

8 Strokes

167 **金 釒** kyung.
Gold, metal. 今

Colloquial, 斜金傍 zia-kyung-paung (2nd form).

168 **長 镸** dzang.
Long. 場

169 **門** mung.
A door, gate. 捫

170 **阜 阝** °veu.
A mound, plenty. 蒀

Colloquial, 左耳朵 tsi°-° nyi-° too (2nd form).

171 **隶** de°.
To reach to, attain. 代

172 **隹** tsoe.
Birds. 錐

173 **雨** °yui.
Rain. 羽

Colloquial, 雨字頭 °yui-z°-deu.

174 **青** ts'ing.
Blue sky, green. 清

175 **非** fi.
Wrong, no. 飛

9 Strokes

176 **面** mien°.
The face. 麵

177 革 kuh.
Raw hide. 隔

178 韋 we.
Leather. 幃

179 韭 °kyeu.
Leeks. 久

180 音 iung.
Sound. 陰

181 頁 yih.
A leaf, the head. 葉

182 風 fong.
Wind. 楓

183 飛 fi.
To fly. 非

184 食 飠 zuh.
To eat. 蝕

185 首 °seu.
The head. 手

186 香 hyang.
Incense, fragrant. 鄉

10 Strokes

107 馬 °mo.
A horse. 碼

188 骨 kweh.
A bone. 汩

189 高 kau.
High. 羔

190 髟 piau.
Hair. 標

191 鬥 teu°.
Quarrel. 鬪

192 鬯 ts'ang°.
Herbs, essences. 悵

193 鬲 lih, kuh.
An urn. 歷

194 鬼 °kwe.
A demon, ghost. 詭

11 Strokes

195 魚 yui.
A fish. 於

196 鳥 °nyau.
A bird. 蔦

197 鹵 °loo.
Salt. 魯

198 鹿 lok.
A deer. 祿

199 麥 muh.
Wheat. 脈

200 麻 mo.
Hemp. 篠

12 Strokes

201 黃 waung.
Yellow. 皇

202 黍 °su.
Millet. 暑

203 黑 huh.
Black. 赫

204 黹 °ts.
Embroidery. 子

13 Strokes

205 黽 °mung.
A frog. 猛

206 鼎 °ting.
A tripod. 頂

207 **鼓** °koo.
A drum. 古

208 **鼠** °su.
A rat. 暑

14 Strokes

209 **鼻** bi°.
The nose. 避

210 **齊** dzi.
Even, regular. 臍

15 Strokes

211 **齒** °t‘s.
Front teeth. 此

16 Strokes

212 **龍** long.
A dragon. 隆

213 **龜** kwe.
A tortoise. 歸

17 Strokes

214 **龠** yak.
A flute. 藥

THE RADICAL ODE

When Dr. Mateer was putting his Mandarin Lessons through the press, he conceived the idea that a rhyme might be useful in learning the meaning and order of the radicals, It was at his instigation, and with the benefit of his helpful criticism, that the following nonsense was perpetrated: in fact, the first stanza was the Doctor's own production. The ode has been found helpful as a mnemonic contrivance, and is printed in Dr. Mateer's Lessons with the following note:—

"The following ode will relieve the student of much labor in learning the meaning and order of the radicals. It will serve as a continuous ladder, with suggestive and ever-varying rounds, which the student can mount with vastly greater ease than he can climb the bare pole of arithmetical numbers. Not only is the first acquirement made easier, but the memory will retain the ode more firmly and recall it more readily than it will the bare number."

HOW TO BEGIN

One Stroke.—Numbers 1—6.

Beginning with *unity* 一, just as you ought,
You next make an *upright* 丨, and then make a *dot* 丶;
Make a *stroke to the left* 丿, then a *curve* 乙, and a *crook* 亅;
And you've summed up the use of one stroke in a book.

A RIDDLE

Two Strokes. —Numbers 7—29.

Two 二 *hats* 亠 on one *man* 人! See, that *tramp* 儿, walking fast,
Enters 入 slyly at *eight* 八, and the *limit* 冂 is passed.
A *cov'ring* 冖 of ice 冫 hides a *bench* 几 and a *box* 凵;
A *sword* 刀 of great *strength* 力 is *wrapped up* 勹 in old socks;
A *spoon* 匕 in a *case* 匚 is *concealed* 匸 with *ten* 十 knives.
Divine 卜 what this means, and then ask the old wives
Why that *seal* 卩 on the *cliff* 厂, made by some *selfish* 厶 hoax.
Should let a *conjunction* 又 end up the two stroked!

CONSOLATION FOR AN UNFORTUNATE WIDOW

Three Strokes. —Numbers 30—60.

Three smacks on the *mouth* 口! an *enclosure* 囗 so sweet
That *earth's* 土 greatest *sage* 士 *follows* 夂 *slowly* 夊 to greet.
This *evening* 夕, *great* 大 *lady* 女, your *son* 子 had a fall
From a *roof* 宀 that was forty-one *inches* 寸 too *small* 小.
He is *lame* 尢, not a *corpse* 尸, and some *sprouts* 屮 from the *hill* 山,
Washed in *streams* 巛 by the *workmen* 工, will keep him quite still.
Wrap *self* 己 in a *napkin* 巾; make *shields* 干 for the *tender* 幺;
Give *shelter* 广 to orphans; *move* 廴 on, their defender!
Joined hands 廾 follow Cupid's *dart* 弋, shot from his *bow* 弓:
Eat *pig's head* 彐; don *plumage* 彡; his *footsteps* 彳 you know.

SUNDRY REFLECTIONS

Four Strokes. —Number 61—94.

If your *heart* 心 be once pierced by a *spear* 戈 as you stand,

Then the *door* 户 of eternity's surely at *hand* 手.

When you've mastered this *branch* 支 of the language, be sure

You've but *tapped* 攴 at the portal of *literature* 文.

Though we measure with *bushels* 斗 and *catties* 斤 and *squares* 方,

Yet *without* 无 the *sun's* 日 light we could not sell our wares.

Why *speak* 曰 of the *moon* 月 with such rapture my dove?

To the shade of the *wood* 木 do we *owe* 欠 our first love.

Stop 止, *vicious* 歹 man, *kill* 殳 not! *Deny* 毋 not my prayer(!)

Can life be *compared* 比 with those locks of red *hair* 毛?

One's *family name* 氏 is as dear as his *breath* 气;

Through *water* 水 and *fire* 火 he'll defend it till death.

The *claws* 爪 of a kitten, my *father* 父 once said,

Should never scratch *crosswise* 爻, nor climb on a *bed* 爿;

And a *splint* 片 twixt the *teeth* 牙 puts an end to all jokes,

While an *ox* 牛 and a *dog* 犬 will end up the four strokes.

SAD DEATH OF TWO JEWELERS

Five Strokes. —Numbers 95—117.

Two *sombre* 玄 *gem* 玉 merchants once ate a *cucumber* 瓜:

They slept on some *tiles* 瓦, and how *sweet* 甘 was their slumber!

But to *live* 生 was no *use* 用; in a *field* 田, at their ease,

In *dry goods* 疋 rolled up, they were killed by *disease* 疒.

Back to back 癶 they were laid, dressed in *white* 白,—'twas their wish,—

With the *skin* 皮 of the cucumber placed in a *dish* 皿!

Then an *eye* 目，*lance* 矛 and *dart* 矢 were engraved on a *stone* 石，
As an *emblem divine* 示 of the *foot-prints* 禸 now flown；
This stone，midst the *grain* 禾 in a *cavernous den* 穴，
Was *erected* 立 to finish five strokes of the pen.

AN ECCENTRIC OLD STATESMAN

Six Strokes. —Numbers 118—146.

"Our *bamboo* 竹 and *rice* 米，*silk* 糸 and *crocks* 缶，I am told，
Our *nets* 网，*sheep* 羊 and *quills* 羽 must be taxed as of *old* 老.
And *yet* 而 we *plow* 耒 on for this fool with long *ears* 耳!"
"Stick a *pen* 聿 in his *flesh* 肉!" cried a boatman with jeers.
The *statesman* 臣 *himself* 自 now *arrived* 至 with a *mortar* 臼：
Thu *tongue* 舌 that *opposed* 舛 him he'd smash and make shorter!
The *boat's* 舟 *perverse* 艮 skipper，with red *colored* 色 face，
He tied up with *grass* 艸，and dismissed in disgrace.
But when *tigers* 虍 and *insects* 虫 drew *blood* 血，he thought best
To *travel* 行 for *clothing* 衣 and skip to the *west* 西.

BEWARE OF THE SERPENT

Seven Strokes. —Numbers 147—166.

Seven strokes we now *see* 見，and a *horn* 角，—fateful *word* 言!
In the *valley* 谷 *beans* 豆 grow，and of *pigs* 豕 a whole herd；
Great *reptiles* 豸 their *precious* 貝 young offspring are feeding；
With legs bare and *naked* 赤 a lad *walks* 走 unheeding；
His *foot* 足 gets a sting and his *body* 身 soon dies；
A *coach* 車 brings his mother：how *bitter* 辛 her cries!

'Tis high *time* 辰 to *run* 辵 from a *region* 邑 so vile,
Where *wine* 酉 *plucks* 釆 its victims for many a *mile* 里.

FLEETING RICHES

Eight Strokes. —Numbers 167—175.

Eight strokes! and now *gold* 金, after *long* 長 labor gained,
Doth open the *doorway* 門 of *plenty* 阜 *attained* 隶.
But riches, like *birds* 隹, when the *rain* 雨 hides the *blue* 青.
If I am not *wrong* 非, will fly quickly from you.

FOOLISH ANGER

Nine Strokes. —Numbers 176—186.

Nine strokes on the *face* 面 with a *raw-hide* 革 or *leather* 韋.
Or e'en with a *leek* 韭, will raise *sounds* 音 in all weather.
For *leaves* 頁 in the *wind* 風, when they *fly* 飛 far away,
Don't *eat* 食 off your *head* 首, nor burn *incense* 香 all day.

GOOD ADVICE

Ten Strokes. —Numbers 187—194.

Ten strokes on a *horse* 馬, with a *bone* 骨 raised on *high* 高,
Will wear off his *hair* 髟, and soon cause him to shy.
Don't *fight* 鬥 about *essences* 鬯 cooked in an *urn* 鬲,
Or you'll find yourself doomed with the *demons* 鬼 to burn.

FISHING AND HUNTING

Eleven Strokes. —Numbers 195—200.

Eleven fresh *fish* 魚 and a *bird* 鳥 caught with *salt* 鹵；
A *deer* 鹿 which eats *wheat* 麥，tied with *hemp* 麻，calls a halt.

GOING TO MARKET

Twelve Strokes. —Numbers 201—204.

Twelve *yellow* 黄 *millet* 黍 stalks next you will see，
And *black* 黑 silk *embroidery* 黹 purchased by me.

EXPLOIT OF SOME FROGS

Thirteen Strokes. —Numbers 205—208.

Thirteen little *frogs* 黽 on a *tripod* 鼎 once sat，
But jumped on a *drum* 鼓，when they saw a big *rat* 鼠.

RESULT OF A FIGHT

Fourteen and Fifteen Strokes. —Numbers 209—211.

Fourteen were tho *noses* 鼻，all *even* 齊 in height，
Fifteen were the teeth 齒，which were lost in a fight.

THE DRAGONS END IT

Sixteen and Seventeen Strokes. —Numbers 212—214.

Sixteen *dragons* 龍 sat on a *tortoise* 龜 last June，
Playing seventeen *flutes* 龠；and that winds up my tune.

SHANGHAI VERNACULAR
Chinese-English Dictionary

1 一

一 ih, 1095, G.5342.
One.

丁[1] ting, 903, G.11253.
A person, a brave (soldier).

七 ts'ih, 987, G.1055.
Seven.

丈[2] °dzang, 25, G.424.
Ten feet; an elder.

下 °ya, c. °'au, 183. G.4230.
Below, mean.

| ya°, c. 'au°.
To descend.

三 san, 723, G.9522.
Three.

上 zang°, c. laung°, 741, G.9729. Above, upon (used after a noun).

| c. zaung°. Above, upon (used before a noun)

| °zaung, c. °zaung.
To ascend.

万 mok, c. muh, 1249, G.12484. Character in the surname mok-ji.

| 見萬 van°, c. man°, 1040, G.1284. A myriad.

丐[3] ke°, 307, G.5788.
To beg, a beggar.

不 peh, 717, G.3595.
Not.

与見與 °iui, 1125, G.13521.
By, with, and.

丑 °ts'eu, 52, G.2518.
1—3 o'clock a.m.

丘[4] cheu, 416, G.2310.
A mound.

丕 p'e, 671, G.8818.
Distinguished, first.

丙 °ping, 699, G.9295.
Bright, clear.

世 s°, 763, G.9969. An age, a generation, the world

且 °ts'ien, c. °ts'ia, 974, G.1555. Still, also, yet, if, moreover.

丞[5] dzung, 78, G.760.
To assist.

両見兩 °liang, 526.
Two.

丢 tieu, 909, G.11301.
To throw away.

两[6] 見兩 °liang, 526.
Two.

並[8] bing°, °bing, 700, G.9282. Together, both, also; used to strengthen a negative.

2 丨

丨 °kwung, 494, G.6528. A perpendicular line.

个[2] koo°, c. kuh, 423, G.6077. Of, pertaining to, sign of genitive; a general classifier, a final particle.

丫 ia, c. au, o, 1066, G.12827. Branch, fork.

中[3] tsong, 105, G.2875. The middle, center fitting.

丨 tsong°. To hit the centre, to attain.

丰 fong, 156, G.3561. Luxuriant, fine, graceful.

目[4] °i, 378, G.5467. To aid, by, with, at.

丱 kwan°, 476, G.6366. The two tufts of a child's hair.

串[6] ts'en°, 121, G.2752. To string, connect.

3 丶

丶 °tsu, 87, G.2525. A point.

凡[2] wen, 246, G.5066. A pill, cinnabar, red.

丸見凡 wen, 246, G.12490.

丹[3] tan, 849, G.10618. Red color.

主[4] °tsu, 87, G.2526. Ruler, lord, owner.

4 丿

丿 p'ih, 686, G.9170. A stroke to the left.

乂[1] nyi°, 284, G.5530. To cut, cleave.

乃 °'ne, 612, G.8113. And, is, moreover, but.

久[2] °kyeu, 413, G.2273. A long time, finally.

之[3] ts, 53, G.1787. Genitive sign, it, him, sign of completed action.

乍[4] dzo°, 4, G.145. Suddenly.

乏 vah, 122, G.3378. Destitute, tired, weary.

乎 'oo, 224, G.4911. An interrogative particle of doubt, admiration, etc.; at, in.

乑[5]見眾 tsong°, 108. Many.

丟見丢 tieu, 909, G. 11301. To throw away.

乖[7] kwe, c. kwa, 470, G.6326. Strange, crafty, perverse.

乘[9] dzung, 772, G.770. By, to ascend, to multiply, to ride.

| dzung°.
A classifier of vehicles.

5 乙

乙 ih, 1096, G.5341.
One, a curve.

九[1] °kyeu, 431, G.2263.
Nine.

乞[2] chih, c. chuh, 395, G.1060.
Beg, give.

也 °ye, c. °'a, 1079, G.12988.
Even, and.

| °yan.
A final particle.

乩[5] kyi, 335, G.877.
To divine.

乭 tauh.
Sign of plural(Soochow).

乱[6] 見亂 loen°, 570, G.6747.
Disorder, to confuse.

乳[7] °zu, c. °na, 298, G.5691.
Milk, breast.

亀[9] 見龜 kwe, c. kyui, 481.
A tortoise.

乾[10] jien, 311, G.1742.
Heaven.

| koen.
Dry.

亂[12] loen°, 570, G.6748.
Confused, disorder.

6 亅

亅 kyoeh, c. joeh, 447, G.3248. A barb.

了 °liau, 529, G.7073.
Finished, final particle.

予 °yui, 1120, G.13671.
To give.

| yui
I.

争[5] 見爭 tsung, c. tsang, 29, G.704. To wrangle.

事[7] z°, 764, G.9990.
Thing, affair, business.

7 二

二 r°, c. nyi°, 721, G.3363.
Two.

于[1] yui, 1118, G.13537.
In, to, as, respecting.

云[2] yuin, 1142, G.13805.
Say, speak.

互 'oo°, 226, G.4972.
United, interchangeable.

井 °tsing, 993, G.2151.
Well, pit.

五 °oo, c. °ng, 1060, G.12698. Five.

亙 kung°, 323, G.6011.
To fill, universal.

亘[4] sien, 821, G.4800.
To remove, return.

些 si, 796, G.4363.
Few, sign of pl.; sign of comparative.

況 °hwaung, 254, G.5144.
Furthermore.

亞[6] ia°, c. a, 1068, G.12810.
Deformed, inferior.

亟 kyih, 393, G.858.
Extreme, prompt.

8 亠

亠 deu, 876, G.11449.
A cover.

亡[1] vaung, c. maung, 1044, G.12502. Dead, forgotten, lost.

亢[2] kaung, 320, G.3848.
The neck or throat.

丨 k'aung°.
Unyielding, to oppose.

亥 °'e, 161, G.3757.
9 to 11 p.m.

交[4] kyau, c. kau, 367, G.1297.
Blend, unite, deliver to.

亦 yuh, c. °'a, 1093, G.5395.
Also, and, moreover.

亨[5] hung, c. hang, 169, G.3906. Successful, to influence.

享[6] °hyang, 189, G.4286.
To enjoy.

京 kyung, 403, G.2140.
Capital, exalted.

亮 liang°, 526, G.7035.
Clear, brilliant.

亭[7] ding, 907, G.11276.
Pavilion, a shed.

亳[8] bok, c. bauh, 710, G.9399.
Ancient capital.

亶[11] °tan, 851, G.10641.
Trusty, abundant.

亹[19] °ri, 1051, G.7756.
Determined.

9 人

人 zung, c. nyung, 286, G.5624. Man.

仇 jeu, dzeu, 52, G.2330.
Enemy.

仆 foo°, c. p'ok, 148, G.3740.
To fall, to overthrow.

仁 zung, c. nyung, 287, G.5627.
Humane, benevolent.

仍 dzung, 291, G.5628.
As before, still.

介 kya°, 360, G.1518.
Guest, assistant.

今 kyung, 398, G.2027.
Now, recent.

什[2] zeh, 768, G.9960.
Ten men, sundries.

仃 ting, 904, G.11254.
Alone, without protection.

仄 tsuh, c. tsak, 959, G.242.
Inclined, refracted.

从見從 dzong, 1024, G.11986.
From, to follow.

仗[3] dzang°, tsang°, 25, G.425.
Fight, weapon.

付 foo°, 147, G.3666.
Pay.

以 °i, 278, G.5462. To aid, have, in, by, to, take.

仞 zung°，288，G.5598.
A fathom.

令 ling°，546，G.7199.
Command，rule.

仕 z°，762，G.9993.
Official.

仙 sien，799，G.4449.
Genii，deified spirits.

他 t‘a，840，G.10508.
Other，he.

代 de°，845，G.10547. Substitute，a generation，age.

仝見同 dong，933，G.12287.
Together.

仟 ts‘ien，980，G.1726.
Commander of 1000 men.

仔[3] °ts，1030，G.11493.
Careful，a little thing.

仡 nyih，1096，G.13159.
Able，robust.

仲[4] dzong°，108，G.2876.
Second of three.

伐 vah，122，G.3369.
Chastise，punish.

份 vung°，131，G.3507.
Part，share.

仿 °faung，134，G.3436.
Copy after.

伏 vok，152，G.3691.
Prostrate.

休 hyeu，210，G.4651.
Put away，abandon.

伊 yi，271，G.5337.
He，him.

丨 i.
That.

伙 °hoo，255，G.5327.
Furniture，tools.

任 zung，zung°，c. nyung，nyung°，289，G.5615.
Office，to bear.

伉 k‘aung°，320，G.5918.
Compare with，couple.

伎 ji，341，G.861.
Ability.

企 °chi，349，G.1114.
Straight，steep.

价 kya°，360，G.1519.
A waiter.

件 °jien，386，G.1677. An affair，classifier of things.

伍 °oo，c. °ng，1060，G.12699.
Five.

仵 °oo，c. °ng，1061，G.12770.
Equalize.

仰 °nyang，1073，G.12885.
Look for，hope.

佔[5] tsen°，c. tsien°，45，G.268.
Usurp.

住 dzu°，89，G.2527.
Dwell.

佛 veh，153，G.3589.
Buddha.

何 ‘oo，215，G.3941.
What，who.

伽 kya，ja，c. ka，ga，G.1558.
Character used in names.

估 °koo，433，G.6189.
Estimate.

伶 ling，544，G.7200.
Actor，play.

伲 nyi°，630，G. 8195. We (Soochow and Shanghai).

｜見伱 °'ni.
You.

伱 °'ni，630，G.8212.
You.

佞 nyung°，637，G.8340.
Flattering，artful.

伴 ben°，652，G.8603.
Companion.

体見體 °t'i，656，G.8855.
The body.

伯 puh，c. pak，707，G.8557.
Father's brother.

佈 poo°，713，G.9480.
Scatter.

伸 sung，736，G.9817.
Straighten，stretch out.

似 z°，837，G.9997.
Like，similar.

伺 z°，837，G.10251.
Wait upon，spy，examine.

但 °dan，852，G.10634.
But，only.

低 ti，877，G.10899.
Beneath，low.

佃 dien，896，G.11178.
Cultivate.

佗 doo，911，G.11346.
Another，carry.

佐 °tsoo，1002，G.11754.
Assist，a deputy.

作 tsauh，1005，G.11741.
To do，make.

位 we°，1053，G.12612.
Place，seat，person.

佚 yih，1097，G.5533.
Lazy.

佑 °yeu，yeu°，1115，G.13437.
Help.

余 yui，1120，G.3356.
I，myself.

侈 6 °ts'，65，G.1936.
Profuse，extravagant.

侄見姪 dzeh，68，G.1818.
Foolish，nephew.

侏 tsu，85，G.2545.
A dwarf.

依 i，271，G. 5387. To rely on，trust，to follow.

侃 k'oen°，315，G.5875. Plain-spoken，straightforward.

佳 kya，351，G.1174.
Beautiful，excellent.

佼 °kyau，370，G.1298.
Handsome.

佶 kyih，392，G.910.
Robust.

供 kong，462，G.6572. Minister，to supply，to testify.

｜ kong°.
To offer in worship.

來 le，498，G.6679.
To come.

例 li°, 521, G.7006.
A law, a regulation.

侖 lung, 565, G.7463.
Arrange.

侔 meu, 588, G.8045.
Equal.

佩 be°, 670, G.8785.
To wear as a souvenir.

佰 puh, c. pak, 707, G.9348.
A hundred men.

侍 z°, c. °z, 761, G.9915.
Servant, to serve.

使 °s, 716, G.9896.
To cause, send.

丨 s°.
A messenger.

佻 t'iau, 888, G.11064.
Weak, envious.

侗 t'ong, 933, G.12270.
Stupid.

佯 yang, 1072, G.12843.
To feign, false.

佾 yih, 1097, G. 5534. A mummer, a scholar below sieu-dze.

侑 yeu°, 1115, G.13377.
To help, assist.

併見倂 °ping.
To unite.

俘7 foo, 143, G.3644.
Capture.

侯 'eu, 174, G.4006.
Duke, marquis.

係 °i, 181, G.4062. Connected, is, are, to belong to.

俠 yah, 356, G.1446.
Resolute, magnanimous.

侷 jok, 456, G.2956.
Cramped, bent down.

俚 °li, 519, G.6871.
Common, usual.

俐 li°, 521, G.6886.
Cunning.

侶 °lui, 559, G.7521.
Companion.

俛見俯 °foo, 594, G.3732.
Prostrate.

俄 ngoo, 627, G.8427.
Sudden.

�

佛 na°, 639, G.8361.
You.

保 °pau, 664, G.8711.
To secure, protect.

便 bien°, 688, G.9187.
Convenient, cheap.

信 sing°, 807, G.4587.
Faith, to believe.

俗 dzok, 822, G.4749.
Common, vulgar.

俟 °z, 837, G.1081.
To wait.

俏 ts'iau°, 972, G.1418.
Handsome, similar.

侵 ts'ing, 991, G.2087.
To encroach, invade.

俎 °tsoo, 1007, G.11832.
Sacrificial bowl.

促 ts'ok, 1015, G.11870.
Swift.

俊 tsing°, 1020, G.3277.
Superior, elegant.

侮 roo°, 1061, G.4982.
To despise, to insult.

俑 °iong, 1148, G.13451.
Image, idol.

俞見兪 yui.
Yes, assent.

倀[8] ts'ang, 26, G.451.
Blindly, not knowing.

倡 ts'ang, c. ts'aung°, 28, G.428. A leader, actor.

値 dzuh, 59, G.1847.
Price, value.

倬 tsauh, 82, G.2390.
To exhibit, extensive.

倣 °faung, 134, G.3456.
To imitate.

俯 °foo, 146, G.3683.
To stoop, bow down.

俸 fong°, 159. G.3575.
Salary, wages.

候 'eu°, 176, G.4021. Time, when, to wait, to enquire after.

倖 °yung, 208, G.4593.
Lucky, fortunate.

倪 nyi, 273, G.5429.
Small, decorous, average.

倚 °i, 279, G.5355.
To rely on, trust.

個 koo°, c. kuh, 423, G.6074.
One, a piece.

俱 kyui, 438, G.3019.
All, the whole.

倨 kyui°, 444, G.2988.
Haughty, bold, strong.

倔 joeh, 448, G.3229.
Obstinate, perverse.

倦 joen°, 450, G.3147.
Weary.

倥 k'ong, 465, G.6596.
Rude, clownish.

倌 kwen, 472, G.6342.
Slave, servant.

倆 °liang, 526, G.7009.
Two, still.

們 mung, 577, G.7752.
Plural sign.

倫 lung, 565. G.7464.
Constant, relationship.

俾 pe, 669, G.8760.
To cause, allow.

倍 be°, 670, G.8787.
Double, increase.

俻見備 be°, 677, G.8803.
Prepare.

倂 °ping, 700, G.9285.
To unite.

俶 sok, 779, G.10040.
To begin, fine.

倏 sok, 781, G.10086.
Suddenly.

儵見倏 sok, 781, G.10085.
Suddenly.

修 sieu，811，G.4661.
Repair，mend.

倘 °t‘aung，862，G.10756.
If，supposing.

倒 °tau，866，G.10793. On the contrary，to fall，to reverse，but，still.

丨 tau°.
To pour out.

倉 ts‘aung，949，G.11591.
Granary.

借 tsie°，c. tsia°，973，G.1536.
Borrow，lend.

倩 ts‘ien°，983，G.1758.
Fine looking.

倅 ts‘oe°，1017，G.11834.
Waiter，servant.

倭 oo，1057，G.12558. The Japanese（“the dwarfs”）.

偵 9 tsung，77，G.699.
A spy.

假 °kya，c. °ka，352，G.1160.
False，if，for instance.

偕 kya，358，G.1438.
Together，all at once.

健 jien°，386，G.1593.
Strong.

偭 °mien，595，G.7887.
Accompany，turn back.

偶 °ngeu，626，G.8501. Accidental，suddenly，an image.

偏 p‘ien，689，G.9215.
Partial，inclined to one side（deflected.）

偪 pih，692，G.8913.
Pursue，persecute.

偲 s，843，G.10272.
To exhort.

偷 t‘eu，875，G.11444.
Steal.

停 ding，907，G.11277.
Stop.

側 tsuh，957，G.227.
Oblique，slanting.

做 tsoo°，1003，G.11761.
To do，make，be.

傯 °tsong，1024，G.12015.
Care-worn，wearied.

偉 °we，1051，G.12528.
Rare，fine.

偃 °ien，1086，G.13117.
Sleep.

⿰亻⿱龹女 見 媵 yung°，1104，G.13279.
Concubine.

傖 10 ts‘iang，31，G.11592.
A reprobate.

傅 foo°，147，G.3632.
A teacher，near，to lay on.

傒 yi，178，G.4064.
A servant.

傚 yau°，194，G.4350.
Imitate.

傢 kya，c. ka，352，G.1140.
Vessel，implement.

傑 jih，377，G.1499.
A good person.

傀 °kw‘e，488，G.6495.
An image idol.

傌見罵 moo°, 572, G.7577. To rail at.

傍 baung, 658, G.8660. Support, reliance, the side.

丨 baung°. To stay near (for protection).

備 be°, 677, G.8804. To prepare, perfect.

傘 san°, 724, G.9563. An umbrella.

傞 soo, 815, G.10219. Reeling as a drunkard.

傏 daung, 861, G.10768. Forward, presuming.

傷 tseu°, 962, G.11805. Attendant.

傜 yau, 1075, G.12911. Unstable.

債[11] tse°, c. tsa°, 10, G.232. Debt.

傳 dzen, 119, G.2703. Propagate, spread, hand down.

丨 dzeu°, Records, chronicles, traditions.

僅 jung°, 399, G.2043. Only, barely, exactly.

傾 chung, 408, G. 2196. To overturn, waste, inclined.

僂 leu, 559, G.7513. To bend down.

僇 lok, 564, G.7443. To disgrace, act foolishly.

僈 man°, 576, G. 7627. An actor, negligent, remiss.

傲 ngau°, 625, G.83. Haughty, proud.

傷 saung, 739, G.9742. Wound.

傈 sih, 798, G.4852. Whisperer.

僊同仙 sien, 800, G.4460. To perform antics.

僉 ts'ien, 981, G.1713. All, the whole.

催 ts'oe, 1017, G.11918. Press, urge.

傴 °yui, c. °eu, °heu, 1126, G.13552. Bent down.

傭 yong, 1148, G.13463. Servant.

僎[12] °dzan, 118, G.2715. Master of a village feast.

僨 vung°, 131, G.3535. To overturn, ruin.

僖 hyi, 178, G.4074. Happy, pleased, cautious.

僑 jau, 374, G.1396. An inn.

僱見雇 °koo, koo°, 435, G.6253. To line.

僚 liau, 527, G.7037. An official associate.

僕 bok, 717, G.9439. Slave, servant.

僧 sung, 725, G.9617. A Buddhist priest.

像 °ziang, ziang°, 793, G.4288. Similar, like, image.

僣見僭 tsien°, 893, G.11158. Artful, cunning.

僭同僣 tsien°, 980. To usurp, To be in error.

僮 dong, 935, G.12300. A young servant.

僦 tsieu°, 1000, G.2284. To hire, procure.

偽 we°, 1055, G.12522. Deceitful, false.

僥 °kyau, 1076, G.1329. Deceitful; a pigmy.

儇 gwan, 245, G.4787. Expert, clever.

儀 nyi, 276, G. 5455. Ceremony, form; deportment.

價 kya°, c. ka°, 353, G.1182. Price, value.

僵 13 kyang, 362, G.1222. To lie down, prostrate.

儌 °kyau, 368, G.1364. Fortunate.

儉 °jien, 387, G.1658. Temperate, frugal.

儆 °kyung, 405, G.2145. Warn, caution.

儈 kwe°, 485, G.6467. A broker. To tell by sign.

僾 e°, 619, G.16. Similar; to pant.

儂 nong°, 642, G.8187. Thou, you.

僻 p'ih, 649, G.8789. A quiet place, mean.

儋 tan, 850, G.10622. Burden, weight.

億 iuh, 1092, G.5368. Repose, 100,000.

儕 dze, 11, G.257. A class, sign of plural.

儔 dzeu, 50, G.2491. Companion.

儗 °'nyi, 280, G.5424. To compare, decide.

儒 zu, 297, G.5675. Scholar, literati.

儐 ping°, 696, G.9234. Friend.

儎 tse°, 941, G.11486. Tonnage, to stow cargo.

儘 °tsing, 989, G.2058. Entire, all, the uttermost.

| 見盡 °dzing. All, the end.

儛 °voo, 1062, G.12761. Dance.

償 15 dzang, dzaung, 27, G.448. Pay, recompense.

儡 °le, 511, G.6832. A wooden idol.

儦 piau, 682, G.9105. Swift.

優 ieu, 1110, G.13382. Sufficient, a juggler.

儭 16 ts'ung°, 22, G.673. A helper.

儲 dzu, 93, G.2652. Collect, store up.

儙[17] °kyien, 384, G.1654.
Proud.

儵見倏 sok, 781, G.10087.
Quickly.

儳[18] tsan, ts'an°, 948, G.323.
Irregular.

儁見俊 tsing°.
Valiant, brave.

儽見儡 °le.
In great distress.

儷[19] li°, 524, G.6912.
A mate, companion.

儺 noo, 639, G.8368.
To expel evil spirits.

儹 °tsan, 945, G.11524.
To come together.

儻[20] °t'aung, 861, G.10766.
If, should.

儼 °ngen, 1088, G.13080.
Majestic in appearance.

儽[21] hyau.
A boaster.

儽 °le, 512, G.6844.
Lazy, indolent.

10 儿

儿 zung, 286, G.5622.
A man.

兀[1] ngeh, 1064, G.12781.
Persistent, not secure.

元[2] nyoen, yoen, 1134. G.13744.
Primary.

允 °iuin, 1143, G.5730.
Promise, secure.

充[3] ts'ong, 109, G.2924.
To fill.

兄 hyong, 213. G.4688.
Elder brother.

兆[4] dzau°, 34, G.489.
An omen, a million

兇 hyong, 213, G.4690.
Cruel.

光 kwaung, 478, G.6389.
Light.

先 sien, 799, G.4440.
First, before.

兊[5]見充 ts'ong, 109, G.2923.
To fill.

克 k'uh, 430, G. 6115. To overcome, subdue, repress.

免 °mien, 594, G.7898.
To avoid.

兌 de°, 925, G.12170.
To exchange.

兎見兔 t'oo°, 920.
A rabbit.

兒[6] r. c. nyi, 'eu, 720, G.3333.
A child.

兕 °z, 837, G.4109.
A rhinoceros.

兔 t'oo°, 902, G.12122.
A rabbit.

兗[7] °yien, 1087, G.13115.
A prefecture.

党[8]見黨 °taung, 858, G.10719.
A class.

兜[9] teu, G.11424.
To surround, a cap.

兢[12] kyung, 405, G. 2173. To fear, caution, brambles.

兜見兜 teu, 873. To surround.

11 入

入 zeh, 299, G.3359. To enter.

内[2] ne°, 618, G.8098. Within.

仝[3]見全 dzien, 1013, G.3175. Complete.

全[4] dzien, zen, dzen, 1013, G.3176. All, complete.

兩[6] °liang, 526, G.7010. An ounce, two, tael.

兪[7] yui, 1123, G.13567. Yes, so.

俞見兪 yui. Yes, so.

12 八

八 pah, 647, G.8504. Eight.

兮[2] i, 179, G.4084. Euphonic expletive.

公 kong, 459, G.6568. Public, a duke, just, term of respect.

六 lok, 562, G.7276. Six.

共[4] gong°, 464, G.6571. Together, all.

兵[5] ping, 698, G.9279. Soldiers.

其[6] ji, 342, G.1026. He, she, it.

具 jui°, 440, G. 3018. All, prepared, instruments.

典 °tien, 894, G. 11177. To manage, a rule, dictionary.

兼[8] kyien, 382, G.1630. To combine, together.

龔[11]見冀 kyi°. To expect.

冀[14] kyi°, 338, G.937. Desire, expect.

13 冂

冂 kyong, 422, G.2352. Remote, distant.

冇[2] °voo, Canton c. °m, 1059. G.12764. Not.

冄 zen, 286, G.5555. Tender, weak.

有 dien°, 807. (*Foochow*). Firm, solid.

回[3]見回 we, 261, G.5165. Return.

册 ts'uh, c. ts'ak, 42, G.266. Record, list.

冊見册 ts'uh, ts'ak. Record.

冉 °zen, 286, G.5556. A name, tender.

冋見坰 kyong, 422, G.2353. Remote.

再[4] tse°, 942, G.11494.
Again.

冋[5] kyong, 422, G.2381.
Light.

冐[6] 見 冒 mau°, G.7699.
Jeopardize, to assume, put on.

胄[7] dzeu°, 49, G.2466.
A helmet.

冒 mau°, 582. Jeopardize, to assume, put one.

冔[8] hyui, 229, G.4734.
A crown.

冓 keu°, 330, G.6151.
A quiet place.

冕[9] °mien, 594, G.7903.
A crown.

晟 dzung, 772.
A rice dish.

冐 muh, 604, G.8029.
To burst out upon.

冪[20] li, 517, G.6907.
A white hat.

14 冖

冖 mih, 596, G.7844.
A cover.

冘[2] yeu, 1113, G.13418.
Doubtful.

冗 同 宂 °nyong, 304, G.5763.
Furlough, allowance.

罙[6] mi, 590, G.7804.
Universal, deep.

冠[7] kwen, 473, G.6373.
Crown, ceremonial hat.

丨 kwen°.
To wear a "crown".

冡[8] 見 蒙 mong.
Immature.

冢 °tsong, 107, G.2897.
High, eminent, honorable.

冥 ming, 600, G.7951.
Dark, obscure.

冣 見 聚 dzui°, 1010, G.2059.
Collect.

㒼[9] men.
Level.

冤 同 寃 ioen, 1132, G.13730.
Enemy.

冩[12] 見 寫 °sie, c. °sia, 796.
To write.

冪[14] mih, 596, G.7848.
To cover.

寵[17] 見 寵 °ts'ong, 110, G.2935.
Favor, delight.

15 冫

冫 ping, 698, G.9276.
Ice.

冬[3] tong, 931, G.12246.
Winter.

冲[4] ts'ong, 109, G.2908.
To boil, collide.

决 見 決 kyoeh, 447, G.3218.
Certainly.

沍 ‘oo°, 227, G.4973.
Freeze.

冰4 ping, 698, G.9277.
Ice.

冷5 °lung, c. °lang, 506, G.669.
Cold.

泮 p‘en°, 654, G.8637.
To melt.

冶 °ye, c. °ya, 1080, G.12990.
Iron foundry.

况見況 hwaung°.
Moreover.

泯 °ming.
To destroy.

洌6 lih, 531, G.7082.
Cold.

浼7 °’me, 586, G.7728.
Polluted, soiled.

准8 °tsung, 103, G.2849.
A rule, equalize, approve.

凉 liang, 525, G.7025.
Cold, cool.

凌 ling, 543, G.6861.
To insult, spurn.

凋 tiau, 885, G.11046.
Wither.

淨見淨 zing°, 994, G.2176.
To cleanse.

淒見淒 ts‘i, 966, G.982.
Grief, cold.

凊 ts‘ing°, 994, G.2127.
Cold.

凍 tong°, 932, G.12250.
Congeal.

減9 見減 °kan, 383, G.1609.
To take from.

渫 dih, 892, G.11117.
Clean, pure.

湊見湊 ts‘eu°, 963, G.11817.
To connect, unite.

凭見憑 bing, 702.
Proof.

濂10 °lien, 534, G.7121.
Thin ice.

溧 lih, 539, G.6976.
Cold.

凾 ‘en.
Cracked ice.

溟 °ming.
Clear, cold.

漻11 lieu, 549, G.7278.
Congealed.

滭 pih, 692, G.8995.
Cold wind.

漼 dzoe, 1017, G.11919.
Snow and sleet.

澌12 s, 834, G.10264.
Floating ice.

潔見潔 kyih.
To cleanse.

澿13 °kyung, 401, G.2035.
Cold.

澟 °’ling, 542, G.7188.
Cold feelings.

澤 dauh, 914, G.11318.
Icicles.

[illegible] kyang.
Congealing ice.

凝[14] nyung, 637, G.8339.
To congeal.

瀆[15] 見瀆 dok, 922, G.12058.
Revile.

16 几

几 °kyi, 337, G.837.
A stand, teapoy.

凡[1] van, 126, G.3399.
All, every, each.

凣見凡 van, 126, G.3398.
All.

処[3] 見處 ts'u°, 94.
A place.

凭[6] bing, 700, G.9294.
To lean upon.

凰[9] waung, 251, G.5108.
A phoenix.

凱[10] °k'e, 308, G.5795.
Victory.

凳[12] tung°, 863, G.10874.
Bench, seat.

憑見凭 bing, 702, G.9329.
To trust, evidence.

17 凵

凵 °ken, 315, G.5882.
Receptacle.

凶[2] hyong, 213, G.4689.
Cruel, evil.

凸[3] deh, c. dih, dzah. 892, G.11142. Convex.

凹 ih, c. au, 623, G.106.
Concave.

出 ts'eh, 98, G.2620.
To go out.

函[6] 'en, yan, 163, G.3809.
A letter.

凾[7] 見函 'en, yan, 163, G.3812.
To envelop, a letter, an epistle.

圅見函 'en, yan. To envelop, a letter, an epistle.

18 刀

刀 tau, 865, G.10783.
Knife.

刁 tiau, 885, G.11038.
Bad, perverse.

刃[1] zung°, 288, G.5597.
Sharp-pointed.

办[2] ts'aung, 115, G.2790.
To wound, cut.

分 fung, 129, G.3506.
To divide.

| vung°.
A part, division.

刈 nyi°, 284, G.5531.
To cut.

切 ts'ih, 976, G.1057.
All, to divide.

刊[3] k'oen, k'an, 314, G.5862.
To carve.

刋見刊 k'an, G.5861.
To engrave.

刑 yung, 206, G.4621.
Punishment.

划 wo, 240, G.5011.
To pole a boat.

列 lih, 531, G.7081.
To arrange, each, every.

刎 4 °'vung, 1042, G.12655.
To cut transversely.

刖 yoeh, 1130, G.13769.
To cut off the feet.

初 5 ts'oo, 91, G.2624.
The beginning.

刦 kyih, 377.
To capture.

刧 見 刦 kyih, 377, G.1175.
To capture.

利 li°, 521, G.6885.
Profit, interest, acute.

刡 °'ming, 598, G.7909.
To scrape off, to turn in.

判 p'en°, 654, G.8638.
To punish.

刨 bau, 665, G.8700.
To plane.

刜 p'i, 678, G.9033.
To plane.

别 bih, 684, G.9155.
Other.

| pih.
To divide, separate.

删 san, 733, G.9694.
To explain, amend.

刮 °tien, 894, G.11163.
To recommend.

刹 ts'ah, 9, G.213.
A spire on a temple.

創 見 刱 ts'aung°, 116, G.2791.
To invent, the first.

制 6 ts°, 59, G. 1910. To invent, to control, put on mourning.

刯 kyih, 357, G.1465.
To brand, tattoo.

刻 k'uh, 430, G.5971.
To carve, cut.

刳 k'oo, 436, G.6269.
To cut open.

券 choen°, 453, G.3159.
Deed, note, proof.

刮 kwah, 469, G.6287.
To scrape.

刲 kw'e, 487, G.6501.
To cut.

刺 ts°, 1035, G.1115.
A thorn, to spy out.

刵 r°, 721, G.3338.
Cut off the ears.

刷 seh, 785, G.10099.
To brush off.

刬 sien, 801, G.4441.
To castrate a fowl.

到 tau°, 867, G.10792.
To arrive at, to reach.

刟 t'iau, 887, G.11073.
To carve.

刑 見 刑 yung.
Punishment.

剄 7 °kyung, 406, G.2118.
Cut off the neck.

剋 k'uh, 430, G.6116.
To subdue.

剌 lah, 498, G.6653.
Perverse, to cut in two.

削 siak, 810, G.4309.
Cleave off.

剃 t'i°, 884, G.10988.
Shave.

則 tsuh, 956, G.11652.
Then, plan, rule.

前 zien, 981, G.1737.
In front of, before.

剉 ts'oo°, 1004, G.11778.
To file.

剗 °ts'an, 14, G.376.
To cleave, spade.

剛 kaung, 318, G.5895.
Hard.

剞 °kyi, 335, G.799.
A carver, to chisel.

剠 jung, 408, G.2199.
Branded, as a criminal.

剖 °p'eu, p'oo°, 673, G.9454.
Cut open.

剝 pok, 708, G.9353.
To flay.

𠜴 tiau, 885, G.11047.
To carve.

剔 t'ih, 903, G.10982.
Scrape off.

剜 'wen, c. wah, 1038, G.12432.
To cut, gouge out.

剦 ien°, 1083, G.13053.
Eunuch.

剡 °ien, 1088, G.13070.
Sharp point.

副 9 foo°, 148, G.3705.
To assist.

剮 °kwo, 466, G.6301.
Cut in pieces.

剩 dzung°, c. dzang°, 772, G.9891. Overplus, remainder.

剬 toen, 936, G.12137. To trim even, correct deportment.

剪 見 翦 °tsien, 978, G.1618.
To shear.

𠝤 ts'ah.
Sound of cutting.

𢦏 10 ts'o, 5, G.197.
To take up with a fork.

創 ts'aung°, 115, G.2770.
Create.

剴 ke, 307, G.5782.
To sharpen, influence.

割 koeh, 428, G.6055.
To cut, reap.

剼 ts'en, 821, G.4831.
A chisel, to prune.

剷 11 °ts'an, 14, G.361.
A cleaver, knife.

𠠃 si, 64, G.1986.
Cut open.

𠠫 °ts'iang, 116, G.2783.
Cut the skin.

剸 doen, 117, G.2704.
To mutilate.

剽 p'iau, 684, G.9120.
Cut off.

剿 °tsiau, ts'au, 971, G.1360.
To destroy.

剹見戮 lok.
To kill.

劃[12] wak, 257, G.3975.
To rive, mark off.

劂 kyoeh, 446, G.3199.
To carve.

劀 kwah, 469, G.6315.
To remove pus and blood.

劆 ling, 541, G.7169.
Pare off skin.

嫳 p'ih, 686, G.9161.
To split.

劗 °tsen, 753, G.9728.
To trim, cut out.

劄見箚 tsah.
Hook.

劍[13] kyien°, 388, G.1659.
Sword.

劇 juh, 395, G.905.
True, reliable.

劊 kwe°, c. kw'e°, 485, G.6468. Decapitating knife.

劌 kwe°, 485, G.6480.
A sharp knife.

劉 lieu, 548, G.7270.
To kill.

劈 p'ih, 694, G.9018.
To split.

劏 taung, 860, G.10765.
To kill, dissect.

劕[14] zah, 8, G.184.
To cut or chop up.

劓 yi°, 284, G.5541.
To cut off the nose.

劑 tsi°, 964, G.812.
A dose.

劔見劍 kyien°.
Sword.

劕 tsien.
To cut.

劋 tsauh.
A cleaver, knife.

劗[15] tseh, 68, G.1894.
A ticket, a pass.

劙 li, 515, G.6943.
To split.

劚 li°.
Sharp edge.

劖[17] tsan, 13, G.324.
A knife, a cleaver.

劗[19] tsan.
A knife, a cleaver.

劘 moo, 585, G.7747.
To cut, pare, dissect.

劙[21] li.
To divide.

劚 tsauh.
To reap, mow.

19 力

力 lih, 536, G.6980.
Strength.

劝[2]見勸 choen°, 453.
Exhort.

加 kya, c. ka, 350, G.1144.
Add.

功[3] kong，460，G.6554.
Merit，works.

劤[4] kyung°，jung°，401，G.2020.
Great strength，brawny.

劣 loeh，c. lih，560，G.7101.
Weak，mean.

劥 k‘ang.
To resist.

劦 yah.
Combine strength.

助[5] dzoo°，90，G.2600.
To help.

劬 jui，443，G.3105.
Labor，distress.

努 °noo，641，G.8389.
Effort.

劭 zau°，746，G.9773.
Effort，tired.

劫見刦 kyih，377.
Rob，plunder.

効[6] yau°，193，G.4344.
Exertion.

劾 ‘eh，220，G.3963.
Investigate.

劼 kyih，c. gah，392，G.911.
To press，crowd into.

劻 kw‘aung，480，G.6401.
To help.

劵見倦 joen°.
Proof，a bond，deed.

劳見勞 lau，507.
Weary.

勅[7] ts‘uh，72，G.1943.
Imperial decree.

勁 kyung°，jung°，407，G.2024.
Strong.

勉 °mien，594，G.7900.
Persuade，encourage.

勃 beh，718，G.9425.
Suddenly.

勇 °iong，1148，G.13457.
Brave.

勑見勅 le(ts‘uh).
Imperial decree.

勑[8] le，72，G.1945.
Imperial decree.（=勅 ts’uh).

勍 jung，408，G.2200.
Strong，violent.

務[9] voo°，1062，G.12790.
Business，duty，function.

勘 k‘en°，315，G.5858.
To examine.

勒 luh，509，G.6814.
Coerce，bridle.

勗見勖 hyok，825，G.4740.
To persuade.

勖 hyok，825，G.4741.
To persuade.

動 °dong，932，G.12256.
To move，motion.

勛[10]見勳 hyuin，212，G.4905.
Loyal.

勞 lau，507，G.6793.
Weary.

勝 sung°，771，G.9876.
To overcome，surpass.

丨 sung.
Adequate to，to bear.

劽 lui°.
To be strong.

募 11 moo°, 606, G.8059.
To enlist, a call for aid.

勠 lok, 564, G.7444.
United strength.

勡 p'iau°, 684, G.9121.
To stab, pierce.

勢 s°, 765, G.9991. Strength, form, configuration.

勣 見 績 tsih, 986, G.829.
Merit.

勤 jung, 402, G.2097.
Diligent.

勥 °jang, 366, G.1294.
Strong.

勦 °tsiau, ts'au, 971, G.1361.
To cast out, destroy.

勩 12 yi°, 282, G.5529.
Merit.

勪 kyoeh, 446, G.3200.
To urge.

勰 13 yah, 196, G.4393.
Union of purpose.

勱 me°, 574, G.7618.
To exert strength.

勮 kyui°.
Urgent.

勯 tan.
Exert.

勳 14 hyuin, 212, G.4855.
Merit.

勵 li°, 523, G.6967.
To incite, animate.

勴 15 lui°, 560, G.7529.
To aid, advise.

勷 17 zang, 290, G.5565.
To aid.

勸 18 choen°, 453, G.3189.
To exhort.

20 勹

勹 pau, 663, G.8695.
A spoon.

勺 1 tsak, c. dzauh, 81, G.9767. A hook.

勾 2 keu, 328. G.6135.
To mark, check off.

勽 °'vung, 665, G.8696.
To brood eggs.

勿 feh, c. 'veh, 1065, G.12774.
Not.

匀 yuin, 1142, G.13821.
To equalize.

匃 3 ke°, 307, G.5779.
To beg.

包 pau, 663, G.8699.
To wrap.

匄 見 匃 kc°.
To beg, a beggar.

匆 見 忽 ts'ong, 1024.
Excited, hurried.

匈 4 hyong, 214, G.4692.
The bosom, affections.

匊 6 kyok, 457, G.2961.
A handful.

匋 dau, 869, G.10821.
A furnace for pottery.

匍7 boo, 715, G.9496.
To crawl on the ground.

匏9 bau, 667, G.8750.
A gourd, squash.

匐 bok, vok, 711, G.9437.
To crawl.

21 匕

匕 °pi, 674, G.8941.
A ladle, stiletto.

七見**化** hwo°.
To alter.

化2 hwo°, 240, G.5001.
To alter, change, digest.

丨 hau°.
In, among, many.

北3 pok, 709, G.8771.
North.

匙9 z, dz, 760, G.1954.
Key.

22 匚

匚 faung, 133, G.3458.
A basket.

匜3 yi, 274, G.5444.
A basin.

匝見**帀** tsah, 939, G.11460.
To revolve, a circuit, a side.

匟4 k'aung°, 320, G.5919.
A bench, table, bed.

匡 kw'aung, 479, G.6400.
Correct, square.

匠 ziang°, 968, G.1246.
An artificer.

匣5 yah, c. 'ah, 185, G.4213.
A box.

匧7 kyah, 380, G.1570.
A case, box.

匪8 °fi, 137, G.3479.
Vagabond.

匭9 °kwe, 483, G.6452.
A casket, to box up.

匬 °yui, 1125, G.13568.
Ask, a measure.

匯10 °we, we°, 263, G.5189.
To deposit, accumulate.

匱12 gwe°, c. jui°, 486, G.6465.
A chest, box.

匳見**奩** lien.
Lady's toilet box.

匲13見**奩** lien.
Lady's toilet box.

匵15 dok, 923, G.12059.
A receptacle.

23 匸

匸 °yi, 180, G.4175.
A case.

匹2 p'ih, 695, G.9029.
A piece.

医5 i, i°, 281, G.5375. A quiver for an arrow. 又見醫

匾9 °pien, 687, G.9173.
Flat.

匿 nyuh, 635, G.8217.
To conceal.

區 chui, 442, G.3088.
Small, a hamlet.

匳[13] 見 奩 lien.
Lady's toilet box.

24 十

十 zeh, seh, 768, G.9959.
Ten.

卂[1] sing°.
Swift.

千 ts'ien, 980, G.1725.
A thousand.

廿 seh, c. nyan°, 300, G.5692.
Twenty.

卅[2] seh, c. san-seh, 721, G.9533. Thirty.

升 sung, 771, G.9879.
To ascend, a measure.

午 °oo, c. °ng, 1061, G.12769. Noon.

卉[3] °hwe, 263, G.5214.
A fragrant plant.

半 pen°, 651, G.8602.
Half.

卍[4] man°, 1040, G.12485.
Antique, mystic element.

卓 tsauh, 82, G.2389.
Eminent.

協 yah, 195, G.1508.
Combined strength.

卑[6] pe, 668, G.8759.
Mean, vulgar, low.

卒 tsoeh, 1013, G.11833.
Soldiers, last, to die.

单 見 單 tan, 849.
Single, a bill.

南[7] nen, 614, G.8128.
South.

博[10] pok, c. pauh, 706, G.9372.
Wise, sage.

25 卜

卜 pok, c. pauh, 717, G.9476.
To divine.

卞[2] bien°, 688, G.9202.
Hurried, all.

占[3] tsen, 43, G.267.
To divine.

丨 tsen°, c. tsien°.
To usurp.

卡 dzeh, c. °k'a, 940, G.1188.
A barrier.

卣[5] °yeu, 1114, G.13440.
Wine pitcher.

卦[6] kwo°, 467, G.6311.
Diagram.

26 卩

卩 tsih, 975, G.1548.
A section, joint, verse.

卬[3] nyaung, 2, G.71.
Great, strenuous.

卭 見 邛 jong, 421.
Infirm, poor.

卮 ts.
Wine dish.

卯 °mau, 581, G.7693.
From 5 to 7 a. m.

夘見卯 °mau, 581, G.7692. 5—7 a. m.

印[4] iung°, 1103, G.13282. A seal, to print.

危 we, 1050, G.12589. Danger.

却[5]見卻 chak, 411, G.2230. But, really, to decline.

卵 °loen, °loo, 570, G.7460. Eggs.

卲 zau°, 746, G.9774. High, virtue.

即見卽 tsih. Then, therefore, otherwise, i. e.

卷[6] kyoen°, 450, G.3146. A scroll.

〡見捲 °kyoen. To roll up.

卺 °kyung, 399, G.2064. Bridal-veil and cup.

卸 sia°, 797, G.4139. To unload, lay aside.

卹 sih, 825, G.4722. To pity.

卻[7] chak, 411, G.2231. Then, truly, certain.

卽 tsih, 984, G. 878. Now, then, if, that is, presently.

卼見𡯁 ngeh, 1065, G.12787. Disquieted, hazardous.

卿[9] chung, 407, G.2198. A high officer.

27 厂

厂 hoen°, 166, G.3843. A cover.

厄[1] uh, 629, G.8170. Impede, cramped.

厎[5] °ts, ti, 878, G.10900. A soft stone, to settle, execute.

厔[6] tseh, 68, G.1820. Windings of brooks.

厓 ya°, 1069, G.22. Mountain base, side.

厚[7] °'eu, 176, G.4024. Thick.

厘見釐 li, 516, G.6872. The thousandth part of a tael, a cash, to rule.

厖 baung, 578, G.7660. A large rock, abundant.

厙 so°. A surname.

厞[8] ri°, 137, G.3161. A quiet retreat.

厝 ts'oo°, 1005, G. 11767. Graven tablet, to engrave.

厜 ts, dzoe, 1029, G.12369. Mountain peak.

原 nyoen, 1133, G.13700. Original.

厠[9] t's°, 1035, G.1993. A privy, dirty gorge.

厥[10] kyoeh, 445, G.3198. Direction to, he, she, it, that.

厦 so°, c. ‘au°, 184, G.4228. A hall.

厨見廚 dzu, 93. A kitchen, a case for books, etc.

厩[11]見廄 kyeu°, 415, G.2290. A stall.

厪 jung°, 400, G.2044. A hut, careful.

廠[12]見廠 °ts‘ang, 28, G.444. Depôt, depository.

厨見廚 dzu, 93. G.2633. A kitchen, a case for books.

厮 s, 834, G.10265. Servant.

厭 ien°, 1089, G.13031. Dislike, disgust.

厲[13] li°, 522, G.6966. Grindstone, severe.

28 厶

厶 s, 836, G.8049. Private, selfish.

么[1]見幺 iau, 1075, G. 12944. Small, tender.

去[3] chui°, c. chi°, 445, G.3068. Go.

| °chui, c. °chi. To dismiss, cast off.

参[6]見參 ts‘en.

叁 san, 723, G.9553. Three.

參[9] ts‘en, c. ts‘an, 946, G.9824. To blend, mixed.

|同蓡 sung. A star, second zodiacal constellation, ginseng.

|見叁 san. Three.

叅[10]見參 ts‘en, 946, G.11549. Blend.

29 又

又 yeu°, c. yi°, 1114, G.13428. Again, also.

叉[1] ts‘o, 5, G.186. Interlace the fingers.

叉[2]見爪 °tsau, 34, G.503. Claws.

反 °fan, 126, G.3413. To turn, reverse.

及 jih, c. ji°, 394, G.841. To effect, to come to, and.

叟 meh, 607, G.8015. To dive.

友 °yeu, 1113, G.13429. Friend.

双見雙 saung, 787. A pair.

収見收 sen, 754. To receive.

受[6] °zeu, 756, G. 10016. To receive, to suffer, bear.

叔 sok, 779, G.10039. An uncle.

敒同刷 seh，785，G.10101. To brush，scrub.

取 °ts'ui，1010，G.3118. To take.

叕 tseh. United，obedient.

变見變 pien°，689. To change.

叚[7] ya，183，G.4194. A surname，to borrow.

丨見假 °kya. To borrow.

叛 ben°，652，G.8609. To rebel.

敘 °dzui，°zu，819，G.4766. To converse together.

叟 seu°，729，G.10223. An old man.

叠[11]見疊 deh，892，G.11137. To pile up.

叡[14] soe°，301，G.5729. Wise.

叢[16] dzong，1025，G.12039. Thick，bushy.

30 口

口 °k'eu，331，G.6174. The mouth.

召[2] dzau°，35，G.464. To order，call.

只 °tsz，c. tsuh，tseh，67，G.1863. Only.

丨見隻 tsak. A classifier.

叱 ts'eh°，72，G.1947. To cry out，scold.

叶 yah，195，G.1506. Harmonious sound.

叩 k'eu°，333，G.6175. To strike.

叫 kyau°，c. kau°，371，G.1377. To call.

呑 jeu，417，G.2332. Vapor rising high.

可 °k'o，°k'oo，c. °k'au，425，G.6078. Can.

古 °koo，432，G.6188. Old.

句 kyui°，440，G.2947. A sentence.

丨 keu. To mark，check off.

另 °kwo，466，G.6299. Cut from the bone.

另 ling°，546，G.7240. Furthermore，dwelling.

叭 pah，c. pa，646，G.8505. A sound.

叵 °p'oo，705，G.9433. Ought not.

史 °s，760，G.9893. History.

司 s，835，G.10250. A mechanic.

台又見臺 t'e，de，847，G.10583. Eminent，venerable.

叨 t'au，868，G.10784.
Long for，desire.

叮 ting，904，G.11255.
Command，order.

右 yeu°，1115，G.13436.
At the right hand.

号見號 'au°，'au，173.
Sign.

后3 °'eu，175，G.4027.
Queen.

向 hyang°，190，G.4283.
Toward，formerly.

合 'eh，217，G.3947.
Collect，correspond，unite.

| keh.
A gill.

吁 hyui，228，G.4733.
Sigh，groan.

吰 hong，235，G.5263.
Clamor.

吉 kyih，391，G.909.
Luckily.

吃又見喫 chuh，chih，395，G.873. To eat.

各 kauh，426，G.6026.
Each，every.

吏 li°，522，G.7004.
Magistrate，to rule.

名 ming，600，G.7940.
One's given name.

吊見弔 tiau°，886，G.11058. To condole，pity，a string of cash.

吐 °t'oo，t'oo°，920，G.12100.
To spit.

同 dong，933，G.12269.
Together.

吆 iau，1075，G.12946.
Brawling.

吠 da°.
Used in names.

吐 °z.
Used in names.

吆見吆 iau，1075. The brawling of peddlers.

吓 'a.
Used in names.

呃4 uh，2，G.36.
To hiccough，chirp.

吵 °ts'au，37，G.507.
Noisy.

呈 dzung，79，G.751.
A petition，to reveal.

吹 ts'oe，c. t's，101，G.2825.
To blow，exhale.

吨 °dung，103，G.2846.
Grumbling.

吩 fung，129，G.3508.
Command，order.

吠 vi°，140，G.3499.
To bark as a dog.

否 °feu，c. va°，141，G.3596.
Interrogative.

含 'en，162，G.3818.
Hold in the mouth.

吭 'aung，168，G.3849.
Bird's throat.

吼 heu°, 175, G.4022.
Lowing of cows.

吸 hyih, 203. G.4124.
Inhale, suck in.

呟 ʻong, 237, G.5273.
Sound of bells.

咿 i, yi, 271, G.5336.
Hum of study.

告 kau°, 326, G.5952.
To tell, petition, indict.

呌見叫 kyau°, 371, G.1376.
To call.

君 kyuin, 418, G.3269.
A prince.

吝 ling°, 542, G.7194.
Stingy.

呂 °lui, °li, 559, G.7520.
Musical scale.

吪 ngoo, 627, G.8444.
To move, influence.

吶 neh, c. na, 640, G.8371.
To stutter.

吧 po, 644, G.8511.
To open the mouth.

吞 tʻung, 929, G.12228.
To swallow.

咂 tsah, 939, G.11457.
Suck in as a child, fish.

吮 °tsing, c. °zung, zien, 1012, G.1667. To suck, lick.

吻 °vung, 1042, G. 12657.
Corners of mouth, to speak.

吾 ngoo, 1060, G.12700.
I myself.

吽 iung, c. hong°, 238, G.5288.
Lowing of cows.

吳 woo, c. ng, 1060, G.12748.
To brag, put on airs.

呀 ia, ya, c. ʻa, 1066, G.6.
Final part.

吆 iau, c. au, 1074, G.12902.
Word of assent, yes.

吟 nyung, 1100, G.13258.
To read, intone.

听 yung, 1101, G.13255.
To laugh. Used also for 聽.

吜 °tsʻeu.
To speak.

吱 ts, 55. A particle denoting certainty.

吸 °fan. Noisy, to be ashamed, strong.

吰 kong.
Sound of a multitude.

吤 kya.
One by one, single one.

呆見獃 nge, 619, G.12.
Foolish, stupid.

呔 tʻa°.
Used in names.

吡 °pi.
Used in names.

咋 5 tsuh, 4, G.146.
A loud noise.

周 tseu, 47, G.2450.
To surround.

呪 tseu°, 49.
To swear.

咒見呪 tseu°, 49, G.2476.
To swear.

咐 foo°, 147, G.3667.
To command.

咈 veh, 154, G.3656.
To object.

呷 hyah, c. hah, 185, G.1530.
To drink.

呵 hoo, c. hau, 215, G.3935.
To call.

呼 hoo, 221, G.4912.
To call.

吰 ʻong, 237, G.5283.
Low of cattle.

和 ʻoo, 254, G.3772.
Peace, harmony.

| ʻoo°.
To mix, conciliate.

呭 yi°, 282, G.5524.
Loquacious.

咕 °koo, G.6189.
Used in names.

咎 jeu°, 415, G.2292.
A fault, error.

命 ming°, 601, G.7962.
Command, law, order.

呶 nau, noo, 616, G.8094.
Laugh, scold.

呢 nyi, 630, G.8196.
Sign of question, sound.

咆 bau, 666, G.8734.
The cry of a tiger.

呸 p'e, 671, G.8819.
To draw in the breath.

咇 pih, 692, G.8924.
To talk, pleasant taste.

呻 sung, 736, G.9818.
To sing.

呞 s, 759, G.2016.
To chew the end.

呾 tan, 852, G.10635.
To call to each other, how.

咄 teh, 921, G.11340.
Joking talk.

呰 °ts, 1031, G.12326.
Slander, molest.

呱 koo, 1036, G.6214.
Child's cry.

味 vi°, c. mi°, 1053, G.12607.
Taste, flavor.

咉 iang, 1070, G.12861.
To vomit.

呦 ieu, 1110, G.13394.
The call of deer.

咏 iong°, 1149, G.13505.
To sing.

呚 °i.
Used in names.

咖 ka.
Used in names.

呫 chien°. Pouch of a monkey, to peck.

咙 vah.
Shield.

听 ngoen°. A sound to call attention.

含見含 ʻen. To hold in the mouth.

呯 bing.
Sound of voices.

咏 ping.
Used in Seraphim.

哜見嗜 z°.
To relish(as food).

呥 zen.
It is.

呧 °ti.
Loquacious.

昭 ts'au.
The call of birds.

哎6 e, e°, c. ah, 1, G.33.
Word of surprise.

咤 °ts'o, 6, G.219.
Sputter when angry.

哆 °t's, c. too, 40, G.577.
Open the mouth.

咥 hyi°, 181, G.4159.
Happy, pleased.

咸 yan, 198, G.4498.
All, everywhere.

咻 hyeu, 211, G.4652.
A shriek, clamor.

哈 ha, 218, G.3754.
Drink, laugh heartily.

咺 °hyoen, 231, G.4801.
To grieve.

哄 °hong, 238, G.5251.
Sound of revelry.

咿 i, 271, G.5338.
Giddy laughter.

咳 k'eh, 429, G.3758.
To cough.

| 'e.
Smile of a child.

咾 °lau, 508, G.6785.
And, also.

咧 lih, 531, G.7083.
The call of birds.

咯 lauh, 553, G.6027.
Contend, dispute, so.

| kauh. Cackling of a fowl, to cough, hack.

咪 °mi.
The bleating of sheep.

哀 e, 619, G.11.
Grief, pity.

咢 ngauh, 628, G. 8453. To strike the drum, to startle.

品 °p'ing, 697, G.9273.
Rank, character.

咡 r°, 721, G.3339. The sides, corners of the mouth.

哂 °sung, 738, G.9855.
A smile.

咲見笑 siau°, 795, G.4357.
To laugh.

咷 dau, 870, G.10806.
Prolonged crying.

哉 tse, 940, G.11482. Final particle denoting completed action.

咨 ts, 1028, G.12344.
Plans, calculations.

哇 'wo, 1036, G.12422.
To vomit.

咬 °iau, °yau, c. °ngau, 1077, G.103. To bite.

咽 ien, 1090, G.12981.
The throat.

丨 ien°.
To swallow.

咟 pak.
To open the mouth.

咣 kwaung.
Loquacious.

咦 yi.
Call loudly, used in names.

咦見咄 yi°.
Talkative.

咙 °kwe.
Cunning speech.

咴 hwe.
Sound of a voice.

咹 oeh.
To eat.

咶 oeh, hwe°.
Sound of reviling.

响見響 °hyang, 190.
Noise, sound.

哲7 tseh, 41, G.553.
Wisdom.

哈見含 ʻen, 166, G.3819. To hold in the mouth.

哼 hung, c. hang, 169, G.3332.
To groan.

唏 °hyi, 180. G.4050.
To smile.

哮 hyau, c. hau, 192, G.3867.
Roar, voice of tigers.

唍 °ʻwen, 247, G.5058.
Laugh.

哽 °kung, 322, G.5991.
Clogged throat, to sob.

唧 chih, 379, G.1566.
To capture.

哿 °kʻoo, 423, G.6043.
Excellent, to be able.

哥 koo, 423. G.6045.
Elder brother.

咯 kok, 454, G.6240.
The cluck of a hen.

哭 kʻok, 455, G.6263.
To cry.

哰 lau, 507, G.6807.
Loquacious, therefore.

哩 li°, 518, G.6873.
Surely, so.

唎 li°, 521, G.6887.
Noise, final particle.

哴 liang°, 527, G.6756.
Grief.

唪 baung, 578, G.7661.
Jargon, hubbub.

咩 me, mi, 583, G.7869.
The bleating of sheep.

哪 na, c. nau, 611, G.8091.
Final particle of certainty.

唉 ʻe, 619, G.7.
An interjection.

哦 ngoo, 627, G.3314.
To chant.

唰 pah, 647, G.8508.
Sound of animals.

哺 boo°，714，G.3625. To feed an infant with a spoon.

哱 beh，718，G.9357. A trumpet.

哨 ts‘iau°，c. sau°，747，G.1419. To cry(of guards)，to patrol.

哷 sok，779，G.10032. To inhale，absorb.

唇又見脣 (zung)，tsung，783，G.2870. To startle.

唆 soo，815，G.10197. To indicate.

唐 daung，861，G.10767. Boasting talk.

唔 ngoo，1060，G.12701. To read.

唁 nyien°，1090，G.13026. To condole，mourn.

唈 ih，1096，G.13170. Short breath.

員 yoen，1132，G.13733. Officers.

哫 tsok. To stir up envy.

哷 lih. Sound of fowls.

唊 kyah. Much talk.

唌 yien. Mourn.

唔見否 va°. Interrogative particle.

啄見啄 tsauh，c. zauh. To peck.

唱 8 ts‘aung°，28，G.429. To sing.

啁 tsau，32，G.501. To boast. Also used for 朝.

丨 tau. Talkative.

啄 tsauh，c. zauh，82，G. 2400. To peck.

啜 tseh，83，G.2421. Sipping noise，sob.

唪 °fong，158，G.3576. Loud laughing.

唬 hya，192，G.4240. The voice of a tiger.

啟 °chi，347，G.1110. To explain，begin.

啓 °chi，347，G.1111. To explain，begin.

啌 chang，366，G.1268. Sound of coughing.

啩 kwen，472，G.6343. Response of birds.

唻 le，499，G.6682. Melody of song.

啉 len，502，G.6740. To drink to the full.

唳 li°，523，G.6988. Cry of a heron.

唵 ien°，621，G.49. To hold in the mouth.

唸 ne°，640，G.8379. Final particle of certainty.

啊 ah，oo，644，G.2. Interjection，interrogative particle.

商 saung，739，G.9738. To consult，a merchant.

售 dzeu°，756，G.10020. To sell.

啐 ts'oe°，tsoeh，828，G.10414. Call to.

啖 °dan，853，G.10645. To masticate.

啕 dau，870，G.10822. Verbose.

唾 t'oo°，913，G.11394. Spittle.

啍 t'ung，929，G.12229. To move slowly.

啑 sah，977，G.1574. Sound of ducks eating.

問 vung°，c. mung°，1042，G.12650. To ask，question.

啥 sa°. What.

唻 mung. Indistinct voice.

唯 vi，1052，G.12594. Think，only.

| °'we. To answer.

啞 °ia，c. °au，°o，1066，G.12812. Dumb.

啀 ya，1069，G.12835. Noise of fighting dogs.

啘 ye°，1080，G.12971. Evening twitter of birds.

唫 又見 吟 nyung，1100，G.13259. To intone，to shut.

啰 zeu°. To communicate to.

喽 oo，°'we. Cry of a child.

唷 yok. Light laughter.

唹 yui. Light laughter.

唺 °t'ien. Spit out.

啣 'en. Wrathful talk.

啗 見 歐 °eu. To spit.

啒 hweh，10. Anxious.

啯 見 胡 woo. Lowering the head.

啫 deh. Uncertain talk.

啶 lok. Sound of birds eating.

啵 poo. Used in names.

啦 la°. Used in names.

啡 fah. Used in names.

啡 fi. Used in names.

喆9 見 哲 tseh，41，G.572. Wise.

喘 °ts'en, °ts'oen, 120, G.2733. Short breath, asthma.

喊 han°, 164, G.3831. To call.

喉 'eu, c. 'oo, 174, G.4007. The throat.

喉見喉 'eu, 174. The throat.

喜 °hyi, 180, G.4073. Happy.

啣見銜 'an, 199, G.4552. To hold in the mouth.

喝 hoeh, 216, G.3930. To call out, rebuke.

煦 °hyui, 229, G.4757. Expel breath.

喧 hyoen, 231, G.4806. A hubbub.

喚 hwen°, 248, G.5079. Call, summons.

喤 waung, 251, G.5109. Clamor of children.

喙 hwe°, 266, G.5216. Beak, bill, snout.

喏 °zo, 293, G.3358. Salute with folded hands.

| c. nau, nau°. Lo, behold.

喈 kya, 358, G.1439. Twitter of birds.

喬 jau, 374, G.1395. Exalted, lofty.

喫 chuh, 396, G.1054. To eat.

喀 k'uh, c. k'ak, 429, G.6122. Clear the throat.

喟 k'we°, we°, 488, G.6516. Breathe heavily, moan.

喇 lah, c. la, 498, G.6654. Cracking sound.

喨 liang°, 527, G.6782. Speak clearly.

喃 nen, 615, G.8129. The voice of birds.

喦 nyih, 633, G.8293. To quarrel.

喪 saung, 725, G.9565. To bury, mourn.

| saung°. To lose.

善 °zen, 752, G.9710. Good, virtue.

| zen°.

啻 t's°, 765, G.9996. Only, a surplus.

單 tan, 849, G.9699. Single.

| zen. A district, a famous chief.

啼 di, 883, G.11013. To crow, as a fowl.

喋 dih, 891, G.11118. To chatter.

喞 tsih, 984, G.879. The sound of insects.

嗽 ts'ieu, 998, G.2250.
The voice of a child.

喂 'we, c. iui°, 1054, G.12550.
To feed, care for.

喔 ok, 1064, G.12740.
The sound of a hen.

喓 iau, 1075, G.12891.
The sound of insects.

喭 nyien°, 1090, G.13108.
Course, condole.

喑 iung, 1100, G.13210.
Continuous crying.

喻 yui°, yui, 1129, G.13569.
A parable, to know.

喩見喻 yui°.
A parable.

喁 nyong, 1147, G.13500.
Gasping, as a fish.

噎見咽 iung.
To swallow.

啼見嗁 dz, di, z°.
To cry.

嘝 ieu.
The voice of deer.

噩見齶 hauh, ngauh.
Roof of the mouth.

喠 °tsong.
Unable to speak.

嘩 kuh, c. kak. To separate, pheasant's call.

喦 ts'ih.
Many voices speaking.

嗏10 ts'o, 5, G.209.
A final particle.

嗔 dien, 19, G.644.
To bluster, bully.

| ts'ung.
To get angry.

嗤 t's, 63, G.1951.
To ridicule.

嗐 'e°, 161, G.3769.
Word of surprize.

嗅 hyeu°, c. hong°, 211, G.4685. Pheasant's call.

嗑 keh, 218, G.3960.
Verbose.

嗛 chien°, 389, G.1717.
The pouch of a monkey.

嗎 °mo, 572, G.7578.
To revile, slander.

嗓 °saung, 724, G.9567.
Throat, larynx.

喿 sau°, 727, G.9588.
Twitter of many birds.

嗇 suh, 728, G.9603.
Avaricious, frugal.

嗄 °so, c. au°, 731, G.9645.
A hoarse voice.

嗜 z°, 765, G.9957.
To relish food.

嗍 sauh, 779, G.10098.
To suck in, inhale.

嗉 soo°, 817, G.10350. Crop of a bird, skin on the throat.

嗣 z°, 838, G.10258.
To succeed to, posterity.

嗁 di, 883, G.3996.
To cry.

嗆 ts'iang, c. ts'iang°, 970, G.1256. Bird food.

嗟 tsien, 973, G.1464. Moaning sound.

嗡 ong, 1046, G.12668. Lowing of cattle.

嗚 oo, 1058, G.12723. To lament.

嗌 iuh, 1092, G.13162. To swallow.

嗃 hauh. Loud voice.

嗯見頷 'en. Affirmative response.

嗀 keu°. Pheasant's call.

嗓見噪 tsau°. Chirping of birds.

嗙 pok. The call of hens.

嗶見嘩 kuh. Call of the pheasant.

嘗[11] dzang, c. zaung, 27, G.449. To taste, formerly.

嘑 hoo, 221, G.4914. To howl at.

嘘 hyui, 227, G.4099. To expel the breath.

嘒 hwe°, we°, 265, G.5192. Sound of insects.

嘅 k'e°, 309, G.5803. Alas.

嘉 kya, c. ka, 351, G.1158. Excellent.

嘏 °kya, °koo, 352, G.1166. Great prosperity, strong.

嘎 kyah, c. kah, 357, G.4. Singing of birds.

Used in names.

嘐 hyau, 368, G.4328. Boasting, cackling.

嗷 ngau, 624, G.85. Wail of beggars.

嘔 eu, 626, G.4738. Sound of retching.

| 同歐 °eu. To vomit.

嘌 p'iau, 683, G.9122. Rushing, lawless.

嗶見咇 pih, 692, G.8996. Cease talking.

嗽 seu°, G.10246. Cough.

嗾 °seu, c. °hyo, ts'ok, 729, G.10216. Bite of dogs.

嗦 seh, 774, G.10208. To taste.

嗔 t'en, 856, G.10691. Many voices.

嘆見歎 t'an°, 857, G.10692. A groan, to praise.

嘈 zau, 955, G.11637. To chatter.

嘖 tsuh, 958, G.11660. To bawl, wrangle, praise.

嗊 hong. Much talk.

嚦 li.
Much talk.

嗹 lien.
Used in names.

嗽見嗽 seu°, 729.
To cough, hack.

嘂 kyau°.
A great noise.

嘑同嘑 hoo.
To menace.

嗷 hyau.
To quarrel.

嘖 tseh.
Verbose.

嗔 °ien.
Loud laughing.

嘛 mo.
Used in names.

嘽 °kyien.
A sound of the voice.

嘕 man°.
Used in names.

嘶 kyi.
Used in Seraphim.

嘊 ya.
Dogs quarrelling.

嘲12 tsau, 32, G.479.
Ridicule, jest.

嘬 ts'e°, c. tsoeh, 112, G.2701. To sip, as flies.

嘷 'au, 171, G.3885.
Voice of a tiger.

嘻 hyi, 178, G.4075.
Joyful sound, laughter.

噏 hyih, 203, G.4133.
Inhale.

嘩 hwo, 240, G.5006.
Clamor, noise.

嘵 hyau, 191, G.4312.
Afraid to speak.

噐見器 chi°, 349, G.1124.
A dish, utensil.

嘹 liau, 527. G.7038.
Clear note of birds.

嘪 °me, c. °ma, 574, G.7607.
Bleating of sheep.

嘿同默 muh, 605, G.8020.
Dark, retired, meditation.

噃 fan, 653, G.8627. To trouble others by abusive talk.

嘶 s, 789, G.4100.
Neigh of a horse.

嘯 siau°, 795, G.4317.
A whistling sound.

噀 sung°, 830, G.10442.
To spirt from the mouth.

噉同啖 °dan, 853, G.10649.
To masticate.

嘽 t'an, 854, G.10684.
To pant, snort.

噋 t'ung, dung, c. tung°, 927, G.12204. To gulp down.

噌 tsung, 952, G.11737.
Turmoil, noise.

噈 ts'ok, 1014, G.11854.
To kiss, smack the lips.

嘴 °ts, 1016, G.11905.
The mouth.

噂 °tsung, 1019, G.11947.
Converse together.

噁 oo°, 1063, G.12780.
To be angry, scold.

噎 ih, 1080, G.12980.
A clogging in the throat.

噊 yoeh, 1140, G.13680.
Danger.

噔 ioeh, 1141, G.13692.
A noise in the throat.

嘰 kyi.
Filthy talk.

噣見嚼 tsok, 96.
To order, charge.

嘳 kw'e°.
Groan.

嘸 °foo, c. m.
Response, answer.

嘾 °den.
Hold in the mouth.

噄見喫 chuh.
To stutter, to eat.

噌 ts'ah.
To tell minutely.

噅 hwe.
Untrue talk.

嚁 seh.
Unable to speak.

噍 dziau°.
To chew.

噫 13 i, 271, G.5369.
A groan, to mourn.

器 chi°, 349, G.1123.
An instrument, tool.

噭 kyau°, 371, G.1365.
Sound of crying.

噤 kyung°, 400, G.2036.
Speechless from disease.

噱 jak, juh, 410, G.2227.
Loud laughing.

噲 kw'e°, 471, G.6338.
Happy, to swallow.

嘓 koo, 489, G.6623.
To sing.

嚕 °loo, 557, G.7393.
Sound of calling pigs.

噯 e°, 620, G.17.
Warm breath.

噩 ngauh, auh, 628, G.8465.
To dread, fear.

噥 'nong, 642, G.8410.
To spit out.

噴 p'ung, 656, G.8853.
To overflow.

噪 sau°, 727, G.9589.
Noisy talk.

噬 z°, 759, G.9949.
To bite.

噢 yok, 1126, G.13648.
To cry from pain.

噰 iong, 1145, G.13469.
Sound of birds.

噠 dah, tan.
Used in names.

噡 tsen.
To eat.

嘬 dien°.
Used in names.

嘼 hyoo.
Send out the breath.

嘽 loo°.
Used in names.

嘾 ke.
Used in names.

嗛14 見銜 'an, 199, G.4507.
To hold in the mouth.

嚇 hya°, c. hak, 219, G.3970.
To fear.

嚅 zu, 298, G.5676. Chatter, hesitating speech.

嚀 nyung, 637, G.8330.
To order, charge.

噠 dah, 842, G.10539.
To swallow whole.

嚎 de, 848, G.10579.
Continuous talk.

嚌 tsi°, 965, G.813.
To taste.

嚂 ia°, e°, ke°.
Test by tasting.

嚶 °lui.
Sound of calling dogs.

嚊 bi°, c. hong°. To breathe from the nose.

嚘 nyih.
An understanding child.

嚋 dzeu.
A lie.

嚗 pok.
Gainsay.

嚏15 t'i°, 880, G.10948.
To sneeze.

嚱 tsih, 984, G.973.
The squeak of mice.

嚙 見齩 °iau, c. °ngau, 1080, G.8296. To gnaw.

嚚 nyung, 1101, G.13283.
Foolish talk.

嚛 juh.
Unrestrained laughter.

嚖 hwe°.
The call of insects.

嚗 pok.
Sound of merriment.

嚮16 hyang°, 190, G.4265.
Over against, until now.

嚦 lih, 537, G.6926.
Splitting noise.

嚧 loo, 554, G.7400.
Sound of talking.

嚨 long, 568, G.7481.
The throat.

嚬 bing, 697, G.9250.
To grin, knit the brows.

嚥 ien°, 1090, G.13049.
To swallow.

嚪 見啖 °dan.
To bite, swallow.

嚱 hyui, 227, G.4715.
To breathe softly.

嚭 °p'i.
Name of a person.

囔[17] °zung, 291, G.5566.
To scold, bluster.

嚳 k'ok, 456, G.6268.
A king's name.

讕 lan, 501, G.6711.
Intelligence, talk.

嚲 °too, 552, G.7334.
Hanging down.

嚴 nyien, 1084, G.13088.
Severe, austere, dignified.

嚶 iung, 1105, G.13319.
Sound of birds.

嚺 se°.
Used in names.

嚼[18] ziak, 997, G.1357.
To chew, bite.

囀 °tsen, 118, G.2712.
Sound of birds.

囂 hyau, 191, G.107.
Clamorous talk.

囁 nyih, 632, G.8270.
Hesitating talk.

嚵見饞 dzan, 14, G.325. To sip, to peck at, greedy.

嚾見喚 hwen°.
Calling sound.

囃 iong.
Sound of birds.

囅[19] °tsen, 47, G.353.
Laughing.

囈 nyi°, 283, G.5518.
Laughing, talking in sleep.

囉 loo, 551, G.7293.
Fretful, annoying.

囊 naung, 615, G.8149.
A bag, sack.

囐[20] nyih.
Condemn.

囑[21] tsok, 96, G.2578.
To command, order.

囓同齧 nyih.
To bite.

嚰 moo.
What.

囕[22]同嵌 k'an°. Name of a mountain.

31 囗

囗 we, 1048, G.5162.
Enclosure.

囚[2] dzieu, 811, G.2336.
Imprison, a prison.

四 s°, 836, G.10291.
Four.

囘見回 we, 261.
Return.

回[3] we, 261, G.5163.
Return, a time, once.

囝 noen, 384, G.1686.
Child.

囡 noen°, 633, G.8291.
Female child.

囟 sing°, 808, G.4634.
Shade for the forehead.

因 iung, 1098, G.13215.
Because.

囱[4] ts'aung, c. ts'ong, 115, G.2774. Window.

囬見回 we, 261, G.5164.
Returning.

囫 weh, 267, G.4924.
Whole, not divided.

困 kw'ung°, 496, G.6542.
To sleep.

囤 °dung, 928, G.12213.
Round bin for rice.

囮 ngoo, 'oo, 1111, G.13443.
To decoy, interpret.

囥 k'aung°.
To conceal.

国見國 kok, 491.
A kingdom.

囷 5 °chuin, 420, G.3092.
A spiral bin for rice.

固 koo°, 435, G.6204.
Firm.

囹 ling, 544, G.7201.
A prison.

囿 6 yeu°, 1115, G.13378.
A garden.

圅 7 見函 'en, 163, G.3808.
Envelop.

圂 wung°, 248, G.5245.
A sty, privy.

圃 °poo, 712, G.9458.
Vegetable garden.

圄 ngoo, 1126, G.12702.
A prison.

圈 8 choen, 451, G.3148.
A circle.

| joen°.
A pen for animals.

國 kok, 491, G.6609.
Kingdom.

圇 lung, 565, G.7465.
Whole, not divided.

圉 °nyui, 1126, G.13629.
A horse boy, a stable.

圍 9 we, 1048, G.12529.
To surround, encircle.

圔 10 ih, 1098, G.13201.
Shrill note of a flute.

圓 yoen, 1132, G.13734.
Round, a dollar.

園 yoen, 1133, G.13740.
A public garden.

圖 11 doo, 918, G.12128.
A plan, map, to plot, reckon on.

團 doen, 938, G.12155.
A bunch, collection.

圝見囮 ngoo, 'oo, 1111, G.13444. To interpret.

圛 13 yuh, 1094, G.13178.
To go in a circle.

圜 yoen, wan, qwan, 245, G.5039. Round, go around.

圞 19 loen, 570, G.7451.
Spherical, round.

32 土

土 °t'oo, 920, G.12042.
Earth.

圠 1 tsah, 1069, G.12821.
Dust hardening.

圣[2]見聖 sung°, 773, G.6265. Holy.

圢 °t'ing, 908, G.11272. A path between rice fields.

圯[3] yi, 276, G.5465. A bridge.

圭 kwe, 481, G.6434. A sceptre, measure.

圮 °p'i, 681, G.9085. Destroyed, prostrated.

地 di°, 879, G.10956. Earth, the ground.

在 °dze, 941, G.11481. In, at, on.

圬 oo, 1058, G.12717. To plaster a wall.

圩 yui, 1120, G.13539. Bank of a stream.

圪 nyih, chih. An earth wall.

圴 tsak. An impression in the soil.

址[4] °ts, 56, G.1838. A foundation.

坂 °fan, 127, G.3414. A mountain path.

坋 °vung, 131, G.3509. Dust.

坌 bung°, 131, G.3510. Dust.

坊 faung, 133, G.3437. An alley, hamlet, store.

坹 kyah, 186, G.4248. A pile of rubbish.

坎 °k'en, 315, G.5870. A hole in the earth.

坑 k'aung, c. k'ang, 323, G.6015. A pit, hole.

圻 ji, 346, G.1011. Boundary.

均 kyuin, 418, G.3293. Equalize, all.

坏 p'e, 671, G.8815. A mound, model, mould.

坒 bi°, be°, 677, G.8949. Boundary, to meet.

坍 t'an, 853, G.10697. To collapse, thrown down.

坉 °dung, 927, G.12214. Mound of earth.

坐 zoo°, 1002, G.11756. A seat, to sit.

坄 yoh, 1095, G.13187. The door of a kiln.

圾 kyih, c. si°, seh. Refuse, offal.

坟見墳 vung, 130. Grave, tomb.

坸[5] °keu. Refuse, offal.

坻 dz, 64, G.1976. Embankment, an islet.

垂 dzoe, 102, G.2829. To hang down, pendant, nearly.

坵見邱 cheu, 416, G.2311. A high mound.

坰 kyong, 422, G.2354. A common.

坷 k'oo, 425, G.6079.
Rough, unfortunate.

坤 kw'ung, 495, G.6540.
What is inferior, the earth, a wife.

坴 lok, 562, G.7429.
A clump of earth.

坳 au, 623, G.120.
A depression, undulation.

坭見**泥** nyi, 630, G.8207.
Soil.

坯見**坏** p'e, 671, G.8820.
Mound.

坪 bing, 701, G.9311.
Level ground.

坡 p'oo, 704, G.9408.
The slope of a hill.

坦 °t'an, 856, G.10703.
Level, composed.

坫 tien°, 895, G.11171.
Earthen stand.

坼 ts'uh, ts'ak, 960, G.11693.
Fissure in the earth.

坱 °iang, 1070, G.12862.
Dust.

坢 °p'en.
A plane.

坥 tsui.
A common.

坧 tsuh.
Foundation.

坍見**坍** t'an.
Thrown down.

坲 veh.
Floating dust.

坌見**坋** °vung.
Dust.

坶 mok.
Name fo a place.

坹 yoeh.
Deep pit.

坺 rah.
Name of a place.

坿見**附** voo°.
Near to.

垀 hoo.
Name of a place.

垃 c. leh. At.
c. la. Dirt.

垗[6] dzau°, 35, G.491. Elevated path about a field or grave.

型 yung, 206, G.4620.
A mould, casting, precedent, example.

垓 ke, 306, G.1511.
Boundary.

垢 °keu, 330, G.6163.
Dust.

垝 °kwe, 483, G.6457.
Ready to fall.

垤 dih, 890, G.11134.
A pile of earth.

垛 °too, 910, G.11327.
A buttress.

垜 °too, G.11337.
A buttress.

埌 nyung, 1101, G.13252.
A bank, shore.

堙 iung, 1099, G.13231.
Earthwork, to restrain water.

垣 yoen, 1135, G.13762.
Wall.

垐 t'sº. To heighten a road with earth.

垑 ºt's.
To cultivate.

埱 roh.
Pile up earth.

垙 kwaung.
A field.

垚見**堯** yau.
A pile of earth.

垞 dza.
A small mound.

城7 dzung, 77, G.763.
A walled city.

埕 dzung, 79, G.752.
Earthen jar.

垾 'oenº, 165, G.3797.
A small dam.

垸 wen, 246, G.12458.
Lime and varnish mixed.

埂 kung, 322, G.5992.
A pit.

埌 laungº, 505, G.6757.
A desert, tomb.

埒 lih, 560, G.7094.
A dike, low dike.

埋 me, c. ma, 573, G.7603.
To bury.

埃 e, i, c. ye, 619, G.8.
Dust, particles.

埧 peº, c. poº, 645, G.8532.
A dam.

埔 p'oo, 712, G.9459.
Wharf.

埻 beh, 718, G.9358.
Flying dust.

埏 yien, 1085, G.9667.
A limit, all around.

埇見**甬** ºiong, 1148, G.13452.
A raised walk.

埣 sing.
Black earth.

埌 ' lieuº. A mow (one-sixth of an acre).

堷 me.
Dust.

埾見**序** ºdzui.
Rank.

埀見**垂** dzoe.
To hang down.

埅見**防** baung.
Defend.

埉 kyah.
Excavation of earth.

埁 longº.
Shore, bank.

埐 ts'ing.
Name of a place.

埑見**哲** tseh.
Wise.

埿見**沙** so.
Sand.

埮 de°.
Bank, shore.

埲 pang.
Canal.

埴[8] dzuh, 66, G.2003.
Mud, sticky soil.

執 tseh, 67, G.1795.
To take, grasp.

埶見**藝** nyi°, 283, G.5513.
Skill.

埳見**坎** °k'en, 315, G.5872.
A pit.

埛 kaung, 319, G.5896.
Water kong.

基 kyi, 336, G.850.
Foundation.

堅 kyien, 380, G.1622.
Firm, secure.

堇 jung, 399, G.2042.
Vigilant, adhesive soil.

堁 °k'oo, 425, G.6091.
Dust.

垻又見**壩** jui°, c. po°, 440, G.3020. Fence.

堀見**窟** kw'eh, 455, G.6274.
Cave, hole.

堃見**坤** kw'ung, 495, G.6541.
Thick, what is inferior.

堊 auh, 628, G.8451.
Colored earth.

埿見**泥** nyi, 630, G.8208.
Soil, dirt.

堋 bung°, 659, G.8861.
To bury.

培 be, 672, G.8806.
To add, increase.

埤 bi, 680, G.9076.
Low wet land.

埠見**步** boo°, 713, G.3608.
Wharf, harbor.

埽 °sau, 727, G.9573.
To sweep.

埭 de°, c. da°, 846, G.10560.
A column.

堂 daung, 860, G.10760.
Hall, church.

埵 °too, 910, G.11341.
Firm ground.

堆 te, 924, G.11907.
Pile up.

埜見**野** °ye, c. °ya, 1097, G.13022. Wild.

埸 yuh, 1095, G.5498.
Boundary path.

淤見**淤** iui, 1119, G.13517.
To silt up.

域 yok, 1141, G.13662.
Boundary.

棐 fi.
Dust.

埞見**隄** di.
A bank dike.

塚 ts'ok.
Earth trodden by cattle.

埡 °oo, Mud wall, dry dock (for 塢).

埂見**腆** °t'ien.
Abundant.

埣 se°.
Loose soil.

埦 °'wen.
Earthen bowl.

埨 °lung.
A pit.

埲 °bong.
Flying dust.

埼 ji.
A winding shore, bank.

堄 nyi°.
Wall.

堉 yok.
Fertile soil.

堌 koo°.
Name of a place.

場 9 dzang, 26, G.459.
Place, spot.

塬 dzen°, 118, G. 2722. To plow, turn over the soil.

堠 'eu°, 176, G.4008.
Earthen mound.

堭見隍 waung, 251, G.5110.
City moat.

堪 k'en, 314, G.5854.
Able, fit, worthy.

堦見階 kya, c. ka, 358, G.1441. Stairs.

堷 °en, 621, G.54.
To conceal.

堨 oeh, 629, G.8487.
A hole in a wall.

堡 °pau, 664, G.8712.
Battlement, breastwork.

報 pau°, 665, G.8731. To recompense, messenger, report.

堤見隄 di, 877, G.10914.
A dike, bank.

堞 dih, 890, G.11119.
Battlement, breastwork.

堵 °too, 916, G.12045.
Wall.

塿 °doo, 917, G.12090.
To fill up.

堗 deh, 921, G.12078.
Cooking range.

堲 tsih, 984, G.880.
Quick, fast.

堯 yau, 1076, G.12907.
Elevated, lofty.

堰 ien°, 1090, G.13118.
A dike, a moat.

堙 iung, 1099, G.13232.
Stoneless mountain.

堬 yui, 1124, G.13570.
A grave.

堛 pih.
Narrow.

堣 nyui.
Name of a mountain.

堥 meu.
Small alley.

堒見墾 °k'ung.
To plow.

塍 10 dzung, c. dzang, 79, G.778. A piece of land.

塚 °tsong, 107, G.2898.
Grave.

堚見壎 hyuin, 231, G.4828.
Musical instrument.

塏 °k'e, 309, G.5796.
High, dry land.

塊 k'we°, 471, G.6340.
A piece, slice.

塞 suh, 728, G.9541.
To stop up.

塰 se°.
A boundary.

塒 z, 759, G.9922.
Hen house.

塐 soo°, 817, G.10351.
Mould in clay.

塑見塐 soo°, 817, G.10364.
To mould in clay.

塌 t'ah, 843, G.10512.
A land slide.

塔 t'ah, 843, G.10525.
Pagoda, tower.

塘 daung, 861, G.10769.
Dyke, dam.

塡 dien, 898, G.11182.
To fill.

塗 doo, 918, G.12053.
Road, soil.

墾見垦 °k'ung, 927, G.12226.
To plow.

塟見葬 tsaung°, 949, G.11579.
To bury.

塢 °oo, oo, 1061, G.12724.
A dry dock.

塋 yung, 1107, G.13298.
Cemetery.

堳 sih.
Fine dust.

墀見墀 dz.
A porch.

塛 lih.
To stop up.

塚見塳 bong.
Dust.

塠 c. te. To fall.
c. teh. To throw.

塡見塡 dien.
To fill.

塵[11] dzung, 20, G.661.
Dust.

墇 tsang, 25, G.392.
A dike, drain.

塲見場 dzang, 26, G.460.
A place.

墀 dz, 64, G.1987.
A porch, court.

墌 tsak, 69, G.1913.
Foundation.

堅 i, 27, i, G.5377.
Dust.

墈 °k'en, 316, G.5859.
A cliff, ledge, bank.

墍 kyi°, 339, G.950.
Rest, stop.

墐見堇 jung°, 399, G.2046.
To daub.

境 °kyung, 405, G.2167.
Boundary, border, region.

塿 °leu, leu, 514, G.7388.
Small mound.

墁 men°, 576, G.7628.
To plaster (as a wall).

墓 moo°, 606, G.8060.
A tomb.

塳 bong, 661, G.8900.
Dust.

墅 °zu, 777, G.10046. Temporary house, a field shed.

塾 zok, 780, G.10050.
Anteroom, study, school.

墖見**塔** t'ah, 843, G.10528.
A tower.

墊 tien°, c. dien°, 896, G.11203. To sink, a cushion.

塹 ts'ien°, 983, G.1764.
A pit, gutter.

墄 ts'ih, 987, G.1019.
Embrasures.

墉 yong, 1148, G.13464.
Small city.

塷見**鹵** °loo.
Saltish land.

塸 °eu.
Earth, mounds, graves.

塼 doen.
Round.

|見**甎** tsen.
Brick.

塽 °saung.
High land.

⿰土張 tsang°.
To pile up soil.

⿸虍土見**罅** hya°.
A seam.

塿 loo.
A straw basket.

墎 kwauh.
A grave, tomb.

墜12 dzoe°, 101, G. 2818. Extravagant, to fall into ruin.

墦 van, 124, G.3384.
A cemetery.

墳 vung, 130, G.3536.
Grave.

⿰土壹 i°, 282, G.5346.
Dust.

墝 chau, 373, G.1391.
Poor soil.

墟 hyui, 443, G.3098.
Site of ancient city.

⿰土尞 liau°, liau, 530, G.7039.
Circular wall.

墨 muh, 604, G.7740.
Ink, block.

墠 °zen, 753, G.9700.
Undulating land.

墡 °zen, 753, G.9712.
White soil.

墰 den, 855, G.10673.
Name of a place.

墮 °doo, 910, G.11335.
To fall down.

墩 tung, 927, G.12205.
Mound.

墪見**墩** dung, 927.
An earth mound.

增 tsung, 951, G.11718.
To pile up, add.

塯 lieu°.
Earthenware.

𡒊 見 圻 ji.
Border.

壆 13 yak, 210, G.4639.
Firm soil.

𡓽 gwan, 246, G.5040.
Earth wall.

𡒪 見 坎 °k'en, 315, G.5880.
A hole in the earth.

墾 °k'ung, 318, G.5987.
To dig the soil.

壁 pih, 691, G.8956.
Thin wall.

𡒈 見 隧 dzoe°, 828, G.10403.
A tunnel.

壇 dan, 854, G.10705.
Altar.

墻 ziang, 969, G.1284.
A wall.

壅 iong°, °iong, 1148, G.13470.
To stop up, prevent.

墿 yuh.
Carriage road.

壀 見 埤 bi.
Low wet land.

壃 見 彊 kyang.
Ginger.

壂 dien°.
Foundation.

𡓞 14 dzeh, zeh, 73, G.2014.
Low land.

壕 'au, ngau, 171, G.3876.
City moat.

壑 hauh, 219, G.3957.
A ditch.

壎 hyuin, 231, G.4830.
A wind instrument.

壐 見 璽 °si, °sui, 790, G.4144.
Emperor's seal.

壔 °tau, 866, G.10794.
A wall of earth.

壓 iah, c. ah, k'ah, 1069, G.12828. To press, oppress.

壗 c. han.
Place.

壙 15 °kw'aung, 480, G.6413.
A vault for the dead.

壘 °le, 511, G.6833.
To pile up, a fort.

壞 16 we°, c. wa°, 244, G.5031.
Ruined.

壚 loo, 554, G.7401.
Black clods of earth.

壟 °long, 568, G.7482.
A grave, to monopolize.

壠 見 壟 °long, 568.
A grave.

壜 den, 855, G.10701.
A piece.

壝 °we, we°, 1051, G.12615.
An altar.

壤 17 °zang, 291, G.5567.
Border, boundary.

壩 21 po°, 645, G.8534.
A dam.

33 士

士 °z，762，G.9992.
A scholar.

壬1 nyung，287，G.5610.
Great，full.

壯4 tsaung°，114，G.2757.
Robust，stout.

壳 k'auh，412，G.2245.
Husk，shield.

声見**聲** sung，c. sang，771.
Sound，voice.

殼5見**壳** k'auh. Shield，a hard covering.

壷8同**壺** 'oo.
A pot，a jug.

壺9 'oo，223，G.4954.
A pot，a jug.

壻 sui°，c. si°，790，G.4158.
Son-in-law.

壹 ih，1096，G.5345.
One，all.

壼10 k'wung°，495，G.6551.
Female quarters，room.

壽11 zeu°，757，G.10019.
Longevity，age.

壽見**壽** zeu°.
Longevity.

34 夂

夂 °ts，56，G.1924. A primitive，denoting progressing.

夆4 vong，156，G.3563.
Push，butt（as cows）.

35 夊

夊 se，826，G.10428.
Walking slowly.

夋4 dzing，1001，G.3309.
To go mincingly.

夏7 ya°，'au°，183，G.4227.
Summer.

夐11 °kyong，214，G.4703.
Pre-eminent.

夔20 gwe，488，G.6507.
Name of an officer.

36 夕

夕 dzih，804，G.4110.
Evening.

外2 we°，c. nga°，1037，G.12442.
Outside，beyond，foreign.

夘見**外** we°，c. nga°.
Outside.

夙3 sok，822，G.4747.
Early dawn.

多 too，c. ta，909，G.11302.
Many，much.

夜5 ye°，c. ya°，1080，G.12970.
Night.

够8 keu°，331，G.6150.
Enough，sufficient.

夠見**够** keu°.
Enough.

夢10見**夢** mong°，c. maung°.
Dream.

夢11 mong°， c. maung°， 610， G.7779. A dream，to dream.

夢 見 夢 mong°, c. maung°, 610, G.7780. Dream.

夤 yung, 1101, G.13250. To respect.

夥 °hoo, 255, G.3967. A partner, a classifier of bands of men.

37 大

大 da°, c. doo°, 839, G.2688. Great, much, noble, full grown.

夫 1 foo, 142, G.3612. Husband, scholar, laborer.

丨 voo. Initial particle, now, then, as, to, therefore.

夬 kwe°, 470, G.6327. Divided, certain.

太 t'e°, c. t'a°, 848, G.10573. Too, very.

天 t'ien, 897, G.11208. Heaven.

夭 iau, 1074, G.12901. Fair.

丨 °iau. Premature death.

夯 2 haung, 168, G.3866. The asthma, to pant.

失 seh, 769, G.9951. To loose.

夲 °pung, 869, G.10836. Origin(wrongly used for 本).

央 iang, 1070, G.12860. In the center.

夷 3 yi, 276, G.5397. Barbarian, to destroy, equalize.

夸 kw'o, 468, G.6316. Bragging.

夾 kyah, c. kah, 356, G.1132. To squeeze, doubled, lining.

奉 5 vong°, 159, G. 3574. To offer, receiving, to serve.

奇 ji, 344, G.798. Wonderful.

奈 ne°, 613, G. 8121. How, what, resource, to meet, occur.

奄 °ien, 1088, G.13052. To cover, furthermore.

奐 6 hwen°, 248, G.5078. Great.

契 chi°, 349, G.1053. Land deed, document.

丨 chih. A statesman.

丨 sih. To sunder, separate.

奎 kw'e, 487, G.6502. The 15th constellation, regarded as auspicious to students.

奔 pung, 655, G.8838. To flee.

奏 tseu°, 962, G.11813. To report to the throne.

奕 yuh, 1093, G.5396. Great.

奘 7 tsaung°, 113, G.2758. Large, powerful, robust.

奚 yi，178，G.4063.
Why，a slave.

套 t'au°，871，G.10839. To wrap，clothe，snare，a classifier of suits.

奋 °pung.
A dish for dust and dirt.

奣[8] °hwaung.
Dawning light.

奡[9] ngau°，625，G.123.
Haughty，a name.

奢 se，747，G.9782.
Extensive，glory.

奠 dien°，896，G.11205.
To offer libations.

奣 °'mung，1107，G.13346.
Flourishing and clear opening year.

𦈢見缺 choeh.
Lack，want.

㚾見報 pau°. To report，recompense.

奥[10] au°，625，G.109. Retired，deep，mysterious.

奩[11] lien，533，G.7137.
A lady's toilet-box.

奪 doeh，913，G.11320.
To snatch，take，serve.

奬 °tsiang，968，G.1214. To exhort，praise，to command.

獘[12]見弊 bi°，676，G.8971. To fall down suddenly.

奭 suh，769，G.10003.
To flourish，a name.

奮[13] fung°，132，G.3549.
Spirited，arouse.

奯 hwah.
Rafters of a house.

奰[15] bi°，678，G.9010.
Robust，great.

38 女

女 °nyui，641，G.8419.
A woman.

丨 nyui°.
To give in marriage.

丨見汝 °zu.
You.

奶[2]見嬭 °ne，c. °na，613，G.8114. Milk.

奴 noo°，640，G.8387.
Servant，slave.

奵 ting.
Fair-faced girl.

奼[3] °ts'o，6，G.216.
Fair girl.

妁 tsak，81，G.10166.
A mediator，go-between.

妃 fi，137，G.3482.
Royal concubine.

好 °hau，171，G.3889.
Good.

丨 hau°.
To love.

如 zu，297，G.5668.
Like，as，similar.

奸 kyan, c. kan, 381, G.1628. Crafty.

妄 vaung°, c. maung°, 1045, G.12503. False, reckless.

奷 'ong. Name of a girl.

妝[4] tsaung, 113, G.2755. Adorn.

妨 faung, 133, G.3438. To hinder, harm.

妦 fong, 156, G.3562. Slender girl.

妊 zung°, 287, G.5611. Pregnant.

妓 ji°, 341, G.862. A prostitute.

妞 °hau, 638, G.8348. A lass.

妗 kyung°, 401, G.2028. Wife's sister.

妙 miau°, 592, G.7857. Good, rare.

妠 neh, 612, G.8099. To take a wife, to get.

妣 °pi, 674, G.8943. Name of deceased mother.

妥 °t'oo, 912, G.11344. Repose, peaceful, safe.

妒 too°, 917, G.12083. Jealousy.

妖 iau, 1074, G.12903. Phantom, entice.

妤 yui, 1120, G.13673. Female official.

妜 kyoeh, 1131, G.13803. Fine looking.

姸見妍 nyien, 1085. Beautiful, elegant.

妔 k'ang. A beautiful girl.

妯[5] dzok, jok, 96, G.2464. Younger brother's wife.

姁 hyui, 229, G.4755. Beautiful woman.

姑 koo, 432, G.6209. Unmarried lady, a nun, for the time being.

妹 me°, 586, G.7730. Sister.

妺 meh, 604, G.8000. Wife of 桀.

姆 °moo, c. °m, 606, G.8068. Mrs, a female teacher, governess.

妳見嬭 °ne, c. °na, 613, G.8118. Nipples, to nurse.

妮 nyi, 630, G.8198. Maid servant.

姍 san, 733, G.9695. Fine, good, to ridicule.

始 °sz, 761, G.9982. Beginning.

妬見妒 °too, 917, G.12084. Jealous.

妻 ts'i, 966, G.981. Wife.

| ts'i°.
To give in marriage.

姐 °tsi, c. °tsia, 973, G.1435.
Virgin.

妾 ts'ih, 977, G.1572.
Concubine.

姊 °tsi, c. °ts, 1031, G.12359.
Elder sister.

姉 °tsi, 1031, G.12364.
Elder sister.

委 °'we, 1051, G.12557. To entrust, delegate, responsibility.

姓 sing°, 810, G.4599.
Surname.

姒 °z, 837, G.10290.
Wife.

妲 tah, 840, G.10490.
Name of ancient queen.

妼 °iau.
A beautiful woman.

姈 ling.
Intelligent woman.

妠見妞 °zen.
Actress.

姘 bing.
Concubine.

姎 iang.
Appellation of humility.

姙見孕 yung°.
Pregnant.

要 kyi. Men committing incest with men.

姹[6]見奼 °ts'o, 6, G.220.
Handsome lady.

姪 dzeh, 68, G.1819.
Brother's child.

姝 chui, 92, G.2625.
Handsome virgin.

姮 'ung, 170, G.3918.
Handsome woman.

姨 yi, 277, G.5399.
Wife's sister.

姙見妊 zung°, 287, G.5616.
Pregnant.

姸 nyien, G.13099.
Beautiful.

姤 keu°, 330, G.6164.
To unite.

姬 kyi, 336, G.876.
Name.

姜 kyang, 362, G.1233.
Name.

姣 kyau, 369, G.1300.
Good, beautiful.

姦 kyan, c. kan, 381, G.1647.
Fornication.

姞 kyih, 392, G.912.
Concubine.

姱 k'wo, 468, G.6318.
Beautiful woman.

姥見姆 °moo, c. °m, 606, G.6786. School-mistress.

娀 song, 831, G.10465.
Name.

姿 ts，1028，G.12339. Countenance，expression.

娃 'wo，1036，G.12423.
A lady's beautiful hair.

威 'we，1046，G.12582.
Severe，stern.

姚 yau，1076，G.12935.
Name，handsome lady.

姻 iung，1098，G.13216.
Relatives，kindred.

姘見嬪 ping. Female accomplishments.

娟見娟 kyoen.
Handsome.

姽 °kwe.
Sedate，proper.

娱 °too.
Beautiful.

娙[7] kyung，207，G.4628.
Tall and beautiful.

娟 kyoen，449，G.3127.
Beautiful，comely.

娌 °li，518，G.6874. Sister-in-law，brother's wife.

娥 ngoo，627，G.3315.
Beautiful woman.

娘 nyang，631，G.8241.
A girl，young lady，mother.

娜 noo，639，G.8363.
Beautiful，fair.

娉 p'ing°，701，G.9325.
Handsome.

娠 sung，tsung°，736，G.638.
To be pregnant.

娑 soo，814，G.10195.
To dance，to be at ease.

娣 di°，880，G.10951.
Younger sister.

娩 °'wan，1039，G.7901.
Agreeable，to bring forth.

娓 °vi，1051，G.12602.
Attentive to，handsome.

娛 nyui，1122，G.13606.
Happy.

娒見姆 °moo，c. °m.
A governess，matron.

妝見妝 tsaung.
To adorn.

娬見嫵 °voo.
To please，to flatter.

娼[8] ts'ang，c. ts'aung，26，G.431. A prostitute.

婦 voo°，149，G.3592.
Married lady.

婚 hwung，268，G.5223.
A relative，to marry.

婪 len，502，G.6742.
To covet.

婁 leu，513，G.7335.
To trail along，frequent.

姘 p'ung，c. p'ing，661，G.8908. Illicit intercourse.

婢 bi°，675，G.8761.
Maid servant，mean，base.

婊 °piau，682，G.9116.
A prostitute.

婆 boo，704，G.9412. Grandmother，a dame，motherly.

婕 tsih, 976, G.1484.
A female official.

娶 ts'ui°, 1011, G.3119.
To take a wife.

婭 ia°, 1068, G.12813.
Brother-in-law.

婣見姻 iung, 1098, G.13241.
A bride, female relatives.

婉 °'wen, 1136, G.13721.
Yielding, docile, winning.

婬見淫 yung, 1101, G.13243.
Fornication.

媧[9] oo, 466, G.6302.
The woman who repaired heaven and invented the organ.

媢 mau°, 582, G.7700.
To be jealous.

媒 me, 585, G.7723.
Go-between.

媚 me°, 586, G.7715.
To follow, to keep near.

婿見壻 si°, sui°, 790, G.4706.
Son-in-law.

媟 sih, 798, G.4415.
To insult females, outrage.

婷 ding, 908, G.11278.
Beautiful looking.

婺 voo°, 1062, G.12788.
A star in Capricorn.

媮 yui, 1123, G.13571.
Wasteful, pleasure seeking.

媛 yoen°, 1135, G.13754.
A beauty, winning.

婚見婚 hwung.
A wife.

媗 hyoen.
Name of a woman.

媸[10] ts, 63, G.1952.
Ill-looking woman.

嫌 yien, ien, 197, G.4471.
Suspect, dislike, slight.

媾 keu°, 330, G.6152. A second marriage, affection.

嫁 kya°, c. ka°, 354, G.1141.
To marry a husband.

媿見愧 gwe°, 484, G.6431.
Ashamed.

媽 °mo, c. 'ma, 572, G.7579.
Mother, matron.

嫋 °'nyau, 632, G.8249.
Graceful.

媲 bi°, 680, G.9063.
Equal, matched.

嫂 °sau, 726, G.9583.
Sister-in-law.

媳 sih, c. sing, 804, G.4035.
Daughter-in-law.

嫉 dzih, 984, G.919.
To envy, hate.

媼 °au, 1042, G.119.
Elderly lady.

媱 yau, 1075, G.12913. Handsome, to play and please.

媵 yung°, 1104, G.13280.
Bride's attendants.

嫈 iung, 1109, G.13299.
Good style in a woman.

嫄 yoen，1133，G.13702. Concubine of a sovereign.

嫪[11] lau°，509，G.6800. Lustful，envious.

嫠 li，516，G.6935. A widow.

嫚 man°，576，G.7629. To despise，reproach.

嫩 nung°，642，G.8138. Tender，soft.

嫖 biau，piau，683，G.9123. Trifling，lewd.

嫦 見 姮 ʻung，c. dzang，740，G.441. Goddess in the moon.

嫡 tih，901，G.10920. The proper wife.

嫣 ien，1083，G.13044. Smiling countenance.

嫗 iui°，1127，G.12795. Elderly woman.

嬉[12] hyi，178，G.4076. To play，sport.

嫺 yien，198，G.4489. Quiet，refined，polished.

嬌 kyau，368，G.1334. Tender，delicate.

嬀 kwe，482，G.6418. Water，place，name.

嫽 liau，528，G.7040. To trifle，dally，pretty.

嬋 zen，751，G.346. Beautiful woman.

嫵 °voo，1062，G.12754. To flatter，to win the affections.

嫻 見 嫺 yien. Quiet.

嬖[13] pi°，675，G.8957. Depraved，mean-minded.

嬗 見 襢 zen，751，G.374. Beautiful and graceful.

嬙 ziang，969，G.1285. Good looking，name.

嬴 yung，1107，G.13328. Surname，a place.

嬝 見 嫋 °ʼnyau. Graceful in movement.

嬭[14] °ne，c. °na，613，G.8126. Elderly woman.

嬲 °nyau，c. gah，632，G.8169. To play with women.

嬪 ping，697，G.9235. King's concubine，servant girl.

嬰 iung，1105，G.13318. A young child.

嬸[15] °sung，738，G.9852. An aunt.

嬢[16] 見 嫋 °ʼnyau，632，G.8256. Graceful，slender.

嬾 見 懶 °lan. Lazy，indolent.

孃[17] 見 娘 nyang，631，G.8242. A mother.

孅 sien，800，G.4475. Slender woman.

孀 saung，787，G.10121. A widow.

孌19 °len, lien°, loen°, 561, G.7558. Fair countenance.

[illegible] chang, 354, G.1197. Pretty.

39 子

子 °ts, 1030, G.12317. Child, one, you.

孑 kyih, 377, G.1505. Alone, orphan-like.

孔1 °k‘ong, 465, G.6605. Face, a hole, excellent, Confucius, through, by.

孕2 yung°, iung°, yuin°, 1104, G.5629. To be pregnant.

存3 dzung, 1020, G.11972. To maintain, continue.

孖 ts, 1030, G.12319. Twin children.

字 z°, 1032, G.12324. A character, to protect, love.

孚4 foo, 142, G.3643. Agreeing, the same as.

孝 hyau°, c. hau°, 193, G.4334. To reverence, respect.

孛 beh, 718, G.9356. A star, to grow, as grass.

孜 ts, 1029, G.12321. Diligent.

斈見學 yak, c. ‘auh, 209. To learn, learning.

季5 kyi°, 339, G.944. A season, the last of a series.

孤 koo, 431, G.6222. Orphan, alone.

孟 mung°, c. mang°, 580, G.7795. The first of a class.

孥 noo, 641, G.8391. Descendant.

孩6 ‘e, 160, G.3759. Child, male child.

孫7 sung, 829, G.10431. Descendants.

孬 hwa°, c. cheu, 1037, G.12444. Bad, defective.

孰8 zok, 780, G.10049. Who, what.

孱9 dzan, 119, G.2736. Weak, timid.

㝅10 keu°, 618, G.8386. To suckle, give milk.

孳 ts, 1029, G.12348. To produce, affectionate.

學13 yak, c. ‘auh, 209, G.4338. To learn, learned.

孺14 zu, 298, G.5678. A weaned child.

孼16 nyih, 1081, G.13010. Sin, a concubine’s son.

孽17 同孼 nyih, 1081, G.8282. See above.

孿19 loen, 570, G.7452. Twin children.

40 宀

宀 mien, 594, G.7907. A roof, a cover.

宁[2] °zu，91，G.2602.
Space behind the throne.

宂 °nyong，304，G.5764.
Duties，affairs，gypsy-like.

宄 °kwe，483，G.6449.
A traitor.

它見他 t'a，911，G.11345.
That，another，to change.

宊[3] kyeu°，416，G.2274.
Poor，diseased.

安 oen，620，G.44. To rest，quiet，to place，how?

守 °seu，755，G.10012.
To receive.

宅 dzuh，c. dzak，959，G.240.
Dwelling，residence.

宇 °iui，1126，G.13540.
House，canopy of heaven.

宏[4] 'ong，237，G.5275.
Great，large.

宋 song°，831，G.10462.
Name，to dwell.

完 wen，246，G.5057
Finished，perfect，wholly.

宙[5] dzeu°，49，G.2465.
All ages，canopy.

宜 nyi，273，G.5353.
Ought，adapted，suitable.

官 kwen，472，G.6341.
To rule，govern.

宓 mih，596，G.3724.
Quiet，tired.

宕 daung°，c. dang°，859，G.10741. To let down，cave.

定 ding°，905，G.11248.
Certain，fixed.

宗 tsong，1021，G.11976.
Ancestor，example.

宛 °'wen，1136，G.12465.
Similar，to yield，same as.

宝見寶 °pau，663.
Precious.

宧[6] wan°，248，G.5085.
Official，eunuch.

客 k'uh，c. k'ak，429，G.6121.
Friend，visitor.

室 suh，770，G.9974.
House，wife，kindred.

宣 sien，820，G.4805.
Promulgate.

宥 yeu°，1115，G.13380.
To forbear，forgive.

宸[7] zung，21，G.653.
King's palace.

害 'e°，161，G.3768.
To hate，harm.

家 kya，c. ka，351，G.1139.
Family，household.

宮 Kong，462，G.6580.
A mansion，palace.

宵 siau，794，G.4296.
In the night，few.

宰 °tse，941，G.11490.
To rule，a ruler，to kill.

宴 ien°，1090，G.13125.
Evening，late，happy.

容 yong, 1146, G.5754. Appearance, easy, to allow.

寄[8] kyi°, 339, G.803.
To send.

寇 k'eu°, 332, G.6180.
Thieves, tyrannical.

寇見寇 k'eu°.
Thieves, tyrannical.

密 mih, 596, G.7835.
Retired, close, compact.

密見密 mih, 596, G.7832.
See above.

寍見寧 nyung, 637, G.8328.
Quiet, at rest.

宿 sok, 823, G.4671.
Dwelling, old.

| sieu°.
A star, a night.

宿見宿 sok.
Dwelling, old.

| sieu°.
A star, a night.

寀 °ts'e, 944, G.11507.
Fellow-officers.

寁 °tsan, 945, G.11545.
Promptly, quickly.

寂 dzih, 985, G.931.
Retired, quiet.

寅 yung, 1100, G.13246. 3—5 a.m. To reverence, officer.

冤同冤 ioen, 1132, G.13729.
Enemy, to oppress.

富[9] foo°, 148, G.3711.
Rich, abundant.

寒 'oen, 163, G.3825.
Cold, fear.

寐 me°, 587, G.7739.
To sleep.

寍見寧 nyung, 637, G.8326.
Quiet, peaceful.

寔見實 zeh, 769, G.9942.
Solid, really, true, sincere.

寓 nyui°, 1128, G.13557.
Inn.

寘[10] ts°, 60, G.1853.
To place.

寖見浸 tsing, 989, G.2079.
Increasingly, name.

察[11] ts'ah, 9, G.200.
To examine.

寨 ze°, c. za°, 10, G.247.
A military station.

| suh.
Peaceful.

寡 °kwo, 467, G.6306.
Few, solitary, friendless.

寥 liau, 528, G.7063.
Idle, vacant.

寞 mok, 603, G.7981.
Alone, desolate.

寧 nyung, 637, G.8190.
Quiet, at rest.

實 zeh, 769, G.9947. Truly, indeed, fruit, firm, hard.

寢 °ts'ing, 991, G.2091.
To sleep, bed room.

寤 ngoo°, 1063, G.12713.
To awake.

寬[12] kw'en, 477, G.6382.
Broad, to be liberal with.

寮 liau, 527, G.7041. A hut, shanty, fellow-student.

審 °sung, 738, G.9851.
To examine, judge.

寫 °sie, c. °sia, 796, G.4404.
To write.

寰[13] gwan, 245, G.5041.
Rotunda, emperor's domains.

寵[16] ts'ong, 110, G.2934.
Mercy, grace.

寳 見 **寶** °pau, 663.
Precious.

寶[17] °pau, G.8720.
Precious.

41 寸

寸 ts'ung°, 1021, G.11965.
Inch.

对[2] 見 **對** te°, 924. To pair, a pair, opposite to.

寺[3] z°. 837, G.9914.
Temple, hall or court.

封[6] fong, 157, G.3582. Appoint to office, seal, canonize.

尅[7] 同 **剋** k'uh, 430, G.6117.
To deny one's self, to repress.

射 ze°, 749, G.5538.
To issue forth as light.

丨 zuh, c. zauh. To shoot.
yuh. To dislike.

專[8] tsen, 116, G.2702. One, specially, one purpose.

將 tsiang, 967, G.1212.
About to be.

丨 tsiang°.
An official, general.

尉 we°, 1055, G.12621.
To harmonize.

丨 iok.
Military official.

尋[9] zing, 807, G.4581.
Seek, commonly, briefly.

尊 tsung, 1019, G.11945.
Eminent, noble, you.

對[11] te°, 924, G.12165.
Agreeing, opposite, a pair.

丨 eh, c. t'eh.
To.

導[13] dau°, 867, G.10781.
To lead, exhort.

42 小

小 °siau, 795, G.4294.
Small.

少[1] °sau, 746, G.9746.
Few.

丨 sau°.
Young.

尔[2] 見 **爾** °r, 720, G.3361.
You.

尒 見 **爾** °r, 720, G.3360.
You.

尖[3] tsien, 977, G.1627.
Pointed, sharp.

尗見叔菽 sok.
Uncle.

尚[5] zang°, c. zaung°, 741, G.9733. Still, yet, besides.

尟[10] °sien, 801, G.4557.
Few, rare, seldom.

尠見尟 °sien, 801, G.4558.
Few, seldom.

43 尢

尢 'waung, 1043, G.12519.
Weak, crooked in the leg.

尤[1] yeu, 1110, G.13413.
More than, hatred, blame.

尨[4] maung, baung, 578, G.7659.
Shaggy dog, mixed.

尬 kya°, c. ka°, 361, G.1520.
Going wrong, nonplussed.

尪 'waung, 1043, G.12494.
Feeble, weak, crooked.

就[9] dzieu°, c. zieu°, 999, G.2283.
To complete, to come to, immediately, then, thereupon.

尰 °tsong, 107, G.2882.
To swell, as the legs.

尷[14] kan, 383, G.1641.
Going wrong, nonplussed.

44 尸

尸 s, 757, G.9898. Effigy of an ancestor, a corpse, master.

尺[1] ts'uh, c. ts'ak, 71, G.1992.
A foot of 10 inches.

尹 °iung, 1102, G.13270.
To rule, a director.

尻[2] k'au, 327, G.5961.
End bone, rump.

尼 nyi, 630, G.8194.
Nun, name of Confucius.

尼 nyuh.
Near.

尽[3]見盡 °dzing, 989.
Extreme, limit.

局[4] jok, 456, G.2955. A club, office, aspect, affair.

尿 nyau°, c. s, 632, G.8253.
Urine.

屁 p'i°, 681, G.9046.
To part, break wind.

尾 °vi, c. °nyi, 1051, G.5473.
Tail, to follow.

屆[5] kya°, c. ka°, 361, G.1539.
To arrive at a time or a place, period.

届見屆 kya°, c. ka°, 361, G.1538. To arrive at a time or place, a period.

居 kyui, 437, G.2987.
Dwell, a home.

屋見居 kyui, 437, G.2986.
To dwell.

屈 choeh, 458, G.3078.
Bent, stooped, afflicted.

屄 pi, 679, G.9011.
The vulva, vagina.

屜 t'i°, 884, G.11029.
A pad, a buffer.

屍[6] s, 757, G.9902.
A carcase, corpse.

屎 °s, c. oo°, 760, G.9900.
Filth, secretion.

屋 ok, 1064. G.12737.
House, house top.

展[7] °tsen, 44, G.293.
To open.

屐 jih, c. juh, 392, G.864.
Wooden clogs.

屑 sih, 798, G.4369.
Fragments, crumbs, clean.

屏[8] bing, 702, G.9291.
A screen.

丨 °ping.
To expell, reject.

屠[9] doo, 918, G.12129.
To kill, butcher.

属見屬 zoh, 780.
Relating to.

屢[11] 'lui°, 559, G.3037.
Continuous, often.

屣 °si, 789, G.4120.
A shoe.

履[12] °li, °lui, 520, G.6952.
To walk, a shoe.

層 dzung, zung, 952, G.11738. A story, layer.

屧[13] sih, 798, G.4417.
The filling in shoe soles.

屨[14] kyui°, 442, G.3039.
Shoes of leather.

屩[15] kyak, 411, G.1345. Wooden and hemp shoes or clogs.

屬[18] zok, 780, G.10061. Belonging to, subject to, a rank.

丨 tsok.
Attached to, entrust to.

45 屮

屮 ts'eh, 42, G.584.
Sprouting, budding.

屯[1] dung, 929, G.2845.
Difficult, a resident camp.

46 山

山 san, 733, G.9663.
Mountain.

屺[3] °chi, 347, G.1071.
Sterile mountain.

屼 ngeh, 1065, G.12783.
A bare hill.

屹 nyih, 1096, G.13160.
Imposing mountain.

岔[4] ts'o°, 7, G.212.
Diverging, forked road.

岑 dzung, 21, G.11708.
A peak.

岐 ji, 345, G.1103. Hill with two peaks, headland.

岌 kyih, 394, G.843.
A lofty peak, hazardous.

岵[5] °'oo, 226, G.4968.
A verdant mountain.

岡 kaung, 318, G.5894.
A peak, a summit.

岷 ming, 597, G.7910.
A mountain in the west.

岸 ‘oen°, c. ngoen°.622, G.63.
Shore, bank.

岫 zieu°, 812, G.4682.
A cave.

岱 de°, 845, G.10548.
A mountain in Shantung.

岨 tsui, 1009, G.2973.
Rocky slope.

岩見巖 ngen, 1084, G.13095.
A precipice.

岳同嶽 ngauh, 1118, G.12909.
A high mountain.

峙 6 °z, 58, G.1900.
Lofty mountain.

峕 chang. A hanging (used wrongly for 峕 and 時).

峒 dong, 933, G.12271.
Up and down, as a defile.

峯 7 fong, 156, G.3564.
Mountain peak.

峰見峯 fong.
Mountain peak.

峽 yah, c. kyah, 185, G.4218.
Chasm, gorge, stream.

峨 ngoo, 627, G.8430. Mountain in Szechuen province.

峩見峨 ngoo, 627, G.8431.
Lofty.

峻 tsing°, 813, G.4897.
High, lofty, dangerous.

島 °tau, 866, G.10790.
Island.

峭 ts‘iau, c. siak, 972, G.1420.
High, dangerous.

崇 8 dzong, 110, G.2930.
Height, exalted.

崤 yau, 193, G.12930.
Name of mountain.

崎 ji, 342, G.993.
Uneven, undulating.

崛 joeh, 448, G.3230. Undulating mountains, eminent.

崑 kw‘ung, 494, G.6518.
A mountain in Thibet①.

崐見崑 k‘wung.
See above.

崙 lung, 565, G.7466.
Mountains north of Thibet.

崘見崙 lung, 565.
See above.

崩 pung, 659, G.8865.
Fall from a height, death of emperor.

崒 ts‘oeh, ts‘oe, 1015, G.11867. High, hazardous.

崔 ts‘oe, 1017, G.11917.
Great, high, name.

崖 ya, 1069, G.23.
Mountain slope.

嵇 9 yi, 179, G.4117.
Mountain in Nganhwui.

嵆見嵇 yi.
See above.

① Thibet:西藏,现今其英文译名采用汉语拼音 Xizang。——编者注

嵌 k‘an°，389，G.1709.
To inlay，fill.

嵐 len，502，G.6749.
Vapor on hills.

嵋 me，585，G.7716.
Name of a mountain.

崽 °tse，941，G.11495.
To give birth to.

嵒見巖 ngen，1084，G.13093.
A precipice.

嵎 nyui，1119，G.13558.
Mountain recess.

嵗見歲 soe°.
Year.

嵩10 song，830，G.10458.
High mountain in Honan.

嵯 ts‘oo，1003，G.11771.
Uneven，rough.

嵬 we，1050，G.12571.
Mountain，high，uneven.

嶄11 °tsan，14，G.357.
High，sharp.

嶂 tsang°，25，G.394.
A range of peaks.

嶇 chui，443，G.3089.
Uneven，rough.

嶔12 chung，402，G.2113.
High peaks.

嶞 °doo，910，G.11336. Long narrow range of hills.

嶧13 yuh，1094，G.5491.
Connected hills，name.

嶷14 nyi，275，G.5425.
Mountain name，lofty.

嶸 yong，237，G.5287.
High，majestic，dignified.

嶺 °ling，546，G.7220.
Mountain pass.

嶼 °zui，819，G.4762.
Island.

嶽 ngauh，1117，G.12953.
A high mountain.

巉 dzan，14，G.326.
High，dangerous.

巍18 we，1050，G.12568.
Very high.

巒19 loen，570，G.7453.
Mountain on mountain.

巔 tien，894，G.11196.
The top，the beginning.

巖20 ngen，1084，G.13090.
Precipice.

47 巛

巛 ts‘en，119，G.2727.
Flowing water.

川 ts‘en，119，G.2728.
Much water.

州3 tseu，48，G.2444. A district，a foo，a continent.

巡4 dzing，813，G.4883.
Police，to search.

巢8 dziau，37，G.520.
A nest.

巤12 lih，532，G.7102.
Bristly hair，name.

48 工

工 kong, 460, G.6553. Time, work, fine wrought.

左[2] °tsoo, c. tsi°, 1002, G.11753. At the left, not upright.

巧 °chau, 374, G.1411. Skilled, cunning, sharp.

巨 °jui, 440, G.3003. Great, chief.

巫[4] voo, 1059, G.12735. Mountain name, a sorcerer.

差[7] ts'e, c. ts'o, 5, G.196. Error.

| ts'a. To send.

| t's. Uneven.

49 己

己 °kyi, 337, G.921. Self, one.

已 °i, 278, G.5464. Already, completed action.

巳 °z, 838, G.10284. 9—11 a.m.

巴[1] po, 644, G.8510. Hope, diligent, about.

巵 ts, 55, G.1858. A cup.

巷[6] yang°, c. 'aung°, 190, G.3861. Alleyway.

巽[9] sung°, 830, G.4900. Fifth of the eight diagrams, north-east, mild.

50 巾

巾 kyung, 397, G.2041. Napkin, cap.

布[2] poo°, 713, G.9479. Cloth, disperse.

市 °z, 762, G.9905. Market.

帆[3] 見帆 van, 126. A sail.

帆 van, G.3400. A sail.

帋[4] 見紙 °ts, 56, G.1885. Paper.

希 hyi, 176, G.4048. To look for, wonderful.

帚[5] °tseu, 49, G.2470. A broom.

帙 dzeh, 69, G.1881. Book cloth. Cover.

帘 lien, 533, G.7134. A curtain.

帕 p'o°, p'ok, p'ak, 646, G.8538. A handkerchief, veil.

帛 buh, c. bak, 707, G.8558. Silk, wealthy, money.

帑同孥 noo, 862, G.10776. A child.

| °t'aung. Imperial treasury.

帖 t'ih, 893, G.11149. A card, settled, decided.

帥[6] se°, 785, G.10107.
Military commander.

| soeh.
To follow.

帝 ti°, 880, G.10942.
Ruler, sovereign.

帮[7] 見幫 paung, 657, G.8650.
To assist.

師 s, 758, G.9909.
A teacher, to learn.

帨 soe°, 782, G.10133.
Handkerchief, girdle.

席 dzih, zih, 804, G.4130.
Matting, a feast.

帩 ts'iau°.
Bind tight.

帳[8] tsang°, 24, G.409.
Curtain, reckon, account.

常 dzang, 740, G.440.
Constant, the five relations, a flag, common.

帶 te°, c. ta°, 846, G.10554.
A bend, to take, girdle.

帷 we, 1049, G.12595.
Curtain, screen, apron.

幅[9] fok, 150, G.3706.
A scroll, map, strip.

帽 mau°, 582, G.7701.
A cap.

幇 見幫 paung, 657, G.8656.
To assist.

幃 we, 1049, G.12530.
A perfume bag, curtain.

幋[10] ben.
A cloth wrapper.

幗[11] kok, 492, G.6611.
A woman's mourning cap.

幔 men°, c. man°, 576, G.7630. Curtain, veil.

幕 mok, c. moo°, 603, G.7983.
Tent, screen.

幟[12] ts°, 66, G. 1963. A long and narrow flag, pennon.

幢 dzang, c. dzaung°, 116, G.2786. Streamer, flag, curtain.

幡 fan, 124, G.3385. Streamers in temples, a duster.

幣 bi°, 676, G.8972.
Presents, wealth, money.

幨[13] 見幨 lien, 534, G.7131.
Door, curtain.

幪[14] mong, 608, G.7764.
A covering.

幫 paung, 657, G.8659.
To assist.

幬 dzeu, 868, G.10795.
The sky, a curtain, veil.

| dau°, dau.
To cover.

幭[15] mih, 596, G.7817.
A sheet, carriage cover.

51 干

干 koen, 309, G.5814.
To seek, how many, to oppose, a bank.

平[2] bing, 701, G.9310.
Plane, a place.

年[3] nyien, 634, G.8301.
Year.

并見幷 °ping, 700, G.9289.
To unite, however.

幷[5] °ping, 700, G.9258.
Together, place.

幸 °yung, 208, G.4592.
Luckily, fortunate.

幹[10] koen°, 313, G.5810. Affairs, capable, tree trunk.

52 幺

幺 iau, 1075, G.121945.
Small, tender.

幻[1] wan°, 248, G.5088. Deception, trick, changeable.

幼[2] ieu°, 1116, G.13393.
Young, tender.

玆[6]見玆 ts, 1029, G.12346.
This, here.

幽 ieu, 1109, G.13391.
Retired, quiet.

幾[9] °kyi, 333, G.786.
How many.

| kyi.
About, nearly.

53 广

广 °yien, 1087, G.13148.
Spacious covering.

庀[2] °pi, 681, G.9042.
To regulate, prepare.

庄[3]見莊 tsaung, 12, G.2753.
Stem, a village, an affair.

床[4]見牀 zaung, 115, G.2778.
A bed.

庇 pi°, °pi, bi°, 677, G.8944.
Protect, shelter.

序 °dzui, 819, G.4771.
A series, order, preface.

府[5] °foo, 145, G.3682. Prefecture, home, official treasury.

庚 kung, c. kang, 321, G.6001.
A stem, age.

庙見廟 miau°, 592, G.7850.
A temple, court.

庖 bau, 666, G.8735. Place of killing and dressing food.

底 °ti, 878, G.10902.
Bottom, below.

店 tien°, 895, G.11173.
A shop.

庥[6] hyeu, 211, G.4653.
To protect, guard.

庠 dziang, 792, G.4276.
A college, gymnasium.

度 doo°, 917, G.11305.
A degree, to measure.

| dauh.
To calculate.

庫[7] k'oo°, 436, G.6279.
Treasury.

庭 ding, 907, G.11286.
Court of a palace.

座 zoo°, 1003, G.11758.
A place of sitting.

康[8] k'aung, 320, G.5908.
Joy, peace, health.

庵見菴 en, 621, G.50. Nunnery, thatched cottage.

庳 °bi, bi°, 669, G.8762.
Humble, mean.

庶 su°, 778, G.10078.
Multitude, concubine.

庾 °yui, 1125, G.13595.
A hungry prisoner.

庸 yong, 1147, G.13462.
Common, respect.

廂[9] siang, 791, G.4250.
Side rooms of a house.

廁 t's°, 1035, G.10297.
Small house, privy.

庽見寓 nyui°.
Tavern, to dwell.

廈[10] ya°, 184, G.4229
Mansion.

廊 laung, 504, G.6778.
A verandah, gallery.

廉 lien, 534, G.7128.
Pure, frugal, by the side.

廋 seu, 755, G.10226.
To conceal, hide.

廐[11] 見廄 kyeu°, 415, G.2291.
Horse stable.

廄 kyeu°.
Horse stable.

廓 k'wauh, 493, G.6127.
The outer wall, spacious.

廖 liau, 530, G.7064.
A surname.

廒 ngau, 624, G.86.
A granary.

廕 iung°, 1103, G.13228.
A cover, to cover.

廣見廣 °kwaung.
Spacious, Canton.

廠[12] °ts'ang, 28, G.443.
Shed, depôt, warehouse.

廛 dzen, 46, G.335.
House for a market.

廚 dzu, 93, G.2634.
Sleeping apartment.

廢 fi°, 138, G.3487.
To abandon.

廣 °kwaung, 478, G.6397.
Broad, extensive, Canton.

廟 miau°, 592, G.7867.
A mansion, temple.

廡 °voo, 1062, G.12755.
Side houses.

廨[13] kya°, c. ka°, 360, G.1516.
Public building.

廩 °ling, 542, G.7189.
Store house.

廬[16] lui, 558, G.7402.
A strawhouse, dwelling.

廳[22] t'ing, 906, G.11300.
Parlor, drawing room.

54 廴

廴 °yung, 1102, G.13285.
To journey, to move on.

廷[4] ding, 907, G.11284.
Imperial palace, court.

延[5] yien, 1084, G.13080. To prolong, to pass along (as water, or fire).

廹見迫 puh, p'eh, p'uh, 708, G.9342. To urge, harass.

廸見迪 dih, 902, G.10938.
To lead, direct.

廻[6]見回 we, 262, G.5175. To curve, bend, remove.

建 kyien°, 386, G.1592.
To establish, set up.

55 廾

廾 °kong, 463, G.6593.
Join hands.

廿[1] seh, c. nyan°, 300, G.5693.
Twenty.

弁[2] bien°, 689, G.9197.
A leather hat, a leader.

异[3]見異 yi°, 278, G.5466.
Strange, wonderful.

弄[4] long°, 569, G.7507.
To trouble, annoy.

弃見棄 chi°.
To discard.

弇[6] °ien, 1088. G.13066.
To cover, hide.

弈 yuh, 1093, G.13176.
Game of chess.

弊[12] bi°, 676, G.8973. Deteriorate, tricky, vicious.

56 弋

弋 yuh, 1094, G.5343.
A spear, dart.

弌[1]見一 ih, 1095, G.5344.
One.

弍[2]見二 r°, c. nyi°, 721, G.3364. Two.

弎[3]見三 san.
Three.

式 suh, 767, G.9984.
Pattern, example, kind.

弒[9] s°, 765, G.9989.
To murder a superior.

57 弓

弓 kong, 461, G.6566.
A bow.

弔[1] tiau°, 886, G.11060.
To condole, to suspend.

引 °yung, 1102, G.13265. To lead, induce, preface of books.

弗[2] feh, 153, G.3653.
Not, nor.

弘 'ong, 237, G.5282.
Liberal, large.

弛[3] °s, 761, G.9931.
To relax, cast off.

丨 c. sa.
Tired, fatigued.

弟[4] °di, di°, 879, 10950.
Younger brother.

丨 di°. To act as a younger brother.

弦[5] yien, 197, G.4480. A string(as of a bow).

弧 ‘oo, 223, G.4955. Pointed.

弩 °noo, 641, G.8392. A broken bow.

弢 t‘au, 869, G.10840. A bow.

弤 °ti, 879, G.10903. Bow of Emperor Shun.

弥 見 彌 mi. Full.

弭[6] °mi, 591, G.7827. Unbent, to stop, cease.

弱[7] zak, 295, G.5588. Weary, tired.

張[8] tsang, 22, G.416. To open, enlarge, a sheet.

強 jang, 366, G.1235. Strong, violent.

丨 °chang, °jang. To force, compel.

弼[9] bih, 693, G.9007. To assist.

强 見 強 jang, 366, G.1293. Strong, violent.

丨 °chang. To force, compel.

彀[10] keu°, 331, G.6167. Enough, able.

彈[12] dan°, 852, G.10603. A ball.

丨 dan. To strike a string, or instrument.

彊[13] 見 強 jang, 366, G.1231. Strong, violent.

丨 °chang. To compel.

彌[14] mi, 589, G.7812. To pervade, to stop, very, still more.

彎[19] ’wan, 1038, G.12477. To curve, bent.

58 彐

彐 kyi°, 339, G.977. Hog’s head.

归[2] 見 歸 kwe, 480. To return, go home.

彖[7] t‘oen°, 938, G.12160. Sum or substance.

彗[8] dzoe°, zoe°, c. we°, 828, G.9596. A broom.

彘[9] dz, 58, G.1909. A hog.

彙[10] we°, 1056, G.5215. A hedgehog, a class.

彝[15] yi, 276, G.5443. Libation, cup.

59 彡

彡 san, 734, G.9686. To adorn with feathers.

形[4] yung, 206, G.4617. Shape, form.

彤 dong, 935, G.12315.
Red, rosy, vermilion.

彥[6] nyien°, 1090, G.13106. Elegant and handsome scholar.

彧 iok, 1140, G.13663.
Literary, clever.

彬[8] ping, 696, G.9255.
Literati, scholars.

彪 piau, 703, G.9112.
Striped like a tiger.

彫同雕 tiau, 885, G. 11049.
To carve, withered.

彩 °ts'e, 943, G.11508.
Variegated, brilliant.

彭[9] bung, c. bang, 662, G.8887.
Near, sound of drum.

彰[11] tsang, 23, G.395.
To adorn, manifest.

影[12] °iung, 1108, G.13339.
Shadow.

60 彳

彳 ts'uh, 73, G.2013.
To step.

彷[4] baung, 135, G.3439.
Timid, undecided.

| °faung.
Like, similar.

役 yok, 1095, G.5520.
Serve, one sent, servant.

征[5] tsung, 74, G.689.
To levy tax, to subjugate.

彿 feh, 153, G.3657.
Like, for example.

彼 °pe, 674, G.8768.
That, they, there, him.

徂 dzoo, 1008, G.2628.
To go.

往 °'waung, 1044, G.12500.
To go, formally.

徃見往 °'waung, 1044, G.12501. To go, formally.

很[6] °hung, 167, G.3901.
Disobedient, sulky, rash.

後 °'eu, 175, G.4025.
After in time.

| 'eu°.
Descendants.

徊 we, 262, G.5166.
To pace to and fro.

律 lih, 564, G.7548.
A law, a tune in music.

徇 dzing, 812, G.4867.
All around, to follow.

待 °de, 845, G.10569.
To wait, serve.

徉 yang, 1072, G.12815.
Sauntering about.

徑[7] kyung°, 407, G.2117.
Path, diameter, radius.

徐 zi, 819, G.4748.
A dignified step.

徒 doo, 919, G.12126. A pupil, in vain, to follow, only.

徠[8]見來 le, 500, G.6684.
To come.

徘見俳 be, 672, G.8829.
To walk about.

徜 zang, 740, G.419.
Irresolute, playful.

徙 °si, 789, G.4119.
To remove.

得 tuh, 872, G.10842.
To obtain.

從 dzong, 1024, G.11987.
Through, by, from, follow.

| dzong°. Attendant, follower, clan.

| ts'ong.
Easy, unembarrassed.

御 nyui°, 1127, G.13645.
A ruler, hackman.

復 9 vok, 151, G.3721. Reply, return, again, recover.

| fok.
Answer.

| veu°.
Again.

徨 waung, 251, G.5112.
In doubt.

徤見健 jien°, 386, G.1594.
To be strong.

徧 pien°, 689, G.9174.
Everywhere.

循 dzing, 813, G.4862.
To follow.

徯 10 yi, 178, G.4066.
To wait.

徬 baung°, 658, G.8677. To walk at the side, in doubt.

微 vi, 1050, G.12586.
Little, obscure, fine, not.

徭 yau, 1075, G.12914.
An attendant.

徹 12 ts'eh, 42, G.578.
To penetrate, discern.

徵 tsung, 74, G.720. To levy (as tax), prove, evidence.

德 tuh, 871, G.10845.
Moral, virtue, goodness.

徼 13 kyau, 371, G.1367.
Desiring, seeking.

徽 14 hwe, 261, G.5160.
Excellent, beautiful.

徽見徽 hwe.
Excellent.

61 心

心 sing, 806, G.4562.
Heart, mind.

必 1 pih, 692, G.8922.
Certain.

忉 2 tau, 866, G.10785.
Grieve.

志 3 ts°, 61, G.1918.
Inclination, purpose, will.

忍 °zung, c.°nyung, 287, G.5607. Patience, harsh, severe.

忌 ji°, 340, G.924. To fear, jealous, anniversary of death.

忙 maung, 578, G.7646.
Busy, pressed.

忐 °t'an, °k'ung, 856, G.10702.
Timorous, a fluttering (as when startled).

忒 t'uh, 872, G.10595. Excess, too, error, to doubt.

忑 t'uh, 873, G.10850. Downhearted, timorous.

忖 °ts'ung, 1021, G. 11967. To consider, meditate.

忘 vaung, vaung°, c. maung°, 1044, G.12504. Forgetful, to forget.

忮[4] ts°, 62, G.1874. Dislike, stubborn, froward.

忠 tsong, 106, G.2877. Faithful.

忡 ts'ong, 109, G.2912. Grieved, palpitation.

忿 °vung, 131, G.3513. Angry.

忻 hyung, 204, G.4566. Delighted, happy.

忽 hweh, 267, G.4927. Suddenly, forgetful.

忼見**慷** °k'aung, 320, G.5920. Liberal, generous.

快 kw'e°, c. kw'a°, k'a°, 471, G.6336. Happy, pleased.

念 nyien°, c. nyan°, 635, G.8303. Thoughts, twenty.

忸 °nyeu, 639, G. 8049. Ashamed, abashed.

忭 bien°, 688, G.9203. Happy, delighted.

忱同**諶** zung, dzung, 737, G.9848. Sincerity, pure, candid.

忝 °t'ien, 899, G.11209. Disgraced, ashamed.

忤 oo°, c. ng°, 1063, G.12771. Disobedient.

怀見**懷** we, 243. To think, the bosom.

怔[5] tsung, 74, G.620. Disturbed, grieved.

怵 ts'eh, 99, G.2678. Anxious.

怫 veh, 154, G.3658. Unhappy.

怙 °'oo, 226, G.4969. To trust, a father.

怡 yi, 575, G.5407. Harmonious, happy.

怯 chih, 379, G.1564. Timid.

急 kyih, 393, G.892. Hasty, pressed.

怪 kwe°, c. kwa°, 470, G.6330. Strange, a spirit.

怩 nyi, 630, G.8200. Shamed face, blush.

怒 noo°, 641, G.8393. To be angry.

怕 p'o°, 647, G.8539. To fear, be afraid.

怦 p'ung, 661, G.8893. Disturbed in mind.

怖 poo°, 714, G.9481. Afraid, alarmed.

性 sing°, 809, G.4600. Nature, disposition.

思 s，834，G.10271.
To think.

丨 s°.
Thoughts，meaning.

怛 tah，840，G.10491.
Grieved，anxious.

怠 de°，845，G.10565.
Indolent，lazy，idle.

怗 t'ih，893，G.11150.
To submit to.

怎 °tsung，948，G.11702.
How.

怍 dzauh，dzo°，1005，G.147.
Ashamed，disgraced.

怱見悤 ts'ong，1024，G.12017.
Excited，agitated.

怏 iang°，1073，G.12863.
Anxious thoughts.

怨 ioen°，1138，G.13716.
Dislike，murmur.

恥 6 °ts，65，G.1999.
Disgrace，shame.

恨 'ung°，167，G.3902.
To hate.

恆 'ung，169，G.3916.
Continuous，constant.

恒見恆 'ung，169，G.3919.
See above.

恔 °kyau，194，G.4346.
Wise，sagacious.

丨 yau°.
Cheerful，joy，jovial.

恊見協 yah，196，G.4386.
Union of purpose.

恍同慌 hwaung°，253，G.5136.
Confused，similar.

恚 we°，265，G.5191.
To hate，dislike.

恁 °zung，288，G.5617.
To consider，thus，so.

恝 kya°，chih，357，G.1490.
Unsympathetic.

恰 chak，c. hah，k'ah，357，G.1194. Luckily，just，exactly.

恐 °k'ong，422，G.2370.
Apprehensive.

恐見恐 °k'ong，422，G.2369.
Supposing，if.

恪 k'auh，chak，429，G.6119.
Attentive to duties.

恭 kong，462，G.6574.
To reverence，respect.

恠見怪 kwe°，c. kwa°，470，G.6332. Strange，spirit.

恢 hwe，487，G.5156. Great，liberal，to magnify.

恩 ung，623，G.3330.
Mercy，grace.

恧 °nyeu，nyok，640，G.8377.
Mortified，ashamed.

恃 °z，761，G.1981.
To rely on.

恕 su°，778，G.10077.
Benevolent，to excuse.

息 sih，803，G.4034.
To rest，to stop.

恂 sing, 812, G.4868.
Honest, true.

恤 sih, 825, G.4723.
To pity, compassion.

恬 dien, 899, G.11220.
At peace, quiet.

恫 t'ong, 933, G.12272.
Careful, grieved over.

恣 ts, 1032, G.12340.
Dissipation.

恙 yang°, 1074, G.12846.
A disease, complaint.

怵 cheu.
Bad, vicious.

悍 7 'oen°, 165, G.3798.
Cruel.

患 wan°, 248, G.5090.
Evil, afflicted.

悔 hwe°, 263, G.5178.
To repent, reform.

悁 kyoen, 451, G.3128.
Distressed, anxious.

悖 beh, be°, 671, G.8792.
To oppose, rebel.

悃 °k'wung, 495, G.6543.
Single-minded, sincere.

悉 sih, 804, G.4138. To know, to investigate, all, whole.

悚 °song, 831, G.10459.
Grieved, ashamed.

悌 di°, °di, 879, G.10952. Act with brotherly respect.

悄 °ts'iau, 972, G.1422.
Distressed, grieved.

悛 °ts'ien, 1013, G.3188.
To reform.

悤 °ts'ong, 1024, G.12035.
Pressed, busy.

悟 ngoo°, 1063, G.12704.
Comprehend, to awake.

悞同**誤** ngoo°, 1064, G.12749.
Neglect, to err.

悠 ieu, 1110, G.13389.
Distant.

悅 yoeh, 1131, G.13776.
Happy, rejoicing.

悵 8 ts'ang°, 29, G.410.
Disappointed, vexed.

惆 ts'eu, dzeu, 50, G.2501.
Vexed, annoyed.

惩見**懲** dzung, 79, G.784.
To correct, to repress, govern.

惙 tseh, 81, G.2423.
Disturbed in mind.

悱 °fi, 138, G.3464. Not able to speak from fear or ignorance.

悻 °yung, 208, G.4595.
Anger, vexed.

惑 wok, c. 'ok, 259, G.3990.
To doubt.

惠 we°, 264, G.5199.
Kind, gracious, liberal.

惚 hweh, 267, G.4928.
In doubt, small, confused.

惛 hwung, 268, G.5224.
Confused, stupid.

悸 ji°, kyi°, 340, G.945. Fearful.

惧見懼 jui°, 440, G.3021. To fear, to reverence.

惓 joen, 452, G.3163. Careful, earnest.

悾 k'ong, 465, G.6598. Honest, stupid.

悶 mung°, 577, G.7754. Distressed.

悲 pe, 668, G.8779. Mournful, grief for others.

惜 sih, 802, G.4106. To pity, close, stingy.

惔 dan, 856, G. 10652. The mind much distressed, as though fired up.

悼 dau°, 868, G.10802. To grieve for.

悳見德 tuh, 871, G.10846. Virtue.

惦 tien°, 896, G.11174. To remember, to think of.

惄 nyuh, 636, G.8238. Grieved, hungry.

惧 °t'ien, 900, G.11223. Ashamed, bashful.

惕 t'ih, 903, G.10983. To respect, to fear.

惇 tung, zung, 927, G.2844. Liberal, sincere, to urge.

悽 ts'i, 966, G.984. Sorrowing, suffering.

情 dzing, zing, 996, G.2187. The seven passions, facts, affairs.

悴 dzoe°, 1018, G.11926. Bitterly distressed.

惘 °vaung, 1045, G.12513. Perturbed mind, disconcerted.

惟 vi, 1049, G.12596. Only, meditate.

惡 auh, 1063, G.3326. Evil, sin.

丨 oo°. To hate, to dislike.

丨 oo. Why, how, an interjection of regret.

惴 9 ts'oe°, 101, G.2695. To fear, embarrassed.

惶 waung, 251, G.5113. Fear, terror, hesitation.

惛同惽 hwung, 268, G.5229. Confused, stupid.

意 i°, 282, G.5367. Meaning, mind.

惹 °za, 293, G.5592. To provoke, to induce.

感 °ken, 312, G.5844. To move, excite, grateful.

愒 chi°, chih, 378, G.1454. To cease, to rest a while.

丨 k'e°. Urgent, in a hurry.

丨 hoeh. A mutual fear of one another.

愜 chah, kyah, 380, G.1568. Satisfied.

愆 chien, 389, G.1715. Fault, mistake.

惸 jong, 422, G.2386. Alone, without relatives.

愍 °ming, 597, G.7919. To mourn for, grieved.

惱見**惱** °nau, 617, G.8165. To dislike.

惱 °nau. To dislike.

愛 e°, 619, G.15. To love, love.

愕 ngauh, 628, G.8455. Frightened, startled.

愎 pih, 693, G.8992. Perverse, self-willed.

想 °siang, 792, G.4251. To think, meditate.

惺 sing, 809, G.4603. To awake, comprehend.

惰 doo°, 910, G.11332. Indolent, lazy.

惻 ts'uh, 960, G.11697. Grieved, to pity, to sympathize.

愁 dzeu, 963, G.2498. Grieve, mournful.

愀 °ts'iau, 972, G.1415. Angry look, sad.

慍 'wung°, iuin°, 1043, G.12643. To be angry.

愚 nyui, 1120, G.13559. Stupid.

愉 yui, 1123, G.13573. Contented, pleased.

愈 yui°, 1126, G.13572. To exceed, more.

愴 10 ts'iang°, ts'iang, 116, G.2771. Afflicted in mind.

愾 hyi°, 181, G.4150. A sigh, grief.

慌 hwaung, hwaung°, 253, G.5102. Confused, nervous, excited.

慁 wung°, 270, G.5247. Disturbed, mortified.

愷 °k'e, 308, G.5797. Joyful, gentle.

慊 chien°, chih, 380, G.1571. Happy, satisfied, enraged, angry.

愨 chak, k'ok, 411, G.2244. Guileless, upright, ingenious.

愧 gwe°, kwe°, 484, G.6432. To be ashamed.

慄 lih, 539, G.6976. To fear, tremble.

愽見**博** pok, c. pauh, 706, G. 9378. Intelligent, universal.

愼 zung°, 738, G.9846. Cautious, careful.

慎見**愼** zung°. Cautious, careful.

愬同**訴** soo°, 817, G. 10365. To tell, inform.

態 t'e°, 849, G.10598.
Form, gait, air, habit.

慆 t'au, 869, G.10813.
To rejoice, reckless.

慈 dz, 1033, G.12406.
Merciful, kind.

慇 iung, 1100, G.13239. Sad, sorry, careful, attentive.

愿又見願 nyoen°, 1137, G.13703.
Sincere, honest, would that.

慂 °iong, 1148, G.13461.
Bold, to stir up, to urge on.

慍見愠 iuin°, wung°.
To be angry.

慣11 kwan°, 476, G.6379.
Habitual, experienced.

慧 we°, 265, G.5193.
Wisdom, knowledge.

慵 yong, 304, G.5761.
Lazy.

慨 k'e°, 309, G.5804.
Liberal, hearty in a thing.

慷 °k'aung, 320, G.5910.
Firm, generous.

憩見愒 chi°, 379, G. 1122.
To rest, take breath.

慳 kyien, 383, G. 1623. Sparing, parsimonious, to reduce.

慶 chung°, 409, G. 2211. To congratulate, good wishes.

慮 lui°, 560, G.7527.
Discontent, anxiety.

慢 man°, 576, G.7631.
Rude, sluggish, slow.

慕 moo°, 606, G.7984.
To love.

慠 ngau°, 625, G.87.
Proud, arrogant, hate.

慭見慠 ngau°.
See above.

慝 t'uh, 873, G.10851.
Depraved heart, wicked.

慟 dong°, 932, G.12257.
Sorrowful, grief.

慙 dzan, 947, G.11547.
To be abashed.

慚見慙 dzan, 947, G. 11546.
To be abashed.

慘 °ts'en, 947, G.11552.
To pity, be sorrowful.

慼 ts'ih, 987, G.1021.
Grief, sorrow.

慫 °song, 1023, G.11989.
To stir up the mind.

慰 we°, 1055, G.12622.
To console.

憂 iou, 1109, G.13381.
Grieved, sad, mournful.

慾 yok, 1139, G.13643.
Lust, desirous.

慴 dzih.
To fear, dread.

憤12 °vung, vung°, 131, G.3538.
Excited, urgent.

憨 hen, 162, G.3805.
Idiotic, silly.

憲 hyien°, 201, G.4547. A precept, to publish law.

憍 kyau, 368, G.1333. Bragging, self-indulgent.

憬 °kyong, 463, G.6591. To fear and tremble (as at calamity).

憦 lau°, 508, G.6794. To regret, to repent of.

憐 lien, 534, G.7156. To pity, have compassion.

憫 °ming, 597, G.7930. Lamentable, to mourn.

憑 bing, 702, G.9328. To trust, evidence.

憚 dan°, 852, G.10604. To dread, fear.

憝 de°, 925, G.2820. Dislike, angry with, an adversary.

憯見憯 °ts'en, 948, G.11573. Distressed for, already.

憎 tsung, 951, G.11719. To dislike.

憔 dziau, 972, G.1405. Withered, dried.

憮 °foo, 1062, G.12756. Sigh, to soothe, to comfort.

憩見愒 chi°. To rest.

懈 13 ye°, c. yau°, 187, G.4421. To be indolent.

憾 'en°, 166, G.3832. To hate, remorse.

懇 °k'ung, 318, G.5988. Ask earnestly.

懃 jung, 402, G.2098. Diligent, vigilant.

懍 °ling, 542, G.7190. Careful, respectful.

懋 meu°, 589, G.8043. To make great effort.

懊 'au, 625, G.111. To repent.

憊 bi°, 648, G.8571. Wearied.

懂 °tong, 931, G.12260. To understand.

懆 °ts'au, tsau, 954, G.11615. Anxious, uneasy.

憶 iuh, 1093, G.5370. To recall, reflection.

懌 yuh, 1094, G.5492. Happy.

應 iung, 1106, G.13294. Ought, fulfill.

| iung°. Answer.

懥 14 ts°, 62, G.1927. To hate, be enraged.

懢 lan, 503, G.6726. Covetous, longing for.

懞 mung°, °mung, 577, G.7760. Sad, melancholy.

懦 zu, 'noo°, 640, G.8369. Timid, sluggish, soft.

懟 de°, 925, G.2819. Enemy.

懕 ien, 1083, G.13034.
To hate, dislike.

懲[15] dzung, 79, G.780.
To correct, govern.

懸[16] yoen, 232, G.4819.
To suspend, undecided.

懷 we, c. wa, 243, G.5032.
To think on, cherish.

懶 lan°, c. °lan, 503, G.6751.
Lazy, indolent.

懵 mong°, 610, G.7783.
Dull, not wise, blind.

懿 i°.
Mild, virtuous, admired.

懺[17] °ts'an, 14, G.372.
To regret, repent.

懾[18] seh, 41, G.568.
To subdue, agitated.

懿同懿 i°, 284, G.5352. Mild, virtuous, admired.

懼 jui°, 440, G.3053.
To reverence, to fear.

懽同歡 hwen, 476, G.6356.
Happy, to like, grieved.

戀[19] lien°, loen°, 561, G.7154.
To love ardently.

戇[24] dzaung°, hen°, ken°, c. gaung°, 114, G. 2769. Stupid.

62 戈

戈 koo, 489, G.6061.
A lance, spear.

戊[1] °voo, 1063, G.12792.
Earth.

成[2] dzung, 77, G.762.
Completed.

戎 dzong, 303, G.5746.
Weapons, arms, soldiers.

戍 su°, 777, G.10083.
To guard a frontier.

戌 sih, 825, G.4735.
9—11 p.m.

戒[3] kya°, c. ka°, 360, G.1531.
To warn, a warning, to break off.

我 °ngoo, 627, G.3313.
I, my.

或[4] 'ok, 259, G.3989.
Perhaps.

戕 ziang, 969, G.1276.
A spear, to kill.

戔 tsien, 978, G.1583. Small, narrow, contracted.

戛[7] kyih, 357, G.1171.
A lance, long spear.

戚 ts'ih, 987, G.1018. A pole-ax, to pity, a relative.

戟[8] kyuh, 392, G.928.
A spear, lance.

戡[9] k'en, 314, G.5856.
To kill, to conquer.

戥 °tung, 863, G.10878.
Money steelyard.

戢 ts'ih, 988, G. 1094. To collect, store up weapons.

戤 ge°.
To rely on, trust.

截[10] dzih, zih, 975, G.1513.
To cut, amputate.

戩 °tsien, 978, G.1656.
To finish up, to destroy.

戮[11] lok, 564, G.7445.
To kill, massacre.

戰[12] tsen°, 45, G.314. To battle, fight, to tremble.

戲[13] hyi°, 180, G.4098.
Theatricals, to ridicule.

戳[14] ts'auh, ts'ok, 84, G.2437.
To stab, stamp, seal.

戴 te°, c. ta°, 844, G.10567.
To put on, wear.

63 户

户 °'oo, 225, G.4959.
A door, a family.

房[4] vaung, 134, G.3440.
House, 11th of the zodiacal constellations.

戽 °'oo, c. °hoo, 225, G.4963.
Bale out water, a bucket in slings.

戾 li°, 523, G.6987. To bend down, crime, to reach to.

所 °soo, 817, G.10064.
A place, which.

扃[5] kyong, 461, G.6584.
A door bar, to bolt.

扁 °pien, 687, G.9172.
Flat.

扅[6] yi, 274, G.5412.
The bar of a gate.

扇 sen°, 753, G.9669.
A fan, door leaf.

扈[7] °'oo, 225, G.4965.
To follow, a retinue.

扉[8] fi, 136, G.3465.
A door of one leaf.

扊 °yien, 1087, G.13071.
The upright bar of a door.

64 手

手 °seu, 754, G.10011.
The hand.

才 dze, 942, G.11496.
Talent, materials.

扎[1] tsah, 7, G.125.
To bind.

扔[2] dzung, 291, G.5637.
To throw away.

扒 pe°, 649, G.8506.
To pull up.

丨 c. bo.
To climb, crawl, steal.

扑 p'ok, 710, G.9415.
To strike, to fall.

打 °tang, 839, G.10494.
To strike.

扞[3] 'oen°, 165, G.5816.
To ward off, defend.

扛 kaung, 319, G.5886.
To carry burdens.

扣 k'eu°, 332, G.6176.
To knock, discount.

托 t'auh, 915, G.11366.
To trust, open up.

扦見**搌** ts'ien, 980, G.1727. To graft, put in.

扤 nyeh, 1065, G.12784. To move, shake.

扱[4] ts'ah, 9, G.226. To receive, raise up, help.

抓 °tsau, c. °tsa, 32, G.486. To scratch.

找 °tsau, 34, G.488. To make up, look for.

抄 ts'au, 36, G.508. To copy, take out.

折 tseh, 40, G.550. Break off, stop.

扯見**撦** °ts'a, 40, G.576. To read, tear.

承 dzung, 78, G.761. To receive, undertake, take a charge.

扶 voo, 144, G.3613. To assist, help.

抗 k'aung°, 321, G.5921. To resist, rebel against.

抅見**拘** kyui, 328, G.6137. To grasp, hinder.

技 ji°, 347, G.1104. Skill, ingenuity.

抉 kyoeh, 447, G.3221. To pluck out.

扼 uh, 629, G.8472. To grip, clutch.

扭 °nyeu, 639, G.8350. To grip, twist.

把 °po, 644, G.8514. To take hold.

扮 pan°, 652, G.8599. To dress up.

扳同**攀** p'an, pan, 653, G.8586. To grasp, to drag, pull.

抛見**拋** p'au, 666, G.8752. To cast.

抔 beu, 673, G.8580. A handful.

批 p'i, 679, G.9048. To judge, to beat, to slap.

抃 bien°, 688, G.9204. To beat, keep time.

抒 su, 776, G.10043. To spread out.

抖 °teu, °t'eu, 874, G.11428. To tremble.

投 deu, 876, G.11446. To hit, to throw, become.

抆 vung°, 1042, G.12634. To rub, smooth.

抑 iuh, 1093, G.5532. Moreover, repress, keep back.

扵見**於** yui, 1118, G.13516. At, in, on, by, with.

抈 yoeh, c. nyoeh, 1130, G.13770. To bend, to move.

招[5] tsau, 31, G.466. To summon, call.

抽 ts'eu, 50, G.2486. To take, select, draw out.

拙 tseh, tsoeh, 83, G.2396. Stupid, clumsy.

拄 °tsu, 88, G.2532.
To brace, support.

拊 °foo, 145, G.3670.
To strike, beat.

拂 feh, 154, G.3659.
To dust off.

拑 jien, 389, G.1705.
To pinch, to grasp, to nip.

拘 kyui, 438, G.2948.
To grasp, to hinder.

拒 jui°, 441, G.3606.
Ward off, reject.

抾 chui, 443, G.3070.
To grasp, lift up.

抓 'wo, kwo, 466, G.6284.
To lead, strike, grab.

拐 °kwe, c. °kwa, 470, G.6328.
To seduce, a swindler.

拉 lah, 497, G.6662.
To break off.

| c.'la.
To pull.

| la°.
At, in.

拎 'ling, 544, G.7202. To take, to carry in the hand.

抹 meh, 604, G.7574.
To anoint.

拇 °meu, °moo, 588, G.8033.
The thumb.

拏 na, c. nau, no, 610, G.8092.
To take.

拈 'nyien, 634, G.8297.
Take in the fingers.

拔 bah, 647, G.8527.
To pull out.

拜 po°, c. pa°, 648, G.8569.
To worship, bow.

拚 bien°, c. p'en, p'ing, 124, G. 8633. Flying to brush off.

拌 p'en, °ben, c. p'ing, 654, G.8605. To dust off.

抱 °bau, 665, G.8709.
Infold, carry in the arms.

披 p'i, 678, G.8814. To open, to put on clothes.

拍 p'uh, c. p'ak, 711, G.8576.
To beat, pat.

抪 poo°, 713, G.9482.
To scatter.

抬見擡 de, 848, G.10584.
Carry, lift up.

抵 °ti, 878, G.10904.
To oppose, substitute.

担又見擔 tan, 851, G.10636.
To carry.

| tan°.
Load.

拕同拖 t'oo, 911, G.11347.
To pull.

拖 t'oo, 911, G.11380.
To pull.

拓 tsak, 915, G.1907.
To pick.

|見托 t'auh.
Carry on the hand.

拆 ts'uh, c. ts'ak, 960, G.254. To break, open.

押 iah, c. ah, 1068, G.12825. To pawn.

拗 °iau, c. °au, 1077, G.121. To snap a thing in two, break.

拶 °tsung. To press out.

抛 p'au. To throw.

指6 °ts, c. tsih, 57, G.1791. To finger, to show.

持 z, 64, G.1982. To grasp, hold.

拯 °tsung, 75, G.715. To rescue, save.

揔 ts'ong°, 111, G.2926. To grab, to lift.

拽 yi°, c. yih, 282, G.2693. To drag, take up.

拷 °k'au, 327, G.5967. To bear, strike.

拮 kyih, 376, G.913. Hampered, embarrassed.

挈 chih, yih, 379, G.1561. To raise up, carry.

拳 joen, 452, G. 3161. The fist, to grasp, athletic.

拱 °kong, 463, G. 6575. To place the hands before the breast so that the thumbs come together, as when making a bow.

挂 kwo°, 467, G.6307. Hung up.

括 kwah, 469, G.6288. To embrace, include.

拿見**拏** na, c. nau, no, 610, G.8093. To take.

挐見**拏** na, c. nau, 610, G.8095. To take.

按 oen°, 622, G.45. According to, examine, place on.

拾 zeh, c. zih, 768, G.9963. To collect, ten.

拭 suh, 768, G.9986. To wipe.

拴 ts'ien, 786, G.2731. To select, buy.

挑 t'iau, 887, G.11076. To carry, pick out, select.

拶 tseh, c.°tsan, 945, G.11540. To torture, press.

挖 'wak, 1037, G.12431. Pluck out.

挨7 °ie, ia, 1, G.10. To crowd in.

丨 c. a. Arrange in order.

振 tsung°, 18, G.640. To move, stir up.

捉 tsauh, 82, G.2406. To catch.

捍同**扞** 'oen°, 165, G.3799. To ward off, defend.

挾 yah, c. kah, 356, G.1133. To clasp under the arm, to

help, squeeze.

捃 kyuin°, 419, G.3370.
To pick up, put to rights.

捐 kyoen, 449, G.3129.
To collect, contribute.

挶 jok, 457, G.2957.
A handful.

捆 °kw'ung, 495, G.6544.
To braid, bind, unite.

捋 loeh, 560, G.7095.
To pull off, stroke, milk.

捏 nyah, 633, G.8261.
To seize, hold.

挪 na, c. nau, 639, G.8364.
To bring.

挼 noo, 639, G.8374.
To rub in the hands.

捌 pah, 647, G.8509.
Eight, to divide.

挷 °paung, 657, G.8651.
To bind.

捕 boo°, 714, G.9461.
To capture, arrest.

挱 soo, 745, G.10192.
To rub in the hands.

捒 sok, 815, G.10221.
To bind fast.

挺 °t'ing, 908, G.11287.
To push out, lead out.

挫 ts'oo°, 1004, G.11779.
To file.

挽 °'wan, 1039, G.12480.
To revert, to make good.

挹 ih, 1097, G.5483.
To take, bring.

掭 8 °t'ien, 19, G.680.
To stretch a thing.

掌 °tsang, c. tsaung, 23, G.421.
The hand, authority.

掙 ts'ang, 30, G.707.
To pierce, block up.

掣 ts'eh, 66, G.583.
To obstruct, select.

捶 °tsoe, 100, G.2807.
To cudgel, torture.

捧 °fong, 159, G.3577.
To take in the hands.

掀 hyien, hyung, 196, G.4455.
To push down.

掐 k'ah, 358, G.1191.
To pinch, claw, indent.

拴見**擒** jing, 402, G.2111.
To seize, take in the band.

据 kyui, 437, G.2991.
Embarrassed, pressed.

掘 joeh, 448, G.3231.
To dig up.

捲 °kyoen, 450, G.3152.
To roll up.

掬 kyok, 457, G.2962.
A handful.

控 k'ong°, 465, G.6599.
To indict, sue, check.

掛同**挂** kwo°, 467, G.6312.
To suspend.

掭 li°, c. lih, 523, G.6990.
To wring out.

掠 liak, 547, G.7027.
To rob, plunder, invade.

掄 lung, c. ling, 565, G.7468.
To select.

捫 mung, 577, G.7755.
To touch.

捺 nah, 611, G.8109.
Press the hand on heavily.

捻 nyah, °nyien, 633, G.8266.
To hold in the hand.

捭 °pe, 649, G.8573.
To strike with both hands.

排 be, c. ba, 649, G.8579.
Arrange, a section.

掊 beu, 673, G.9421.
To appropriate, get from.

拼 pung, c. p'ing, 700, G.9290.
To unite.

掃 °sau, 726, G.9574.
To sweep, brush.

捨 °se, c. °so, 748, G.9790.
To give up, lay down.

授 °zeu, c. dzeu°, 757, G.10017.
To give, grant.

探 t'en, c. t'en°, 853, G.10688.
A spy, explore, tempt.

掏 dau, 869, G.10823.
To mix, confuse.

掉 diau°, 887, G.7075.
To interchange, change.

掂 tien, 894, G.11175. To estimate weight with the hand.

揚 t'ih, 903, G.10984.
To expunge.

掇 toeh, 913, G.11314.
To collect, take up.

推 ts'oe, 926, G.2822.
To inter from, to extend.

| t'e.
To decline, refuse.

採 °ts'e, 944, G.11509.
To pick, select.

接 tsih, 975, G.1480.
To accept, receive.

捷 dzih, 976, G.1485.
Swift, victorious.

措 ts'oo°, 1008, G.11768.
To arrange, employ.

捽 dzeh, tsoeh, 1014, G.11836.
To clinch, grasp.

捱 ya, 1069, G.12837.
To crowd in, push.

掩 °ien, c. °en, 1088, G.13057.
To cover.

掖 yuh, 1095, G.5508. Hold up by the arm, lift up.

掮 見 揵 jien.
To shoulder.

揸[9] tsa, tso, 3, G.132. To lay on(as color or paint).

插 ts'ah, 9, G.205.
To stick in.

揣 ts'oe, ts'oen, 112, G.2696.
To guess, find out.

換 wen°, 249, G.5080.
To exchange.

揮 hwe, 260, G.5149.
To drive out.

揉 dzeu, c. nyok, 294, G.5654.
To bend, rub.

揩 cha, c. k'a, 362, G.1575.
To wipe.

揭 kyih, c. hyih, 378, G.1455.
To open.

揀 °kyan, c. °kan, 383, G.1669.
To select, choose.

揵 jien, 390, G.1779.
To carry on the shoulder.

揆 °gwe, 488, G.6487.
To guess, calculate.

描 miau, 591, G.7853.
To trace, copy, sketch.

揞 °en, 621, G.56.
To hide with the hand.

揑見捏 nyah, 633, G.8262.
To hold, seize.

掱 paung, 657, G.8657.
To assist.

揼 bung°, c. p'ang°, bang°, 662, G.8911. To hit upon, meet.

揙見拼 pung, c. p'ing, 700, G.9292. To unite.

掺見搜 seu, 755, G.10239.
To search, rapid.

提 di, 882, G.10915.
To lift up, mention.

揥 t'i°, ti°, 885, G.11014.
A long round hair-pin.

揲 zeh, dih, 893, G.9797.
To fold, cast, pile up.

揫 ts'ieu, 998, G.2252.
To seize with the hands.

揪同揫 ts'ieu, 998, G.2251.
See above.

握 ok, 1064, G. 12692. To lead by the hand, seize.

揠 'wah, 1069, G.12833.
To pull out.

揚 yang, 1070, G.12876.
Spread abroad.

揶 ya, 1079, G.12975.
To play antics.

揜 °ien, 1088, G.13067.
To cover up.

揖 ih, 1097, G.5393.
To unite the hands.

揄 yui, 1124, G.13574.
To draw out, lead.

援 yoen, 1135, G.13755.
To rescue, save.

掾 yoen°, nyien°, 1136, G.11735.
Principal officer.

揔見總 °tsong, 1023.
All, the whole.

搽 10 dzo, 6, G.210.
To rub, to wipe.

搌 °tsen, 44, G.294.
To turn about.

搐 ts'ok, 99, G.4743.
To drag along.

搥 te, c. teh, 102, G.2836.
To throw (as a stone).

丨 dzoe.
To beat.

携見攜 yi, 179, G.4118.
To lead by the band.

掴 'weh, kw'eh, 270, G.5248.
To incommode, dishonor.

搆 keu°, 330, G.6153.
To make, complete.

搴 chien, 389, G.1651.
To join hands, take.

揔 chung°, 403, G.2108. Press down, put the hand on.

搉 chak, 411, G.3262.
To beat, knock.

搕 k'eh, 430, G.6109.
To pat, beat.

搯見抽 ts'eu, 550, G.7257.
Toss in the arms.

搤 uh, 629, G.8482.
To take.

搦 nyuh, 636, G.8215.
To grasp, take hold of.

搬 pen, 650, G.8592.
To move, transplant.

搏 pok, 706, G.9373.
To beat, strike.

搡 °saung, 725, G.9568.
To oppose with the hand.

搔 sau, c. tsau, 726, G.9576.
To scratch.

搜同摎 seu, 755, G.10227. To search, rapid, swift.

搠 ts'ok, 774, G.10178.
To shoot out.

損 °sung, 829, G.10440.
To wound.

搭 teh, c. tah, 841, G.10485.
Joined with, and.

搨 t'ah, 843, G.10495.
To soil, daub.

搪 daung, 861, G.10770.
Presuming, to evade.

搗同擣 °tau, 866, G. 10791.
Pound in a mortar.

搶 °ts'iang, 969, G.1258.
To take by force.

搓 ts'oo, 1003, G.11772.
To rub on.

搲 'wo, 1036, G.12439.
To seize, hold.

搗 °oo, 1061, G.12726.
To hide with the hand.

搖 yau, 1075, G.12916.
To move to and fro.

搅見擋 °taung, 858.
To obstruct.

搿 geh.
To squeeze.

摣 11 tso, 3, G.157.
To seize, clutch.

摺 tseh, 41, G.559.
To fold, wrinkled.

摯 ts°, 61, G.1797.
Great, earnestly.

摭見拓 tsak, 69, G.1914.
To pick up.

摴 chui, 92, G.10094.
To play cards, pleased.

摳 k'eu, 331, G.6171.
To lift up the clothes.

摜又見**慣** gwan°, 476, G.6380.
To beat out.

摟 leu, 513, G.7341.
To carry off, drag off.

摘 t's, 517, G.1970.
To find out, select.

摞 loo, 552, G.7286.
To arrange, pile up.

摩 moo, 602, G.7969.
To rub, polish.

摸 mok, 603, G.7589.
To touch.

摹 moo, 605, G.8064.
To pattern, copy.

摽 °p'iau, 683, G.9096.
To push off.

摻 san, 734, G.4478.
Small, delicate hand.

摧 °ts'an, 734, G.9723.
Separated, picked over.

摏 song, 784, G.2922.
To ram down, to batter.

摔 soeh, 785, G.10106.
To scatter, spread out.

摬 teu, 873, G.11425.
To raise, get hold of, seize.

摶 doen, 938, G.12152.
To make round, to roll.

摲 °dzan, 946, G.309.
To strike, to throw.

摲 san°, 946, G.308.
To cut in two.

摘 tsuh, c. tsak, 959, G.228.
To pick with the hand.

攓 ts'ien, 980, G.1710.
To graft into, stick into.

摧 ts'oe, 1017, G.11920.
To repress, urge, to push.

摠見**總** °tsong, 1023, G.12012.
Collect, all, whole.

樣 yang°, 1073, G.12853.
A rule, pattern.

㨨見**旋** zih, zien, zien°, 821.
Turn around.

撐12見**撐** ts'ung, c. ts'ang°, 30, G.735. To push, pole.

撐 ts'ung, c. ts'ang, ts'ang°, 30, G.736. To push, pole.

撦 °ts'a, 40, G.582.
To tear, force apart.

撤 ts'eh, 42, G.579.
To remove, recall.

撞 dzaung°, 114, G.2766.
To hit, collide.

撰 dzan°, 118, G.2718.
Compose, record, edit.

撫 °foo, 145, G.3735. Soothe, comfort, control, quiet.

撝同**揮麾** hwe, 260, G.5158.
To split.

撬 chau, 375, G.1428.
Pry open.

撅 kyoeh, 485, G.3204.
To strike.

撈 lau, c. liau, 'lau, 507, G.6795. To hook up, dredge.

撩 liau, 527, G.7044. To hook up.

撓 nau, 617, G.3881. Confused.

撚 °'nyien, 634, G.5630. To work over in the fingers.

撆 p'ih, 686, G.9164. To strike a stroke, throw away.

撇 同 撆 p'ih, 686, G.9163. See above.

播 poo°, 703, G.9369. To scatter, sow.

撥 peh, 708, G.8526. To give, from, by.

撲 p'ok, 710, G. 9441. To strike, slap, to fall down.

撒 sah, 721, G.9523. To scatter, spread.

揌 sa, 732, G.9653. To strike.

撏 zing, c. zien, 800, G.4554. To take.

撕 s, 835, G.4102. To rend.

撣 °dan, 852, G.10605. To seize, grasp.

撢 t'en°, c. °toen, 857, G.10662. To dust, a duster, to strike.

摥 t'aung, 860, G.10752. To ward off.

撮 ts'oeh, 1006, G.11750. To pinch, borrow.

撙 tsung, 1019, G.11950. Frugal.

撍 tsung, 1026, G.11536. Quick, swift.

13 撾 tso, 111, G.2680. To strike, beat.

撼 °'en, 166, G.3833. To move, agitate.

擐 gwan°, 249, G.5042. To put on armor.

擊 見 擊 kyuh, 375, G.1425. To whip, to screen.

撿 °kyien, 385, G.1660. To press, examine.

擊 kyuh, 395, G.869. To tap, run against, arouse.

擒 jung, 402, G.2103. To clutch (as a hawk).

擎 jung, 408, G.2205. To raise up, elevate.

據 kyui°, 442, G.3044. Tangible, evidence.

擂 le, le°, 510, G.6825. To crush with the hand.

擄 °'loo, 557, G.7285. To capture, captivity.

擗 p'ih, 694, G.8554. To bend, break, discard.

擘 puh, c. pak, 710, G.8555. To break in pieces.

擌 suh, 723, G.9542. To stop up.

擅 zen°, 753, G.9677. To usurp, unauthorized.

撻 t'ah, 844, G.10474.
To whip.

擔 tan, 850, G.10624.
To bring.

| tan°.
A burden.

擋 taung°, 858, G.10722.
To obstruct, protect.

操 ts'au, 955, G.11646.
To manage, exercise.

| ts'au°.
Principle, purpose.

擇 dzuh, 958, G.238.
Select, pick.

擁 °iong, 1149, G.13471.
To embrace, crowd.

擐 hyau.
To open, lift up.

擢[14] dzauh, 83, G.2411.
To pull out.

擤 °hung, 208, G.4627.
To blow the nose.

擬 °'nyi, 280, G.5426.
To compare, intend, pronounce, decide.

擱 kauh, c. gauh, 426, G.6038.
To put away (on shelves).

擯 ping°, 696, G.9236. To reject, expel, to receive.

擡 de, 848, G.10580.
To exalt, lift up.

擣 °tau, 866, G.10797.
To pound down.

擠 tsi°, c. tsi, 964, G.815.
To crowd, push.

擲[15] dzuh, c. dzak, 71, G.1860.
To throw away.

擄 chui, 92, G.7530.
To capture, take.

擷 yih, 194, G.12979.
To take off, select.

擾 °dzau, °zau, 292, G.5586.
To embarrass, trouble.

擴 kw'auh, 493, G.6129.
To enlarge, extend.

擸 lih, 497, G.6665.
To stroke, smooth.

擺 °pe, c. °pa, 648, G.8562.
To place.

攀 p'an, 653, G.8634.
To pull, drag.

擻 °seu, 729, G.10242.
To lift up.

擿 dzak, tih, 903, G.11037.
To scratch, throw, pick out.

擦 ts'ah, 940, G.201.
To rub, polish.

攉[16] hauh, 257, G. 3980. To move the hand to and fro.

攏 °long, 568, G.7485.
All, the whole, to unite.

攘[17] zang, 290, G.5570. To reject, to appropriate, seize.

攔 lan, c. lah, 501, G.6713.
To fence off, separate.

攖 iung, 1105, G.13321.
To assail, audacious.

攙 ts'an, 13, G.327.
To push off, away.

攜[18] yi, 179, G.4169.
To take in hand.

攝 seh, 750, G.2806.
To take, control, act for.

攛 ts'oen, 1027, G.3172.
To tempt, decoy, stir up.

攤[19] t'an, 854, G.8137.
To spread out.

攣 lien, loen, 561, G.7560.
To tie, dote on.

攞 loo, 552, G.7294.
To collect.

攢 tsan, tsoen, 1027, G.3174.
To pile up, put away.

攪[20] °kyau, c. °kau, 371, G.1375.
To confuse, disturb.

攫 jak, 492, G.6639.
To seize, claw.

攩 °taung, 858, G.10732.
To strike, impede.

攬[21] °lan, 502, G.6736.
To grasp, carry.

攂見**擤** hyau.
To open, lift up.

65 支

支 ts, 54, G. 1873. Branch, tribe, pay out, advance.

攲[8] ji, 342, G.995.
Tripped up, inclined.

𢻎見**散** °san, 724.
To scatter.

66 攴

攴 p'ok, 718, G.9486.
Slight tap, poke.

攷[2]見**考** °k'au, 327, G.5965.
To examine, examination.

收 seu, 754, G.10009.
To receive, collect.

改[3] °ke, 307, G.5783.
To change, correct.

攻 kong, 461, G.6555.
To fight.

攸 ieu, 1110, G.13388. What, which, who, to dart through.

放[4] faung°, 135, G.3455.
To release.

政[5] tsung°, 76, G.692.
To rule, govern.

故 koo°, 434, G.6190.
The cause, reason.

效[6] yau°, 193, G.4349.
To imitate, copy.

敇見**策** ts'uh.
To whip, strike.

敉 mi.
To console, comfort.

敕[7] ts'uh, 72, G.194.
Imperial orders.

教 kyau°, c. kau°, 372, G.1352.
To teach, instruct.

救 kyeu°, 415, G.2281.
To save.

敏 °'ming, 598, G.7933.
Clever, prompt, witty.

敖 ngau, 623, G.82.
Tall, proud.

丨 nyau°.
Proud.

敗 be°, c. ba°, 648, G.8567.
Destroy, defeat.

敘 °dzui, °zu, 819, G.4768.
To arrange, discourse.

敔 °nyui, 1126, G.13625.
Musical instrument.

敞8 °ts'ang, 28, G.442.
High, a plateau.

敢 °ken, 312, G.5841.
Daring.

攲 kyi, °chi, 336, G.804.
Uneven, irregular.

敁 chan, c. k'an, 389, G.1776.
To peek at.

敝 bi°, 675, G.8970.
Spoiled.

散 °san, san°, 724, G.9559.
To scatter.

敦 tung, 927, G.12203.
Generous.

敬9 kyung°, 406, G.2144.
To reverence, respect.

敳10 nge, 619, G.26.
Able to arrange.

敲 chau, c. k'au, 373, G.1389.
To strike.

敷11 foo, 143, G.3638. To diffuse, spread out, sufficient.

敺同驅 chui, 443, G.8491.
To expel, drive out.

數 soo°, 777, G.10075.
Number.

丨 °soo.
To account.

丨 sauh.
Worried, continuous care.

敵 dih, 902, G.10921.
Enemy, foe.

整12 °tsung, 75, G.697.
Adjust, repair.

斂13 lien°, 534, G.7143.
To collect, place in coffin.

斁 yuh, 918, G.5493.
Indolent, lazy.

丨 too°.
Destroyed.

斃14 bi°, 676, G.8976.
To die, struck dead.

斆16 yau°, 194, G.4340.
To imitate, copy.

67 文

文 vung, 1041, G.12633.
Letters, cash, color.

斈3 見舉 °kyui, 439.
To lift up, propose.

斋6 見齋 tse, c. tsa, 10, G.235.
To reverence, retired.

斐8 °fi, 137, G.3462.
Graceful, elegant.

斌同彬 ping, 696, G.9254.
Honesty and polite-

ness blended.

斑 pan，650，G.8597.
Variegated，spotted.

斕17 lan，501，G.6714.
Striped，various color.

68 斗

斗 °teu，874，G.11427.
A bushel，a star，a peck.

料6 liau°，530，G.7070.
Material，to estimate.

斛7 'ok，233，G.4918.
A measure，a picul.

斜 zie，c. zia，796，G.4226.
Diagonal.

斝8 °kya，353，G.1185.
A metallic libation cup.

斟9 tsung，16，G.624.
To deliberate，pour out.

斡10 'wah，475，G.6377.
Supply，deficiency.

69 斤

斤 kyung，397，G.2019.
A catty，an axe.

斥1 ts'uh，c. ts'ak，72，G.1962.
To expel，drive away.

斧4 °foo，147，G.3738.
An axe.

斨 dziang，969，G.1277.
A broad axe，to slander.

斫5 tsak，c. tsauh，81，G.563.
To cut with an axe.

斬7 °tsan，tsan，12，G.307.
To sunder，cut.

斮8 tsauh，81，G.558.
To cut in two.

斯 s，834，G.10262.
To split，this，that.

新9 sing，806，G.4574.
New，last.

斲12 tsauh，83，G.2417.
To cut，a knife.

斷14 °doen，937，G.12149.
To break，cut.

| doen°.
Certainly.

| °toen.
To shorten.

斸21 tsauh，96，G.2582.
To cut，a knife.

70 方

方 faung，132，G.3435.
Square，place，compare，to.

旁4 見旁 baung，658，G.8674.
At the side.

於 yui，1118，G.13515.
In，at，upon，relating.

旆5 見旆 p'e°，671，G.8802.
A flag.

施 s，758，G.9934. Expanded，granted，to give，to do.

| s°.
To distribute.

旃6 tsen，44，G.279.
Banner，staff.

旂 ji，344，G.1017.
A flag.

旅 °lui，559，G.7541.
A stranger.

旄 mau，580，G.7687. Tail of the yak，an old man.

旆 p'e°，671，G.8800.
A flag.

旁 baung，658，G.8675.
Side.

丨 baung°.
To learn，to depend on.

旒[7] 見旒 lieu，548，G.7246. Streamers，pennants.

旎 °nyi，631，G.8210. Fluttering of flags in the wind.

旋 zien，zien°，c. zih，821，G.4780. To turn about.

族 zok，1015，G.11845.
Clan，family，tribe.

旌 tsing，993，G.2150.
A signal，flag.

旐[8] °zau，35，G.492. Banner inscribed with snakes，etc.

旒[9] lieu，548，G.7247.
Streamers，pennants.

旖[10] °i，272，G.5364. The tremulous waving of a banner.

旗 ji，344，G.1045.
A flag.

旛[14] fan，124，G.3395.
Streamer，funeral flag.

旟[15] yui，1122，G.13532.
A triangular flag.

71 无

无 voo，1059，G.12752.
Not，none，destroy.

旡[1] kyi°，339，G.948.
Belching of the stomach.

既[7] kyi°，339，G.949. When，since，already，finish.

72 日

日 zeh，c. nyih，293，G.5595.
Day，sun.

旦[1] tan°，851，G.10633. Morning，excellent，purpose.

旧 見舊 jeu°，414.
Old.

旨[2] °ts，57，G.1790.
Will，good，excellent.

旬 dzing，812，G.4864.
A decade.

旭 hyok，825，G.4760.
Rising sun.

早 °tsau，953，G.11603.
Early，morning.

旱[3] 'oen°，'°oen，164，G.3796.
Dry.

阳 見陽 yang，1071，G.12873.
The sun.

旰 koen°，313，G.5817.
Sunset，dusk.

昂[4] ngaung，2，G.75.
To rise higher，elevate.

昌 ts'ang，ts'aung，26，G.427.
Abundant，prosperous.

昉 °faung, 134, G.3441. Dawning, bright.

昊 °'au, 172, G.3887. Luminous, vast, grand.

昕 hyung, 205, G.4567. Morn, dawn.

昏 hwung, 267, G.5222. Twilight, obscure.

易 yuh, 281, G.5497. To change.

| yi°. Easy.

昆 k'wung, 494, G.6517. Alike same race, brothers.

旻 'ming, 597, G.7927. Autumnal sky, sad feelings.

明 ming, 599, G.7946. Clear, to understand.

昔 sih, 802, G.4105. Formerly, ancient.

昇 sung, 771, G.9880. Rising sun, ascending.

昃 tsuh, 959, G.11683. Afternoon sun.

旺 waung°, c. yaung°, 1045, G.12495. Fervent heat, brilliant.

旹見**時** z, 759, G.10004. Time.

昶5 °ts'ang, 28, G.462. A long day, extended.

昭 tsau, 31, G.473. Bright.

春 ts'ung, 104, G.2854. Spring.

昴 °mau, 582, G.7694. 18th of the zodiacal constellations.

昧 me°, 586, G.7733. Without, light, dumb.

是 °z, 762, G.9940. Is, yes, this, these.

星 sing, 808, G.4602. A star.

昨 dzauh, c. dzok, dzo, zau, zauh, zo, 1005, G.11744. Yesterday.

昜 yang, 1070, G.12874. To open, expand, bright.

映 iung°, 1108, G.13307. Shine out, reflect.

昱 yok, 1139, G.13635. Bright, glorious sun.

昻見**昂** ngaung. To rise higher, elevate.

晁6見**朝** dzau, 32, G.493. A court, dynasty.

晅 hyoen, 231, G.4802. Bright sun or fire.

晃 °hwaung, 253, G.5137. Light.

晌 °hyang, 741, G.9731. Noon.

時 z, 759, G.9921. Time, hour.

晉 tsing°, 990, G. 2670. To grow, enter, a kingdom.

晋見晉 tsing°, 990, G.2069. To enter, a kingdom.

晏 ien°, c. an°, 1089, G.13126. Evening, peaceful, clear sky.

晒見曬 se°, c. so°, 733. To sun, dry.

晨 7 zung, 21, G.655. Morning, dawn.

晝 tseu°, 50, G.2475. Daytime, light.

晢見晣 tseh, 62, G.1928. Bright, clear.

晣 tseh, 62, G.1929. Bright, perspicuous.

晞 hyi, 177, G.4052. To dry by the sun.

晛 yien°, hyien°, 202, G.4538. Winter's sun melting snow.

晦 hwe°, 263, G.5179. Dusky, obscure.

晡 boo, 712, G.9462. Afternoon.

晚 °van, °wan, c. °man, an°, 1038, G.12481. Late, evening, behind.

晤 ngoo°, 1063, G.12706. To see face to face.

晟 zung°, 773, G.9888. Bright.

智 8 ts°, 58, G.1784. To know, wisdom.

景 °kyung, 405, G.2143. Bright, condition, aspect, landscape.

晷 °kwe, 484, G.6442. Sun-dial.

晾 liang°, c. laung, 527, G.7028. To dry in the sun.

暏 pih, 685, G.9144. To dry in the sun.

普 °p'oo, 716, G.9513. Universal, everywhere.

晳 sih, 802, G.4042. Bright.

晰 sih, 802, G.4043. Clear, bright.

晬 soe°, 828, G.10415. Revolution of a complete year in the age of a person.

晶 tsing, 993, G.2149. Crystal, transparent.

晴 dzing, 996, G.2186. Bright, cleared up sky.

暇 9 ye°, c. ya°, 184, G.4196. Leisure, idle.

暄 hyoen, 231, G.4808. Genial, warm.

暉 hwe, 260, G.5150. A sun ray, bright.

暌 gwe, 487, G.6488. Distant from, separated.

暗 en°, 622, G.57. Dark, darkness.

暝見暖 °noen, 643, G.8146. Warm, genial.

暖 °noen, 643, G.8142. Warm, genial.

暑 °su, 776, G.10065. Summer, hot weather.

暘 yang, 1071, G.12877. The sun.

暎 見 映 iung°, 1108, G.13309. To shine in or through.

暈 yuin°, 1145, G.13816. Halo of sun, vapor, fog.

暢 10 ts'ang°, 29, G.461. Contented, happy.

暠 °kau, 326, G.5928. White, hoary.

暝 ming, 601, G.7954. Obscure sun.

暵 11 hoen°, 163, G.3835. Dry, parched.

暮 moo°, 606, G.7987. Sunset, end of life.

暱 nyuh, 635, G.8219. Near at hand, draw near.

暴 bau°, 666, G.8724. Cruel, fierce.

| bok, c. pau°. To show, proclaim.

暩 p'iau°, 684, G.9125. To dry in the sun.

暫 dzan°, 946, G.310. A brief time.

曉 12 °hyau, 193, G.4313. Early light, understand.

曀 ih, 272, G.5347. The sun hidden by clouds.

暨 kyi°, 339, G.956. And, together with.

曆 lih, 537, G.6923. The planets, almanac, calender.

暹 sien, 800, G.4479. Siam, rising sun.

曇 den, 855, G.10700. Overspreading clouds.

暾 t'ung, 929, G.12230. Early sun.

曈 dong, 935, G.12301. The sun about rising.

曖 13 e°, 620, G.18. Dull sun.

燠 iok, 1140, G.113. Heat.

曛 14 hyuin, 212, G.4856. Evening twilight.

曚 'mong, 608, G.7765. Obscure sun.

曙 dzui°, 778, G.10067. Early, sun about rising.

曜 yau°, 1078, G.12954. Splendor of the sun.

矆 hwauh, hauh. Lightning.

曠 15 k'waung°, 480, G.6415. Bright, distant.

曝 bok, 666, G.8726. To dry in the sun.

曦 16 hyi, 177, G.4093. Sun-light.

曨 long, 568, G.7486. Sun about to rise.

曩 17 °naung, 615, G.8148. Formerly, previous.

曬19 se°, c. so°, 733, G.9654.
To sun, dry.

73 日

日 yoeh, 1130, G.13772.
To say.

曳2 yi°, 282, G.5475.
To drag, pull.

曲 chok, 458, G.3062.
Bent, a song.

更3 kung, c. kang, 321, G.2159.
To change, night watch.

| kung°.
More.

曷5 oeh, 216, G.3929.
Why, what reason.

書6 su, 774, G.10024.
A book, to write.

曼7 man°, 575, G.7626.
Long, extended, fine.

曹 zau, 955, G.11636.
A judge, S. plural.

替8 t'i°, 884, G.11018.
Abolish, substitute.

曾 tsung, 952, G.11717.
To add, a name.

| dzung, zung.
Already.

最 tsoe°, 1017, G.11908.
Very, collect.

會9 we°, 264, G.5184.
To assemble, a society.

| 'we°.
Can, able.

| kwe°.
To calculate.

74 月

月 yoeh, c. nyoeh, 1129, G.13768. Moon.

有2 °yeu, 1113, G.13376.
To have.

阴3 見陰 iung, 1099, G.13225.
Shade, the female principle.

服4 vok, 152, G.3727. To use, subjugate, clothing.

朋 bung, c. bang, 661, G.8878.
A friend.

朕6 °dzung, 18, G.634.
Imperial I, a protoplasm.

朔 sauh, 773, G.10176.
First day of the moon.

朗7 °laung, 505, G.6775.
Bright.

朙 見明 ming, 599, G.7950.
Clear, to understand.

望 vaung°, c. maung°, 1045, G.12509. To look, hope for.

朝8 tsau, 32, G.478.
Morning.

| dzau.
A court, dynasty.

期 ji, 344, G.854.
A set time, season.

| kyi.
A full year.

朞見期 kyi, 336, G.852.
A full year.

膧[12] dong, 935, G.12302.
Rising moon.

朦[14] mong, 609, G.7766.
Setting moon.

朧[16] long, 568, G.7487.
Setting moon.

75 木

木 mok, 607, G.8077.
Wood.

札[1] tsah, 7, G.127.
A thin tablet, a letter.

末 meh, 604, G.7999.
End, last, dust.

本 °pung, 655, G.8846. Original, classifier of books.

术 dzeh, 779, G.2577.
Medical herb.

未 vi°, c. mi°, 1052, G.12606.
Not yet, flavor, taste.

朱[2] tsu, 85, G.2544.
Vermilion color.

朽 °hyeu, 211, G.4673.
Rotten, decayed wood.

机見機 kyi, 337, G.838.
Machinery.

朴同樸 p'ok, c. p'auh, 711, G.9416. Bark of magnolia, trusty.

朵同朶 °too, 909, G.10789.
A cluster, flower.

朶 °too, 909, G.10788.
A cluster, flower.

朿 t's°, 1035, G.12410.
A thorn on plants.

杈[3] ts'o, 7, G.188.
Branches, forked.

杈見杈 ts'o.
Branches, forked.

杖 °dzang, 25, G.426.
A staff, to lean on.

杓 piau, c. dzauh, 81, G.9103.
A handle, spoon, ladle.

杏 °yung, c. °'ang, 209, G.4637.
Apricot, plumb.

杆 koen, 310, G.5818.
Flag pole, a paling.

杠 kaung, 319, G.5887.
A small bridge.

李 °li, 520, G.1067.
The plum.

杞 °chi, 347, G.6884.
Alder tree, acid fruit.

杲見梅 me. Plums, prunes, strawberries.

杉 san, 733, G.9638.
A kind of pine.

束 sok, 779, G.10031.
To tie, bind, to rule.

杕 di°, 880, G.10959.
Lone tree, eminent.

杜 °doo, 917, G.12043. Medical plant, a reddish fruit.

材 dze, ze, 942, G.11497.
Materials, ability.

村 ts'ung, 1020, G.11968.
A village.

杅 oo, 1058, G.12718.
A trowel.

杌 nyeh, 1065, G.12785.
A stool.

来見來 le, 498.
To come.

枕[4] °tsung, 16, G.630.
A pillow.

| °tsung.
To pillow.

枝 ts, 55, G.1875.
Branches.

杼 °dzu, 91, G.2611.
A weaver's shuttle.

杵 °ts'u, °su, 93, G.2659.
A pestle, beater.

杶 ts'ung, 104, G.2867.
Sumach, varnish tree.

杭 'aung, 168, G.3856.
Hangchow, ferry boat.

枘 dzoe°, 301, G.5716.
A handle.

杰見傑 jih, 377, G.1500.
Name.

果 °koo, 489, G.6627.
A fruit, truly, indeed.

林 ling, 540, G.7157.
Forest, wood.

枚 me, 584, G.7720.
One, a gag, trunk of tree.

杪 °'miau, 592, G.7858.
A twig, minute, second.

枏 nen, 614, G.8145.
A yellowish fine wood.

杻 °ts'eu, 639, G.2469.
Manacles, hand-cuffs.

| °nyen.
A kind of tree.

杷 bo, 646, G.8544.
A fruit, to rake, a rake.

板 °pan, 651, G.8588.
A board, unyielding.

枇 bi, c. bih, 679, G.9049.
A fruit, the bihbo.

杯 pe, 668, G.8781.
A cup.

柿 °z, 763, G.3496.
The persimmon.

析 sih, 802, G.4040.
To split, discriminate.

松 song, 830, G.10449.
The pine tree.

東 tong, 930, G.12248.
East, landlord.

枉 °'waung, 1044, G.12496.
Illegal, wrong, distorted.

杳 °iau, 1076, G.7868.
Obscure, dark, sombre.

查[5] dzo, 6, G.193.
To examine.

|見楂 tso.
A sour fruit.

柴 ze, c. za, 11, G.258.
Kindling wood.

柘 tso°, 39, G.562.
A kind of tree.

栅 ts'uh, c. sak, 42, G.144.
A bar, barrier.

枳 °ts, 57, G.1864.
A hedge-thorn.

柱 °dzu, 89, G.2533.
A pillar, post.

柙 yah, 185, G.4215.
A cage for beasts.

枵 hyau, 192, G.4326.
Hollow, empty, famished.

染 °zen, c. °nyien, 286, G.5562.
To dye, dye shop.

柑 ken, 311, G.5833.
Loose-jacket orange.

柔 dzeu, 294, G.5653.
Mild, gentle.

枸 °keu, 329, G.6140.
A tree, crooked.

枷 kya, c. ka, 350, G.1145.
A cangue, wooden collar.

架 kya°, c. ka°, 353, G.1157.
A frame of wood, shelf.

柬 °kyien, °kyan, c. kan°, 384, G.1668. To select, a visiting-card.

柩 jeu°, 415, G.2278.
A coffin.

柯 k'oo, 423, G.6039.
Axe handle, a branch.

枯 k'oo, 436, G.6256.
Withered, dried.

柺 °kwe, c. kwa, 470, G.6329.
A cane, staff.

柜 °kyui, 486, G.3007.
A table, counter.

柳 °lieu, 549, G.7251.
Willow tree.

某 °meu, 588, G.8031.
A certain person, a fruit.

柰 ne°, 613, G.8122.
A kind of plum, resource.

柄 ping°, 700, G.9298.
A handle.

枰 bing, 701, G.9312.
Chessboard.

柏 puh, c. pak, 708, G.8559.
Cedar tree.

枲 °si, 790, G.4187.
Hemp plant.

枱見檯 de, 847, G.10309.
A table.

柁見舵 °doo, 912, G.11330.
Rudder of a boat.

柝 t'auh, 915, G.11398.
Watch-man's clapper.

柮 teh, 921, G.12088.
A stump.

| ngeh.
Branchless tree.

柒 ts'ih, 987, G.1056.
Varnish tree, seven.

柞 dzauh, 1005, G.11745.
Hard tree.

柚 yeu°, 1116, G.13408.
The pumelo.

| dzok. The reed or slaie of a loom.

桎6 tseh, 68, G.1824.
Shackles for the feet.

栻 suh, 73, G.2011.
A tree, pattern.

桌 tsauh, 82, G.2393.
Table.

株 tsu, 85, G.2547.
Classifier of trees, a post.

桁 yung, c. ‘ang, 170, G.3859.
Purlines of roof.

丨 ‘aung.
A cangue—at Peking.

栩 °hyui, 228, G.4751.
A sort of oak, soft.

核 ‘eh, c. weh, 234, G.3964.
Kernel, the facts, earnestly.

桓 wen, 246, G.5075.
Martial valor, tomb-stone.

根 kung, 317, G.5974.
A root.

栲 °k‘au, c. k‘eh, 327, G.5968.
A willow-basket or bucket.

枅 kyi, 335, G.887. A short piece of wood on the top of posts.

栔 chi°, 350, G.1052.
To carve.

校 kyau°, kau°, 373, G.1302.
To compare, to collate.

丨 yau°.
A high school or gymnasium.

桔 kyih, 376, G.1467.
A water wheel, a fruit.

桀 jih, 377, G.1498.
Hen-roost, savage, harsh.

桕 °jeu, 414, G.2287.
The tallow tree.

格 kuh, c. kak, 426, G.6029.
Pattern, enquire into.

栱 °kong, 463, G.6577.
A post, tie-beam.

栝 kwah, 469, G.6289.
A kind of tree.

桄 kwaung, 478, G.6390.
The beam of a loom.

框 k‘waung, c. chaung, 479, G.6403. End pieces of coffin.

桂 kwe°, 484, G.6435.
Cinnamon, cassia.

栳 °lau, 508, G.6788.
Willow rice basket.

栗 lih, 539, G.6973.
Chestnut.

案 oen°, 622, G.46.
Table, bench, judge, a case.

栢見**柏** puh, c. pak, 708, G.8561. The pine.

桑 saung, 724, G.9566.
The mulberry.

桒見**桑** saung.
The mulberry.

栖 si, 788, G.4033.
To roast, stop.

栒 °sung, 813, G.4869.
Cross-beam in a temple.

桃 dau, 870, G.10807.
The peach.

條 diau，888，G.11095. A long thing，a section.

桐 dong，934，G.12274. National tree of China from which oil is made.

栽 tse，940，G.11483. To set，plant.

桅 we，1050，G.12591. Mast of ship.

梔7 ts，55，G.1859. Seeds used for dyeing yellow.

棁 tseh，84，G.2419. A small king-post.

椓 tsu，87，G.2590. A dead tree，rotten.

梵 van，127，G.3403. Sanscrit language.

械 ye°，188，4436. Weapons，fetters.

梟 hyau，192，G.4329. A kind of owl，a bandit.

桿見杆 koen，312，G.5827. A flag staff.

梗 °kung，c. °kang，322，G.5994. A tree，wicked，wilful.

桷 kyak，410，G.3237. Square rafters.

梏 kok，454，G.6246. Hand cuffs.

梱 °kw'ung，496，G.6545. Door frame.

梨同棃 li，515，G.6888. Peer tree，a pear.

梁 liang，525，G.7021. A bridge，beam.

梅 me，584，G.7765. Phums，prunes，strawberries.

梆 paung，656，G.8652. Watch-man's cylinder for beating.

桮同杯 pe，668，G.8783. Wooden cup.

梢 sau，745，G.9758. Tip end of a tree.

梳 soo，c. s，775，G.10025. To comb，a comb.

桫 soo，c. so，814，G.10193. Horse-chestnut.

梭 soo，814，G.10199. A shuttle.

梯 t'i，882，G.10990. A ladder，stairs.

梃 °t'ing，908，G.11288. A straight stick.

桶 °dong，935，G.12289. A wooden vessel.

椮 °tsan，945，G.11541. Strips of wood placed between the fingers for torture.

梓 °ts，1031，G.12356. Stately tree，to carve characters.

梧 ngoo，1060，G.12707. A kind of tree.

梛 ya，1079，G.12984. A cocoa-nut.

梦見夢 mong°，c. maung°，610. A dream，to dream.

梹見檳 ping, 695.
Areca-nut.

棧8 °dzan, dzan°, 12, G.298.
A ware-house, inn.

棦 tsung, 30, G.748.
A thorn on a tree.

棖 dzung, c. dzang, 31, G.773.
Door posts.

棹同櫂 dau°, 34, G.494.
An oar for boats.

丨 dzauh, tsauh.
Table.

植 dzuh, 71, G.1849.
To plant, to place.

椓 tsauh, 82, G.2402.
To strike, pound.

椎 dzoe, c. dz, z, 102, G.2823.
Wooden mallet, beetle, to beat.

棼 vung, 130, G.3531.
Confused.

棻 vung, 130, G.3530.
A fragrant wood.

椅 i, i°, 279, G.5357.
A kind of tree.

丨 °i, c. iui°.
A chair.

棋同棊 ji, 343, G.1031.
Chess men.

棊 ji, 343, G.1032.
Chess men.

棨 °chi, 348, G.1112.
A signal flag or board.

棄 chi°, 349, G.1116.
To reject, abandon.

棘 kyuh, 392, G.959.
Thorn, bramble.

極 juh, 393, G.859.
Extreme, ultimate.

椐 kyui, 438, G.2992.
Elm wood, knotty whip.

椇 °kyui, 439, G.3022.
A fruit tasting like a plum.

棬 choen, 452, G.3165.
A wooden cup.

棃 li, G.6941a.
Pear tree, a pear.

棺 kwen, 472, G.6347.
A coffin.

椁見槨 kwauh, 492, G.6616.
Stone or brick work for coffins.

棍 °kwung, 495, G.6520.
Stick, staff.

棱 lung, 506, G.6863.
Cornered, square.

棉 mien, 594, G.7883.
Cotton.

棒 °baung, 657, G.8655.
A staff.

棚 bung, c. bang, 662, G.8880.
Awning, booth.

棅同柄 ping°, 700, G.9306.
Power.

森 sung, 734, G.9616.
Close, thick.

棲同栖 si, ts'i, 788, G.985. To roost, perch, stay.

棠 daung, 861, G.10757. Crab-apple.

棣 di°, 879, G.10965. A kind of plum.

棟 tong°, 932, G.12252. A post.

棗 °tsau, 953, G.11623. The buck-thorn, Chinese "dates."

椒 tsiau, 970, G.1350. Spicy plants, pepper.

椊 ts'oeh, 1014, G.11837. To put in an axe handle.

棕見椶 tsong, 1022, G.11977. Palmetto or palm.

椀同盌 °'wen, 1039, G.12470. A bowl.

椏 ia, c. au, 1066, G.12816. A fork in a tree.

棫 yok, 1141, G.13664. A tree.

棵 k'oo. Classifier of trees.

楂⁹同查槎樝 tso, 3, G.133. Hawthorn, a fruit.

椹同葚 °zung, c. tung, 16, G.625. Larch or juniper, a target.

楨 tsung, 73, G.608. An evergreen tree.

楮 °ts'u, 93, G.2649. Mulberry tree, paper.

楚 °ts'oo, 94, G.2662. Grievous, cleared up.

椿 ts'ung, 101, G.2856. Long lived tree, a father.

椽 dzen, 119, G.2743. Rafters.

楓 fong, 156, G.3555. The maple tree.

楥 hyoen°, 232, G.4817. A last, to form on a last.

楦見楥 hyoen°, 232, G.4809. See above.

楷 °cha, c. °k'a, 362, G.1203. A straight tree, a pattern.

椷 kyan, c. kan, 383. G.1611. A box, wooden bowl.

楇 'oo°, 489, G.6620. A pot for greasing the axle.

楞同棱 lung, 506, G.6868. Square, cornered.

楝 lien°, 536, G.7148. Pride of India, lilac tree.

楣 me, 585, G.7717. Cross stick over a door.

楙 meu°, 589, G.8042. The quince, luxuriant.

楘 mok, 607, G.8084. Leather bands on front of a cart.

楠見枬 men, 614, G.8131. Yellowish fine wood.

楩 bien, 690, G.9228. Yellow wood used in furniture.

楯 °dung, 784, G.10154. The beam of a railing.

楫 ts‘ih, 976, G.941.
To row, an oar.

楸 ts‘ieu, 1001, G.2303.
A kind of tree, chess-board.

椶 tsong, 1022, G.11997.
Palmetto or palm.

楊 yang, 1071, G.12878.
The willow tree.

椰同**梛** ya, 1079, G.12976.
The cocoa-nut.

業 nyih, 1082, G.12991.
Employment, already.

楹 yung, 1107, G.13293.
A pillar, post.

榆 yui, 1123, G.13575.
The elm tree.

楀 °yui, 1125, G.13619.
A kind of tree.

楢 yeu.
A soft kind of wood.

榨[10] tso°, 4, G.154.
An oil press, to press.

槎 dzo, 6, G.198.
Drift wood, a raft.

榛 tsung, 16, G.610.
Chinese hazel tree, thorny.

榰 ts, 55, G.1794.
Wooden base for a pillar.

槌 dzoe, 102, G.2837.
Wooden mallet, to beat.

榧 °fi, 138, G.3480.
A species of yew.

槐 we, c. wa, 243, G.5028.
A tree.

榦 koen°, 313, G.5813.
Central branch of a tree.

槁 °kau, 325, G.5929.
A withered tree.

構 keu°, 330, G.1242.
To make, construct.

榷 chak, 411, G.3243.
A water barrier.

槅 kuh, 428, G.6064.
The yoke of a cart.

榼 k‘eh, 430, G.6110.
A wine cup.

榾 kweh, 454, G.6236.
Fine-grained white wood.

榖 kok, 454, G.6228.
Variety of mulberry tree.

榔 laung, 504, G.6779.
The betel-nut.

榴見**橊** lieu, 547, G.7258.
The pomegranate.

槓見**杠** kaung, 569, G.5893.
Sedan-chair pole.

榜同**[illegible]** °paung, 657, G.8662.
List of graduates.

丨 paung°.
To row a boat.

槃 ben, 654, G.8618.
A wooden tray.

榯 z, 760, G.9923.
Erect(as a tree).

槊 sauh, 773, G.10179.
A great spear, chess board.

榭 zie°, zia°, 797, G.4431.
An arbor fenced room.

榫 °sung, 829, G.10445. To fit a piece of wood into a hole, a tenon.

榻 t'ah, 843, G.10514. A couch, a bed.

槍 ts'iang, 968, G.1259. A spear, a gun.

榱 ts'oe, 1017, G.11935. A square, rafter.

槝 oo, 1058, G.12727. A wood suitable for arrows.

榮 yong, 1146, G.5740. Glory.

樝 11 tso, 3, G.159. A sour red fruit.

樾 °ts'an, 14, G.364. A kind of peach tasting like a plum.

樟 tsaung, 23, G.398. The camphor tree.

樞 chui, 92, G.2623. An axle, hinge, fundamental.

樗 chui, 92, G.2627. A tree. A useless tree with fetid leaves, the ailantus.

樁 tsaung, 113, G.2762. A stake post, an affair.

樊 van, 125, G.3408. A cage, a railing.

槩 ke°, 307, G.5791. A grain striker, to even.

概同槩 ke°, 307, G.5790. See above.

槿 °kyung, 399, G.2047. A tree whose blossom fade in a day, fleeting.

樛 kyeu, 413, G.2272. Pendulous branches.

槨同椁 kwauh, 492, G.6618. Brick-made tomb.

樏 °le, 511, G.6821. Partitions of a tray.

樓 leu, 513, G.7343. A chamber, upper story.

樑 liang, 525, G.7022. A beam, ridge-pole.

樂 yak, ngauh, 554, G.6817. Music.

| lauh. Happy, joyous.

| yau°. To take delight in.

樐同櫓 °loo, 557, G.7425. An oar, paddle.

模 moo, 605, G.7988. A pattern, model.

標 piau, 681, G.9097. Top-most branch, signal.

樨 si, 789, G.4129. A reddish flower.

槥 dzoe°, 829, G.10420. A small coffin.

槽 zau, 955, G.11639. A manger, trough.

槳 °tsiang, 968, G.1216. An oar, paddle.

槧 dzan°, 983, G.1763. Blocks, tablets.

橾 ts'ih, 987, G.1025.
Varnish, paint.

樣 yang°, 1073, G.12854.
Model, rule, pattern.

槱 °yeu, 1113, G.13401. To lay in stores of firewood.

橕[12] ts'ung, c. ts'ang, 30, G.738.
A prop, to prop.

橙 dzung, c. dzang, 31, G.660.
Common or coolie orange.

横 wung, c. wang, 236, G.3915.
Cross-bar, crosswise.

丨 wung°, c. wang°.
To act perversely.

樺 wo, 241, G.5007.
A kind of wood.

橈 nau°, 292, G.5579.
Crooked, bent hook.

丨 zau.
An oar.

橄 °kan, 312, G.5842.
Olive tree.

槔 kau, 325, G.5945.
Water wheel.

機 kyi, 333, G.787. Machinery, loom, occasion.

橇 chau, 373, G.1429.
A sledge, mud-shoe.

橋 jau, 374, G.1398.
A bridge.

橜同橛 kyoeh, joeh, 446, G.3205. A pile, a short piece.

橛 kyoeh, joeh. A post, pile, a short piece.

橘 kyoeh, 457, G.3026.
Orange.

樸 p'ok, c. p'auh, 710, G.9442.
Substance, material, honest.

樲 r°, 721, G.3362.
Small date tree.

樹 zu°, 777, G.10090.
A tree.

丨 zu.
To set up, to establish.

橡 °ziang, 793, G.4289.
Chestnut oak.

橝 den, 855, G.10675.
A hard wood.

橐 t'auh, 915, G.11404.
A sack open at both ends.

樵 dziau, 971, G.1407.
To gather fire wood.

樽 tsung, 1019, G.11951.
Wine jug.

藂見叢 dzong, 1025, G.12038.
Thick (as a forest).

樾 yoeh, 1131, G.13782.
Shade of trees.

橊 lieu.
The pomegranate.

檉[13] ts'ung, 77, G.745.
The tamarisk, or willow.

颾見風 fong, 158, G.3559.
Sound of wind among the trees, hum of priests.

檄 yuh，203，G.4162. Summons to war，hasty.

櫃 °kya，353，G.1183. A kind of wood.

檢 °kyien，385，G.1661. To examine，correct.

檠 jung，°kyung，408，G.2203. A lamp stand，bracket.

檜 kwe°，485，G.6470. The cypress.

樐見櫓 °loo，557，G.7395. An oar for propelling.

檗 puh，710，G.9397. A kind of tree.

檖 dzoe°，829，G.10404. A kind of wood.

檀 dan，854，G.10706. Sandal wood.

檔 taung°，859，G.10723. A cross-piece，rung.

檣 ziang，969，G.1286. Mast of a boat.

檐 yien，1086，G.10625. Eves of roof.

櫂14 dau°，34，G.494. An oar.

檻 °chan，c. °k'an，200，G.1642. Bars，paling，animal's cage.

櫃 gwe°，c. jui°，486，G.6464. A closet，chest.

檬 mong，609，G.7767. Trees like the locust，the mango.

檸 nyung，616，G. 8332. A tree，lemon-syrup.

檳見檳 ping，695，G.9247. The areca-nut.

檳 ping. The areca-nut.

檯 de，847，G.10581. A table.

櫈 tung°，863，G.10875. A stool，seat.

檮 dau，870，G.10832. A useless stick.

檼 iung°，1103，G.13273. A ridge-pole.

櫜15 kau，325，G.5949. The case of a bow.

櫑 le，510，G.6835. A wooden，wine-jar.

櫟 lih，538，G.6997. Scrub oak.

櫓 °loo，557，G.7389. An oar for boats.

櫚 lui，c. li，558，G.7524. A palm tree.

櫝 dok，923，G.12061. A chest，coffin.

櫛 tsih，975，G.1478. To comb，a comb.

櫞 yoen，1136，G.13741. Citron，Buddha's hand，or palm tree.

櫬16 ts'ung°，22，G.675. A coffin.

櫪 lih，537，G.6927. A stable.

櫨 loo，555，G.7398.
A short post，king-post.

櫳 long，568，G.7488.
A cage，a curtain.

櫇 bing，697，G.9270.
A fruit，the apple tree.

欄17 lan，501，G.6715.
Railing.

櫦 sen，786，G.10112.
A door bar，bolt.

櫺 ling，c. lung.
A window bar，paling.

櫻 iung，c. ang，1105，G.13322.
The cherry.

權18 joen，452，G.3190. Steel-yard weight，authority.

欒19 loen，570，G.7458.
A kind of tree.

欓20 °taung，859，G.10734. Cross-piece，round，purloins.

欖21 °lan，503，G.6737.
The olive tree.

欝22 見鬱 ioeh，1139，G.13536.
A date.

欞24 見櫺 ling，c. lung，544，G.7223. A window bar，paling.

76 欠

欠 chien°，391，G.1750.
Deficient.

次2 t'sº，1034，G.12382.
Second，secondary.

欣4 hyung，204，G.4571.
Happy，joy.

欬6 k'e°，c. k'eh，429，G.6101.
To cough，hack.

欷7 hyi，177，G.4053.
To sigh，groan.

欵見款 °kw'en，477，G.6385.
Sincere，true，a section.

欲 yok，1139，G.13642.
Long for，passion.

欹8 i，chi，272，G.5358.
Bravo，good.

歁 °k'en，315，G.5873.
Not full，not satisfied.

欺 chi，342，G.1046.
To cheat，deceive.

欽 chung，401，G.2114. To respect，reverence，imperial.

款 °kw'en，477，G.6384. Sincere，true，a section，kind.

歇9 hyih，195，G.1458.
To stop，a little.

歆 hyung，205，G.4576.
Sacrificial fumes，to taste.

歃 ts'ah，732，G.9636. Confirming an oath with blood.

歉10 chien°，chih，388，G.1633.
Deficiency，lack.

歌 koo，423，G.6046.
A hymn，song.

歐11 °eu，625，G.8492.
To vomit.

歎 t'an°，857，G.10693.
To sigh，moan.

歙[12] hyih，204，G.4134.
To snuff，turn up the nose.

歔 hyui，228，G.4714.
To sigh，moan.

歗同嘯 siau°，795，G.4320.
A hissing sound.

歛[13] han，162，G.3842.
To desire，to beg.

歟[14] yui，1122，G.13525.
A final particle.

歠[15] tseh，83，G.2432.
Drink with a noise，to sob.

歡[18] hwen，244，G.5051.
To reject，like.

77 止

止 °ts，56，G.1837.
To stop，rest.

正[1] tsung°，75，G.687.
Correct，true.

丨 tsung.
Presently，just.

此[2] °t's，1034，G.12387.
This.

步[3] boo°，713，G.9485.
Step.

歧[4] ji，345，G.1105.
Divided，forked.

武 °voo，1061，G.12744.
Military，strong，severe.

歪[5] 'we，c. hwa，'wa，1037，G.12443. Deflected.

歲[9] soe°，827，G.10382.
Year，age.

嵗見歲 soe°，827.
Year，age.

歷[12] lih，537，G.6924.
To pass on，arrange.

歸[14] kwe，c. kyui，480，G.6419.
To return.

78 歺

歺 oeh.
Rotten bone.

丨同歹 °te，844，G.10541.
Bad，evil.

歹 °te.（Generally written as No. 3509.）Bad.

死[2] °s，c. °si，836，G.10280.
To die，dead.

歿[4] meh，606，G.8056.
The end，to die.

殀 °iau，1077，G.12904.
To die prematurely.

殆[5] °de，846，G.10563.
Near，almost，dangerous.

殄 °dien，900，G.11239.
To destroy.

殂 tsoo，1008，G.2629.
To fall down.

殃 iang，1070，G.12865.
A judgement from Heaven.

殊[6] dzu，776，G.10036.
To skill，very，really，different，unlike.

殉 dzing°，dzing，814，G.4870.
To be buried alive with the dead，to follow.

殍7 °p'iau, 684, G.9140.
To die from hunger.

殖8 dzuh, 71, G.1851.
To enrich, merchandise.

殘 dzan, 947, G.11564.
To ruin, destroy.

殛9 kyuh, 393, G.860.
To put to death, punish.

殞10 °yuin, 1143, G.13836.
To perish, die.

殤11 saung, 740, G.9743.
Early death.

殪12 ih, 282, G.5348.
To shoot dead.

殰 °liau, 530, G.7046.
Spoiled.

殫 tan, 850, G.10606.
The uttermost, entire.

殭13 kyang, 363, G.1224.
Death of insects.

殮 lien°, 535, G.7139.
To put in the coffin.

殯14 ping°, 696, G.9237.
To put in the coffin.

殯同殯 ping°.
Same as above.

殲17 sien, 978, G.1580.
To kill, minute.

79 殳

殳 zu, 776, G.10047.
A spear, to kill.

段5 doen°, 937, G.12140.
A piece.

殷6 iung, 1099, G.13238.
Right, diligent.

殺同殺 sah, 731, G.9632.
To kill.

| se°.
To pare off, reduce.

殺7 sah.
See above.

殽8 yau, 193, G.12931.
Mixed food, to confuse.

殼 chak, c. k'auh, 412, G.2216.
Husk, skin of fruit.

毀9 °hwe, 262, G.5196.
Break down, demolish.

殿 dien°, 896, G.11202.
A hall, temple.

| tien°.
The hindermost.

毅11 nyi°, 284, G.5522.
Resolute, firm.

毆 °eu, 626, G.8493.
To strike.

80 毋

毋 voo, 1060, G.12765.
Do not.

母1 °moo, c. °m, 605, G.8067.
Mother.

每3 °'me, 586, G.7704.
Each.

毒5 dok, 922, G.12054.
Poison.

毓9 yok, 1141, G.13693.
To nurture, educate.

81 比

比 °pi, 674, G.8942.
Compare.

| bi°. To harmonize, with, equal.

毖[5] pi°, 676, G.8927.
Fatigue, distress.

毘 bi, 679, G.9051.
Continuous, kind, liberal.

毗 同 毘 bi, 679, G.9050.
See above.

82 毛

毛 mau, 580, G.7679.
Hair.

毡[5] 見 氈 tsen, 43, G.269.
Felt cloth.

毧[6] nyong, 303, G.5749.
Fine fur, felt.

毨 °sien, 801, G.4443. To molt, renew the hair, sleek.

毫[7] ʻau, 171, G. 3873. Long soft hair, a little, 1000th part of a cent.

毬 jeu, 417, G.2320.
A ball.

毸 so, 730, G.9626.
A shaggy surplice.

毯[8] °t'an, c. t'an, 856, G.10653.
A carpet, rug.

毳 ts'oe°, tsoeh, 1018, G.2840.
Down, soft, velvety.

毽[9] kyien°, 386, G.1596.
A shuttle-cock, foot-ball.

毹 yui, 775, G.10028.
A rug for kneeling on.

氅[12] °ts'ang, 28, G.446.
The down of a crane.

氄 °nyong, 303, G.5765. The down on birds and beasts.

氈[13] 見 氊 tsen, 43, G.283.
Felt cloth.

氊 tsen.
Felt cloth.

氍[18] jui, 444, G.3083.
A mat, a carpet.

83 氏

氏 °z, 763, G.9978.
Female name, a family.

氐[1] °ti, 878, G.10898.
To, unto.

民 ming, 597, G.7908.
People.

氓[4] mung, c. maung, 609, G.7790. People.

84 气

气 chi°, 348, G.1062.
Vapor, breath.

氛[4] fung, 129, G.3517.
Vapor, mist, miasma.

氣[6] chi°, 348, G.1064. Breath, anger, air, climate.

氤 iung, 1098, G.13217.
Warm, genial aura.

氳[10] 'wung, 1142, G.13826. Warm, genial aura.

85 水

水 °soe, c.°s, 781, G.10128. Water.

氷[1] 見冰 ping, 698, G.9278. Ice.

永 °iong, 1149, G.13504. Everlasting.

汁[9] tseh, 67, G.1789. Juice.

氾 fan°, 128, G.3425. Inundate.

求 jeu, 416, G.2315. To seek, pray, beg.

汀 t'ing, 906, G.11274. A flat beach or bank.

氽 °t'ung, 930, G.12245. To float on water.

汊[3] ts'o°, 7, G.189. Branched stream.

池 dz, 63, G.1983. A pool, tank.

汎 fan°, 128, G.3402. To float, floating.

汗 'oen°, 165, G.3784. Sweat.

汔 chih, 204, G.4147. Dried up water.

汞 °hong, 238, G.5266. Quicksilver ore.

汝 °zu, 298, G.5666. You, your, a river.

江 kyang, c. kaung, 362, G.1208. River.

汕 san, 734, G.9664. Fish jumping out of water.

汐 dzih, 804, G.4111. Night, tide.

汛 sing°, 808, G.4584. To sprinkle, a guard station.

污同汙 oo, 1058, G.12719. Stagnant, water, foul, to defile.

汙 oo, 1058, G.12716. See above.

沈[4] °sung, dzung, 20, G.649. To sink in water.

沉見沈 dzung, 20, G.649. See above.

沚 °ts, 56, G.1839. Water's edge.

沖 ts'ong, 109, G.2909. To dash, to pour in.

汾 vung, 130, G.3518. Name of a river.

沍 'oo°, 227, G.4974. Frozen, chilly, cloudy.

沂 nyi, 275, G.5438. A river in Shansi.

汭 dzoe°, 301, G.5717. A river in Kansuh.

汲 kyih, 394, G.844. To draw in, imbibe.

決 kyoeh, 447, G. 3219. To decide, certainly, flood.

汩 hweh, 454, G.6249.
To mix, float, confuse.

丨 mih.
Name of a river.

沔 °mien, 594, G.7894.
A flood, overflowing.

沒 meh, 606, G.7713.
To sink, die, not, without.

沐 mok, 607, G.8078.
To bathe the head.

汴 bien°, 688, G.9205.
Name of a river.

沙 so, 730, G.9624.
Shoal, sand, reef.

沓 deh, 842, G.10497. To pile up, rippling water, slowly.

汰 t'e°, c. t'a°, 848, G.10575.
Slippery, to clean, scour.

沌 °dung, 928, G.12217.
Interrupted, chaos.

沁 sing°, 992, G.2110.
To understand, a river.

汪 'waung, 1043, G.12497.
Wide and deep.

汶 vung, 1048, G.12635. Min River, a river in Shantung.

沃 'wok, 1065, G.12697.
To pour.

沅 nyoen, 1185, G.13746.
A large river.

沛 p'e°, 673, G.8834.
Copious, aquatic plants.

沼 5 °tsau, 34, G.467.
Fish-pond, tank.

沾 tsen, 43, G.274.
To moisten, to obtain.

治 dz, dz°, 59, G.1845.
Govern, rule, head.

注 tsu°, 89, G.2542.
To flow, to think on.

法 fah, 123, G.3366.
A rule.

泛 fan°, 128, G.3423.
To float.

沸 fi°, 139, G.3490.
Boiling water.

丨 feh.
To sprinkle.

河 'oo, 215, G.3936.
A stream, river.

泫 °yoen, 232, G.4793.
Dewdrops, falling tears.

況 hwaung°, 254, G.5146.
Ice water, to compare.

泄 sih, 282, G.4411.
To ooze, leak out.

泔 ken, 811, G.5834. Water in which rice has been scoured.

泣 chih, 896, G.1117.
Grieved, to weep silently.

沽 koo, 432, G.6191.
To buy and sell, a river.

泐 luh, 510, G.6815.
A river, split rock.

泪同淚 li°, le°, 512, G.6857.
Tears.

泠 ling, 544, G.7204.
Noise of running water.

泖 °mau, 582, G.7695.
A stream.

沫 meh, c. moo, 604, G.7575.
Froth, foam.

泯 °ming, 598, G.7912.
Exhausted, blown out.

泥 nyi, 630, G. 8197. Mire, mud, to soil, adhesive.

丨 nyi°.
Bigoted, attached to.

泮 p'en°, 654, G.8639.
Provincial college.

泡 p'au, p'au°, 667, G.8736.
Bubble, blubber.

泌 pi°, 677, G.8928.
Rushing water.

泙 bing, 701, G.9317.
The sound of water.

波 poo, 703, G.9336.
Wave.

泊 bok, c. bauh, p'ak, 707, G.9350. To stop, anchor.

泅 dzieu, c. yeu, 811, G.4666.
To swim.

泝同**溯** soo°, 817, G. 10356.
To trace to the source.

泗 s°, 836, G.10292. A river, place where Confucius taught.

泰 t'e°, c. t'a°, 848, G.10596.
Extensive, exalted.

沲同**沱** doo, 912, G.11882.
A river.

沱 doo, 912, G.11349.
A river.

沰 t'auh, c. tauh, 914, G.11343.
To drop, as rain, let down.

沮 tsui, 1009, G.2983. A branch of the Yang-tse.

丨 °tsui.
To stop, destroy, waste.

泉 dzien, 1013, G.3187.
Fountain, spring.

泚 °t's, 1034, G.12391.
Fresh, perspiring.

沿見**沿** yien, 1085, G.13077.
Water's edge, encroaching water.

沿 yien, 1085, G.13076.
A shore, along by.

泱 iang, 1070, G.12866.
The sound of water.

油 yeu, 1111, G.13409.
Oil.

丨 yeu°.
To oil, paint.

泳 °iong, 1149, G.13507.
Swimming fish.

洲6 tseu, 48, G.2445.
A continent, an island.

洙 tsu, 85, G.2548. A river, Confucius' birth place.

洽 yah, 186, G.4233. To soak, permeate, harmonize.

洪 'ong, 236, G.5252.
A flood, vast, immense.

活 weh, 258, G.3958.
To live, life.

洟 yi, 277, G.5403.
Mucus from the nose.

洎 kyi°, 339, G.962.
To reach to, fertile.

洶 hyong, 214, G.4694. Rushing water, clamorous.

洚 kyang°, 364, G.1250.
A food.

洌 lih, 531, G.7085.
Clear water.

洛 lauh, 552, G.6816.
A river.

派 p'e°, c. p'a°, 650, G.8583.
A tribe, clan.

洱 °r, mi, 720, G.3340.
A river.

洒 °se, c. °sa, 731, G.9531.
To sprinkle.

洗 °si, 789, G.4146.
To sprinkle, to wash.

洩 yi°, 798, G.4383.
Peaceful.

| sih.
To leak, ooze, diminish.

洵 sing, 812, G.4871.
To weep, really, even.

洫 hyok, 825, G.4724.
A ditch, drain.

洮 t'au, 869, G.10808.
A river, to wash.

洞 dong°, 931, G.12266.
A hole.

津 tsing, 988, G.2057.
A ferry, ford, mart.

洧 °'we, 1052, G.12603.
A river.

洿 oo, 1058, G.12720.
A pond, pool, foul.

洋 yang, 1072, G.12847. Much, great, ocean, foreign.

浙 7 tseh, 41, G.552.
Chehkiang, a stream.

浮 veu, 140, G.3600. To float, empty, worthless.

海 °he, 160, G.3767.
The sea, vast.

浩 °'au, 172, G.3891.
Vast, great.

浣 °'wen, °wen, 247, G.5061.
To wash, bathe.

涇 kyung, 405, G.2121.
A river, to run straight.

涓 kyoen, 450, G.3130.
A drop of water.

浪 laung°, 505, G.6762.
Waves.

流 lieu, 549, G.7248.
To flow.

浼 °'me, 586, G.7729.
To defile, to annoy.

涅 nyih, 633, G.8263.
Black mud, to blacken.

浜 pung, c. pang, 660, G.8875.
Canal.

浦 °p'oo, 716, G.9500.
A stream, broad.

浡 beh, 718, G.9423.
A river.

涉 dzeh，750，G.9784.
To pass，to concern.

消 siau，793，G.4297.
To destroy，digest，need.

浚 tsing°，818，G.3280. Deep，profound，well read.

涕 °t'i°，t's°，884，G.10991.
Tears.

涂 doo，918，G.12112.
A stream，the 12th moon.

涒 t'ung，929，G.12244.
To vomit.

浹 yah，976，G.1448. Moisten，imbue with，extend.

涎 yien，c. dzan，982，G.1741.
Spittle.

浸 tsing°，989，G.2078.
To immerse，baptize.

浥 ih，1097，G.5484.
Wet，damp.

浴 yok，1139，G.13638.
To bathe，wash.

涌 °iong，1148，G.13460.
Rising，rushing.

涿 8 tsok，82，G.2403.
A river.

涪 veu，140，G.3611.
A river.

涵 'en，168，G.3810.
To submerge，to run in.

淆 yau，193，G.12932.
Mixed，turbid，a name.

涸 hauh，220，G.3893.
Dried up.

淏 °'oo，c. hoo，225，G.4964.
To bale out water.

淮 we，c. wa，243，G.5034.
A river.

混 °wung，269，G.5239.
Mixed，turbid.

淇 ji，343，G.1028.
A stream.

淚 li°，le°，512，G.6856.
Tears.

涼 liang，525，G.7030.
Thin，cool.

淋 ling，540，G.7159.
Dropping water，to souse.

淩 ling，544，G.7230.
A river，galloping.

淪 lung，565，G.7469.
To immerse.

淼 °'miau，592，G.7865.
Vast.

淖 nau°，617，G.8172.
Mud.

淜 p'ing，661，G.8881.
The sound of water.

深 sung，736，G.9823.
Deep.

淑 zok，779，G.10041.
Clear，virtuous，correct.

淳 zung，783，G.2862.
Clear.

涮 seh，786，G.10113.
Wipe with water.

淅 sih，803，G.4044.
To wash rice.

淞 song，830，G.10452.
A stream，Soochow Creek.

淡 °dan，853，G.10646.
Limpid，flat，tasteless.

淘 dau，870，G.10824.
To wash rice.

淂 又見 得 tuh，872，G.10844.
Water，to get，obtain.

添 t'ien，898，G.11212.
To add，supply.

涶 同 唾 t'oo°，913，G.11395.
Spittle.

涷 tong，930，G.12253.
A river，to drench.

淒 ts'i，966，G.983.
Cold.

淺 °ts'ien，982，G.1735.
Shallow.

淨 zing°，994，G.2177.
Clean，undefiled，to wash.

清 ts'ing，995，G.2188.
Clear，lucid.

淬 dzoe°，1018，G.11927.
To temper（as steel）.

淙 tsong，1025，G.2781.
Sound of running water.

淄 ts，1030，G.1805.
A river，dark，color.

涯 ya，1069，G.24.
Bank of river.

淹 ien°，1083，G.13059.
To cloak，to cover.

| ien.
Intelligent.

液 yuh，1095，G.5509. The fluid secretions，nourishment.

淫 yung，1101，G.13244.
Fornication，excess，soak.

淤 iui，1119，G.13519.
Sediment.

淵 ioen，1131，G.13713.
Gulf，abyss.

滂 p'au°.
To steep.

9

渣 tso，3，G.134.
Sediment，grounds.

湛 °dzan，12，G.313.
Clear，to sink，imbued.

渚 °tsu，88，G.2560.
Small stream.

湖 woo，'oo，222，G.4931.
A lake.

渙 hwen°，249，G.5082. To disperse，name of river.

渾 wung，268，G.5231.
Vast，confused，chaos.

港 °kaung，364，G.1245.
A river.

減 °kyan，c.°kan，383，G.1610.
To take from，subtract.

渴 k'oeh，430，G.6126.
Thirst.

渠 jui，444，G.3113.
A ditch，that person.

湄 me，585，G.7718.
The brink of a stream.

湎 °mien，595，G.7890.
To immerse.

渺 °miau, 592, G.7863.
A wide stream.

涅 nyih, 633, G.8263.
Black mud, to defile.

湃 p'e°, 650, G.8584.
Sound of running water.

湓 bung, 656, G.8851.
A stream, to sink.

渤 beh, 718, G.9426.
A sea.

湜 dzuh, 769. G.9948.
Clear, limpid water.

湻同淳 zung, 783, G.2861.
Pure, limpid, honest.

湘 siang, 791, G.4252.
Name of a river.

湏見須 sui, su, 818, G.4718.
Ought, should.

湑 °sui, 819, G.4707.
Pure, limpid.

湯 t'aung, 860, G.10751.
Soup, dressing, gravy.

渧 ti°, 881, G.10943.
To drop, a drop.

渡 doo°, 917, G.12091.
To ferry over.

湍 t'oen, 938, G.12157.
Rapid flowing water.

測 ts'uh, c. ts'ak, 960, G.11698.
To fathom, estimate.

湊 ts'eu°, 963, G.11818.
To accumulate.

湔 tsien, 977, G.1615.
To sprinkle, cleanse.

湫 ts'ieu, 998, G.2253.
A pool, cool, refreshing.

| °tsiau.
To be stopped(as water).

温 'wung, 1040, G.12646.
Tepid, warm, to review.

渨 'we, 1047, G.12552.
Bank of a stream.

渭 we°, 1054, G.12577.
Rapid, tributary.

渥 'wok, 1064, G.12743. To enrich, benefit, moisten.

渰 °ien, 1082, G.13068.
To spread out, cover.

湮 iung, 1099, G.13233.
To sink, lose.

游 yeu, 1112, G. 13421. To swim, to travel, pleased.

渝 yui, 1123, G.13576.
A river, to grow worse.

湧見涌 °iong, 1148, G.13458.
To bubble up, rising.

溱 10 tsung, 16, G.611.
A stream, to reach.

滁 dzu, 92, G.2639.
A river.

準 °tsung, 104, G.2852.
To equalize, to rule.

滑 wah, 242, G.5022.
Slippery.

| kweh.
Sound of flowing water.

滙見匯 we°, 263, G.5190.
To deposit (as mon-

ey), stagnate.

溷 'wung°, 270, G.5249. Turbid, confused.

溽 zok, 300, G.5686. Humid, damp.

溝 keu, 328, G.6155. A ditch, drain.

溪 chi, 341, G.1009. A rivulet.

溧 lih, 539, G.6978. A small stream.

溜 'lieu°, 550, G.7259. To use, flow.

滅 mih, 593, G.7874. To destroy.

溟 'ming, 600, G.7955. Boundless sea, drizzling rain.

溺 nyuh, 635, G.8216. To sink, greedy, excess.

滂 baung, c. p'ang, 658, G.8687. Heavy rain.

溥 °p'oo, 716, G.9498. Large, extensive.

溲 °seu, 756, G.10228. To soak.

| seu. To urinate.

濇 seh, c. sak, 770, G.9937. Wet, damp.

溫同**温** 'wung, G.12733. Tepid, warm, review.

溯 soo°, 817, G.10180. Trace to the source, against.

滕 dung, 864, G.10887. Name of state, empty talk.

滔 t'au, 869, G.10816. To overflow, a torrent.

滇 tien, dien, 894, G.11185. A lake, vast.

滌 dih, 902, G.10941. To purify, cleanse.

滄 ts'aung, 950, G.11593. The sea.

滋 ts, 1029, G.12350. To enrich, taste, flavor.

滓 °ts, 1031, G.12357. Refuse, dregs.

溢 yih, iuh, 1092, G.5486. Full, abundant, run over.

源 nyoen, 1133, G.13704. The origin, source.

滎 yong, 1146, G.5741. Name of a river.

溏 daung. A tank.

漳11 tsang, 23, G.399. Name of a river.

漲 °tsang, tsang°, 24, G.417. Rising water.

滯 dz°, 60, G.1906. Obstructed water.

漢 hoen°, 164, G.3836. A Chinese dynasty, a river.

滸 hoo, 221, G.4917. Bank, name of a river.

滸 °hoo, 225, G.4958. Sloping bank, name.

滬 °'oo, 225, G.4966. Shanghai, to fish by stakes.

漑 ke°, 307, G.952.
To water, irrigate.

滾 °kwung, 494, G.6533.
To boil, to roll along

漏 leu°, 514, G.7360.
To leak.

漓 li, 516, G.6898.
To soak in by drops.

漻 liau, 528, G. 7066. Deep and clear(as the sea).

漣 lien, 533, G.7113.
Ripples on water, clear.

滷 °loo, 556, G.7426.
Salt land or marsh.

滿 °men, 575, G.7622.
Full, complete.

漫 man°, man, 576, G.7633.
Diffuse, an expanse, slow.

漠 mok, 603, G.7989.
Sandy plain, careless.

漚 eu°, 626, G.8494.
To soak in.

| eu.
Bubbles on water.

漂 p'iau°, 683, G.9138.
To whiten, cleanse.

| p'iau.
To float, drift.

滲 sung°, 739, G.9826.
To saturate, soak.

漱 seu°.
To rinse the mouth.

潄見漱 seu°, 757, G.10247.
See above.

漘 zung, 783, G.10147.
Bank of a stream.

漩 zien°, 821, G.4781.
Eddying.

漯 t'ah, 843, G.10540.
Name of a river.

滴 tih, 901, G.10923.
To drip, to drop.

漙 doen, 938, G.12153.
Profuse dew.

漕 dzau°, zau, 955, G.11640.
A canal, channel, convey revenue.

漿 tsiang, 968, G.1210.
A thick fluid.

漸 °dzien, 979, G.1629.
Slowly, gradually.

漆 ts'ih, 987, G.1023.
Lacquer, varnish, paint.

窪 'wo, 1036, G.12428.
A puddle, hole.

漾 yang°, 1073, G.12855.
Floating about.

演 °ien, 1087, G.13130.
Practice, perform, drill.

潁 °iung, 1108, G.13338.
A river.

漁 yui, 1119, G.13512.
To catch fish.

漬 ts°, c. tsih, 1032, G.12366.
Water-soaked, moldy, to soak.

潮[12] dzau, 37, G.519.
The tide.

澈 ts'eh, 42, G.580.
Clear.

澄 dzung, 78, G.775.
Clear.

瀓同澄 dzung, 78, G.779.
Clear.

潴同瀦 tsu, 87, G.2570.
A pool.

潺 dzan, 119, G.2738. Sound of flowing water.

潢 waung, 252, G.5125.
A pool, a dyke.

潰 gwe°, 265, G.5206.
Confused.

潤 zung°, 302, G.5732.
Moisten, enrich, glossy.

澆 kyau, 368, G.1330.
To sprinkle, irrigate.

潔 kyih, 377, G.1491.
To cleanse, purify.

澗 kyien°, c. kan°, 387, G.1603.
Mountain stream.

潦 °liau, 508, G.6803.
Peddles of water, careless.

| liau.
Name of a river.

潾 ling, 541, G.7173.
Clear, rippling water.

潘 p'en, 653, G.8628.
Name of a river.

澀 seh, 728, G.9812. Rough, uneven, stringent taste.

澁同澀 seh, G.9613.
See above.

澎 p'ung, 660, G.8888.
Sound of waves.

潑 p'eh, 710, G.9428. To sprinkle, scatter, vigorous.

潸 san, 734, G.9693.
To weep.

潯 zing, 807, G.4886.
Name of river.

潭 den, 855, G.10676.
A ditch, drain.

潼 dong, 935, G.12305.
Name of a river, damp.

潛 dzien, c. zien, 982, G.1739.
To ford, swim, secretly, carefully.

潜見潛 dzien, 982, G.1740.
See above.

濁[13] dzok, c. dzauh, 83, G.2409.
Turbid water.

澣 °'wen, °wen, 247, G.5077. To wash.

激 kyuh, 395, G.886.
To agitate, move.

澮 kwe°, 485, G.6471.
A drain in a field.

濂 lien, 534, G.7132.
Clear, clean.

澳 iok, 625, G.114.
A bay.

| au°.
A cove, bay.

濃 nyong, c. nong, 642, G.8188. Thick, strong(as tea).

濇同澀 seh, 728, G.9606. Rough, uneven, astringent.

澾 t'ah, 844, G.10533. Slippery.

澹 °dan, 855, G.10626. Thin, weak(as tea).

澡 °tsau, 953, G.11621. To bathe, wash.

澤 dzuh, 958, G.239. A pool, fertile, rich, grace.

澦 yui, 1129, G.13676. A tributary.

濯 14 dzok, 83, G.2412. To wash, cleanse.

濠 'au, c. ngau, 171, G.3878. A pool, pound.

濡 zu, 298, G.5679. To soak in.

濶見闊 kw'eh, 493, G.6124. Wide.

濫 lan°, 503, G.6728. To overflow, excess.

濛 mong, 608, G.7768. Turbid water.

濱 ping. Bank of a stream.

濵見濱 ping, 695, G.9238. Bank of a stream.

濮 bok, 718, G.9510. A river.

濕見溼 seh, c. sak, 770, G.9938. Wet, damp, moist.

濬 tsing°, 813, G.3300. To deepen.

濤 dau, 870, G.10833. Billows, great waves.

濟 tsi°, 964, G.817. To succor, to cross(as a stream).

濆 ben. To overflow.

濾 15 lui°, c. lih, 560, G.7531. To filter, to strain.

瀑 bok, c. bauh, 718, G.8727. A cataract.

瀋 °sung, 738, G.9853. The elements of water, a river.

瀉 sie°, c. sia°, 797, G.4405. To leak, to purge, diarrhoea.

瀆 dok, 922, G.12063. A ditch, sluice.

濺 tsien°, 979, G. 1590. A swift current, to dash up.

瀚 16 'oen°, 165, G.3829. North sea.

瀝 lih, 537, G.6928. To drain out, filter.

瀧 long, 568, G.7490. Name of a river.

| saung. A town.

瀕 bing, 695, G.9251. Edge of a stream.

瀟 siau, 795, G.4323.
Name of a river.

瀛 yung, 1107, G.13329.
Name of a river.

瀾17 lan, 501, G.6716.
Billows, waves, rolling.

瀰 °mi, 589, G.7813. An expanse of water, indistinct.

瀹 yak, 1117, G.13359.
To open through.

灋18 見**法** fah, 123, G.3368.
Plan, way.

灃 fong, 158, G.3580.
Name of a river.

灌 kwen°, 476, G.6358.
To water, pour into.

灑19 同**洒** °se, c. °sa, 731, G.9532. To sprinkle, scatter.

灘 t'an, 854, G.10695.
Bank, shore.

灝21 °'au, 172, G.3895.
Vast, unfathomable.

灞 po°, 645, G.8536.
Stopped, impeded.

灣22 'wan, 1038, G.12478.
To bend, curve, a bay.

灩28 yien°, 1091, G.13144.
Water beautifully moving, rolling sea.

86 火

火 °hoo, 255, G.3966.
Fire.

灰2 hwe, 260, G.5155.
Ashes, dust, mortar.

灰見**灰** hwe, 260.
See above.

灯見**燈** tung, 863, G.10881.
A lamp.

灼3 tsak, 81, G.9769. To burn, roast, brilliant, distinct.

灸 °kyeu, kyeu°, 413, G.2275.
To cauterize.

災 tse, 941, G.11487.
Calamity, misery, plague.

灾同**災** tse, 941, G.11488.
See above.

灶見**竈** tsau°, 954, G.11626.
Cooking range.

炒4 °ts'au, 37, G.509.
To roast, fry, pop.

炙 tsuh, 69, G.1880.
To roast.

炊 ts'oe, c. t's, 102, G.2827.
To cook.

炕 k'aung°, 320, G.5923.
To dry, bake, spread out.

炉見**爐** loo, 555, G.7422.
A stove, grate.

炎 yan, 1085, G.13069.
A flame, to blaze.

灵見**靈** ling, 543.
Spirit, soul.

炸5 tso°, zah, 8, G. 148. To boil, to scald with water.

炤見**照** tsau°, 36, G.468.
To shine upon.

炷 °tsu, 89, G.2534.
Tongues of fire.

炫 yoen°, 233, G.4794.
Brilliant, bright.

炯 kyong°, 422, G.2377.
To twinkle.

炬 °jui, 441, G.3008.
A torch, candle.

炰 bau, 666, G.8738.
To roast on the fire.

炮見炰 bau, 667, G.8737.
See above.

丨見礮 p'au°.
Cannon, an explosion.

炳 °ping, 699, G.9299.
Brilliant, bright.

炭 t'an°, 857, G.10650.
Coal, charcoal.

点見點 °tien, 895. To light, a spark, little.

烝[6] tsung, 74, G.716.
To stream, vapor.

烛見燭 tsok, 97, G.2586.
To light, a candle.

烘 hong, 235, G.5253.
To roast.

烤 °k'au, 327, G.5969.
To toast, grill, char.

烈 lih, 531, G.7086.
Fierce, headstrong.

烙 lauh, 553, G.6808.
To brand, an iron.

烏 oo, 1058, G.12721. A crow, filial, black, nothing.

烊 yang, 1071, G.12848.
To melt.

烟見煙 ien, 1082, G.13029.
Smoke, tobacco, opium.

烽[7] fong, 156, G.3565.
Beacon fire.

焄 hyuin, 212, G.4891.
To roast, toast.

烹 p'ung, 660, G.8907.
To cook.

焉 yien, 1082, G.13042.
Final particle.

丨 ien.
How, why, when.

焚[8] vung, 130, G.3532.
To burn, bright.

焜 °wung, 269, G.5240.
The light of fire.

然 zen, 285, G.5551.
To burn, so, certainly.

焙 be°, 670, G.8788.
To dry over a fire.

焦 tsiau, 970, G.1317.
To scorch, burn, vex.

尉 ioeh, c. yuin°, 1055, G.12620.
To iron, a flat iron.

無 voo, c. m, 1059, G.12753.
Not.

焰 yan°, G.13151.
A flame, burning.

焔見焰 yan°, 1091.
See above.

煠[9] zah, 8, G.182.
To fry, boil in fat, scald.

照 tsau°, 35, G.474.
According to, illuminate.

煑 °tsu, c. °ts. To cook, boil, steam, boiled.

煮見煑 °tsu, c. °ts, 88, G.2562.
See above.

煩 van, 125, G.3411.
To trouble, annoy.

熙 hyi, 177, G.4115.
Bright, ample.

煦 hyui°, 229, G.4759.
Genial, warm.

煥 hwen°, 249, G.5083.
Brilliant, resplendent.

焕見煥 hwen.
See above.

煌 waung, 251, G.5115.
A blaze.

煇同輝 hwe, 260, G.5152.
A blaze.

煢 jong, 421, G.2375.
Desolate.

煖 °noen, 643, G.8143.
Warm.

煉 lien°, 536, G.7150.
To melt, refine.

煤 me, 585, G.7724.
Coal.

煏 pih, 693, G.8917.
To dry by fire.

煞見殺 sah, sa°, 732, G.9637.
To strike, kill, intensity.

煅見鍛 toen°, 937, G.12142.
To forge, hammer out.

煎 tsien, 977, G.1616.
To fry.

煨 'we, 1047, G.12553.
To fire, heat.

煬 yang, 1071, G.12879.
To melt.

煙 ien, 1082, G.13064.
Smoke tobacco, opium.

烟見煙 ien.
See above.

煜 yok, 1139, G.13636.
Bright blaze, glorious.

熌 t'ung.
Light of fire.

熈[10]見熙 hyi, 177, G.4116.
Bright, splendid, to enlarge.

熇 hauh, 191, G.4355.
To dry, to toast, great heat.

熏 hyuin, 212, G.4854.
To roast.

熊 yong, 214, G.4700.
A bear.

煽 sen°, 751, G.9672.
To excite, delude.

熄 sih, 804, G.4036.
To extinguish.

熓 °oo, 1061, G.12729.
Covered embers, to cook.

熒 yong, 1146, G.5744.
A brilliant flame.

熯[11] hoen°, 164, G.3837.
To roast.

熱 zeh, c. nyih, 293, G.5593.
Hot, fever, earnest.

爇見熱 zeh, c. nyih, 293.
See above.

熬 ngau, 624, G.89.
To boil, simmer, disgust.

熟 zok, 780, G.10010.
Ripe, experienced, apt.

熨見尉 ioeh, c. yuin°, 1055, G.12623. To smooth, iron.

熾[12] ts°, 66, G.1811.
The flame of fire, splendor.

燋見爝 dzak, 81, G.481.
To take fire, to burn.

燔 van, 124, G.3386.
To roast, as in sacrifice.

熹 hyi, 178, G.4080.
To roast, bright.

燃見然 zen, 285, G.5552.
To burn.

燎 liau, 529, G.7048.
To light, enlighten.

燐 ling, 541, G.7174.
Will, o'-wisp, ignis fatuus.

燒 sau, 745, G.9766.
To burn, roast.

燖 zien, 800, G.4555.
To scald.

燙 t'aung°, 862, G.10753.
To be hot, burn, to iron.

燈 tung, 863, G.10864.
A lamp.

燉 tung°, 930, G.12208.
To scald.

燋 tsiau, 971, G.1319.
To scorch.

燕 ien°, 1090, G.13048.
To rest, a swallow.

| ien.
A name.

燄 yan°, 1091, G.13152.
A flame, glorious.

燅見燄 yan°.
See above.

燚見燄 yan°.
A flame, glorious.

餡見脂 °'en. Eating but not satisfied.

燭[13] tsok, 97, G.2579.
A candle.

燬 °hwe, 262, G.5197.
Destroy by fire.

燥 sau°, 727, G.9590.
To dry, scorch.

燮 sih, 799, G.4400.
To blend, harmonize.

燧 dzoe°, 828, G.10406.
To burn.

燦 ts'an°, 948, G.11568.
Bright.

營 yung, yong, 1107, G.13305.
A camp, do business, regulate.

燠 iok, 1140, G.115.
Very warm.

燋 dzak.
To ignite, burn.

燻[14] 見熏 hyuin, 212, G.4854.
To roast, toast.

燹 °sien, 801, G.4525.
A fire on the wilds.

燼 tsing°, 989, G.2060.
Ashes, embers.

燿同耀 yau°, 1078, G.12955.
Illuminate, glory.

爕見燮 sih. To blend, harmonize.

爇[15] zeh, 294, G.5594.
To burn, to crack.

爆 pau°, 666, G.8728.
To burn, to crack.

丨 p'au°.
Fire-crackers.

爍 sak, 773, G.10174.
Flames.

爐[16] loo, 555, G.7403.
Stove, fire place, censor.

爛[17] lan°, 503, G.6717. Cooked through, rotten, brilliant.

爟[18] kwen°, 476, G.6359.
To light a fire.

爝 tsiak, 997, G.2221.
Brilliant.

爨[24] ts'oen°, 1027, G.3195.
To cook food.

87 爪

爪 °tsau, 34, G.484.
Claws, nails.

爬[4] bo, 646, G.8545.
To scratch.

爭 tsung, c. tsang, 29, G.703.
To wrangle, contend.

爰[5] yoen, 1135, G.13753.
To lead, therefore.

爮[7] 見管 °kwen, 474.
To rule, to govern.

爲[8] we, 1047, G.12521.
To be, do.

丨 we°.
Because of, for.

為見爲 we, we°.
See above.

爵[14] tsiak, 997, G.1356.
Cup, rank of nobility.

88 父

父 °voo, 147, G.3736.
A father.

丨 °foo.
Husband, a polite term.

爸[4] °po, c. pak, 646, G.8515.
A father.

爹[6] ti, c. tia, 890, G.11109.
A grandfather.

爺[9] ya, 1079, G.12977.
Father.

89 爻

爻 yau, 192, G.4331.
To imitate, compare.

爼5 見**俎** °tsoo.
A sacrificial bowl.

爽7 °saung, 787, G.10125.
Cheerful, bright.

爾10 °r, 720, G.3354.
You.

90 爿

爿 ziang, c. ban, °pan, 115, G.1275. A shop, bed, to crawl.

牀4 zaung, 115, G.2779.
A bed.

牆13 ziang, 969, G.1289.
A wall.

91 片

片 p'ien°, 690, G.9213.
A splinter, slice.

版4 °pan, 651, G.8589.
A board.

牌8 be, c. ba, 649, G.8574.
A card, signboard, tablet.

牋 tsien, 978, G.1585.
A slip of paper.

牒9 dih, 891, G.11122.
A dispatch.

牕11 同**窗** ts'aung, 115, G.2776.
A window.

牖 °yeu, 1114, G.13439. Hole in the wall, window, to lead, instruct.

牘15 dok, 923, G.12064.
A document.

92 牙

牙 ya, c. nya, 1066, G.12797.
Teeth.

牚8 ts'ung, c. ts'ang, 30, G.737.
A prop.

93 牛

牛 nyeu, 638, G.8346.
An ox, cow.

牟2 meu, 587, G.8044.
To bellow, low.

牝 °bing, 697, G.9274.
Female of animals.

牣3 zung°, 288, G.5600.
To stuff, fill.

牢 lau, 507, G.6806. Firm, strong, a cow, stable.

牡 °meu, 588, G.8089.
The male of animals.

牦4 mau, 581, G.7680.
A yak.

牧 mok, 607, G.8073.
To shepherd, a shepherd.

物 veh, c. meh, 1065, G.12777.
Things.

牯5 °koo, 433, G.6192.
A bull, buffalo.

牲 sung, c. sang, 742, G.9866.
Cattle, animals.

牴 °ti, 877, G.10907.
To hook.

牮 tsien°, 979, G.1678.
To prop up.

特[6] duh, 872, G. 10852. Singly, on purpose, specially.

牷 ts'ien, 1013, G.3179.
Perfect, uniform.

牽[7] chien, 388, G.1702.
To lead.

犁見犂 li, 515, G.6889.
To plow, a plow.

犀 si, 789, G.4128.
A rhinoceros.

犇[8]見奔 pang, 655, G.8845.
To flee, run.

犂 li, G.6941.
To plow, a plow.

犒[10] k'au°, 327, G.5958.
Reward, bounty.

犢[15] dok, 923, G.12065.
A calf.

犧[16] hyi, 177, G.4094.
Victims for sacrifice.

94 犬

犬 °choen, 452, G.3192.
A dog.

犯[2] °van, 128, G.3428.
To offend, a criminal.

犴[3] 'oen°, 166, G.3785.
A wild dog.

丨 ngoen°.
A country jail.

狀[4] zaung°, dzaung°, 114, G.2756. Form, appearance, accuse.

狂 gwaung, 479, G.6409.
Wild, mad, daft.

狃 °nyeu, 639, G.8352.
Accustomed to.

狄 dih, 901, G.10930.
Northern barbarian.

狁 °iung, 1143, G.13845.
Scythians.

狎[5] yah, 185, G.4216.
Approach near, desecrate.

狐 'oo, 223, G.4956.
A fox.

狗 °keu, 329, G.6141.
A dog.

狠[6] gwan, 167, G.3904.
Gnaw, sign of superlative.

丨見很 °hung.
Fierce.

狡 °kyau, 369, G.1303.
Crafty, wily.

狩 seu°, 756, G.10013.
To hunt.

狥見徇 dzing, 814, G. 4872.
To connive, to accord.

狹[7] yah, c. 'ah, 186, G.4219.
Narrow.

狷 kyoen°, 451, G.3131.
Hasty, prompt.

狼 laung, 505, G.6764.
A wolf, cruel.

狸 li, 518, G.6878.
A fox, a wild cat.

狽 pe°, 670, G.8796.
To embarrass.

狴 be°, 681, G.9058.
A wild dog, a prison.

猖[8] ts'ang, c. ts'aung, 26, G.488. Fierce.

猙 tsung, 29, G.708.
Hideous, repulsive.

猗 i, 272, G.5366.
Abundant, good.

猛 °mung, c. °mang, 610, G.7797.
Fierce, courageous.

猋 piau, 682, G.9100.
Whirling, spiral.

猜 ts'e, ts'oe, 942, G.11515.
To guess, dislike, to suspect.

猝 ts'oeh, 1015, G.11868.
Suddenly.

猪[9] 見豬 tsu, c. ts, 87, G.2569. A hog.

猴 'eu, 174, G.4011.
A monkey.

猢 'oo, c. weh, 222, G.4933.
A kind of monkey.

猫 見貓 mau, 581, G.7676.
A cat.

猱 nau, 616, G.8160.
A monkey.

猩 sing, 809, G.4605.
An ape.

猥 'we°, 1052, G.12554.
Low, exceeding, many.

猬 we°, 1053, G.12579.
Hedgehog.

猶 yeu, 1112, G.13405.
Like, as, if, similar.

猷 yeu, 1112, G.13402.
A scheme, plan.

猨 yoen, 1135, G.13756.
Monkey.

献 見獻 hyien°, 201.
To offer worship.

猾[10] wah, 242, G.5023.
Confuse, disloyal, artful.

獃 nge, c. te, 619, G.27.
Silly, foolish.

獅 s, 758, G.9911.
A lion.

猻 sung, 829, G.10434.
A monkey.

猺 yau, 1076, G.12917.
A wild dog.

猿 yoen, 1135, G.13741.
A monkey.

獄 nyok, 1139, G.13633.
A prison, hell.

獍[11] kyung°, 406, G. 2168. A feline animal said to eat its dam.

獒 ngau, 624, G.90.
A dog.

獗[12] kyoeh, 446, G.3206.
Fierce.

獝 kyoeh, 447, G.3028.
Violent.

獘 bi°, 676, G.8974.
To fall down, to die.

獧[13] kyoen°, 451, G.3158.
A running dog.

獪 kwe°, 485, G.6472.
Cunning, shrewd.

獨 dok, 921, G.12073.
Only, singly.

獯[14] hyuin, 212, G.4857.
A tribe of Scythians.

獲 wauh, 258, G.3926.
To obtain.

獰 nyung, 616, G.8192.
Distasteful.

獮 °sien, 801, G.4526.
To kill, autumn hunting.

獵[15] lih, 532, G.7104.
To hunt.

獸 seu°, 756, G.10022.
Wild beasts.

獻[16] hyien°, 201, G.4530.
To offer, present.

獹 loo, 555, G.7404.
A dog.

獺 t'ah, 844, G.10530.
An otter.

獼[17] mi, 590, G.7814.
Female monkey.

獾[18] hwen, c. hoen, 244, G.5052. A badger.

玁[20] °hyien, 200, G.4519.
A dog, a pointer.

95 玄

玄 yoen, 231, G.4791.
Sombre, mysterious.

玅[4] 同妙 miau°, 592, G.7859.
Wonderful, excellent.

玆[5] 又見茲 ts, G.12346.
Now, here.

率[6] soeh, 786, G. 10105. To lead, command, approximately.

96 玉

玉 nyok, 1138, G.13630.
A gem, jade stone.

王 waung, 1043, G.12493.
A prince, king.

〡 waung°.
To rule.

玎[2] ting, 904, G.11256.
Sound of metals striking.

玕[3] koen, 310, G.5819.
Inferior gem.

玖 °kyeu, 413, G.2276.
A black stone, mine.

玞[4] foo, 142, G.3615.
A reddish stone.

玠 kya°, 361, G.1521.
A jade tablet.

玦 kyoeh, 447, G.3222.
Jade ear-ring.

玫 me, 584, G.7721.
A red stone.

玩 wan°，1039，G.12455.
To play，trifle.

珍5 tsung，15，G.599.
A pearl，rare.

珎見珍 tsung，15.
See above.

珏 kyak，kok，411，G.2228.
Two gems side by side.

珈 kya，350，G.1146.
A jade ring.

珂 k'oo，424，G.6082.
Quartz crystal.

玲 ling，544，G.7205.
Bright，witty，smart.

珉 ming，597，G.7913.
A valuable stone.

玻 poo，704，G.9333.
Glass.

珀 p'uh，c. p'ak，710，G.9418. Amber.

珊 san，733，G.9558.
Coral.

玳 de°，c. da°，845，G.10551.
Tortoise shell.

玷 °tien，895，G.11166.
A flaw，spot.

珠6 tsu，85，G.2549.
Pearl，precious.

珩 yung，170，G.3910.
Gems，cat's eye.

珪見圭 kwe，481，G.6436.
Jade stone.

珞 lauh，553，G.7321.
Gems for necklace.

班 pan，650，G.8595.
To make known，a class.

珮 be°，670，G.8786.
To gird on.

珥 r°，°r，720，G.3341.
Ear-rings，ornaments.

現7 yien°，201，G.4539.
Now，to manifest.

球 jeu，417，G.2321.
A sphere，ball.

琄 °yoen，449，G.3132.
A scabbard.

琅 laung，504，G.6765.
A whitish stone.

理 °li，519，G.6879. Reason，principle，to regulate.

琉 lieu，548，G.7244.
A pearl.

琇 sieu°，812，G.4676.
A coarse jade.

琮8 ts'ung，sung，19，G.646.
A precious stone.

琤 ts'ung，c. ts'ang，30，G.709. Sound of stones.

琢 tsauh，82，G.2404.
To work in gems，cut.

琥 °hoo，224，G.4922.
Amber.

琪 ji，343，G.1029.
A valuable stone.

琦 ji，344，G.996.
A valuable stone.

琴 jung，402，G.2109.
A lute，harp，organ.

琚 kyui，438，G.2993.
A girdle with gems.

琯 °kwen，475，G.6349.
A stone flute.

琨 kw'ung，494，G.6521.
Pearl，mother-of-pearl.

琳 ling，540，G.7160.
A kind of jade.

琶 bo，646，G.8551.
A guitar.

琫 °fong，660，G.8870.
Ornamented with gems.

琵 bi，679，G.9061.
A large guitar.

琮 tsong，1025，G.12026.
A badge，signet.

琰 °ien，1087，G.13073.
The sparkle of a gem.

琬 °'wen，1137，G.13724.
A jade sceptre.

瑕 9 ya，183，G.4197.
A flaw，blemish.

瑚 'oo，222，G.4934.
The coral.

瑁 mau，me°，586，G.7749.
The tortoise.

瑙 °nau，617，G.8166.
Opal，cornelian，etc.

瑟 seh，728，G.9599.
A large guitar.

瑞 dzoe°，782，G.5726.
A signet of rank，favor.

瑄 sien，821，G.4810.
A stone medal.

瑇 de°，c. da°，845，G.10570.
Tortoise shell.

瑛 iung，1105，G.13310.
The luster of gems.

瑜 yui，1123，G.13577.
A perfect stone.

瑰 10 kwe，482，G.6433.
A reddish pearl.

瑯見琅 laung，504，G.6780.
A whitish stone.

瑠 lieu，548，G.7261.
A precious pearl.

瑪 °mo，572，G.7582.
The cornelian.

瑣 °soo，815，G.10202.
Fragment，fine，petty.

瑣見瑣 °soo.
See above.

瑤 yau，1075，G.12918. Green jasper or quartz，green.

瑩 yong，1146，G.5742.
Luster of a gem.

璋 11 tsang，23，G.400.
A flat stone ruler.

瑾 °kyung，400，G.2049.
A perfect gem.

璃 li，515，G.6899.
Glass.

璉 °lien，535，G.7114.
A sacrificial vase.

璇 zien，821，G.4782.
A revolving gem.

璜 12 waung，252，G.5126.
Oval gem.

璣 kyi，334，G.788.
A globular gem.

璘 ling，541，G.7176.
The veins in a gem.

璞 p'ok，711，G.9443.
A rough unpolished gem.

環13 gwan，245，G.5043.
A ring，a circle.

璧 pih，691，G.8958. A piece of jade with a hole.

璫 taung，858，G.10724.
Ear pendents.

璨 ts'an°，948，G.11569.
The glitter of jade.

璽14 °si，c. °sui，790，G.4143.
The royal signet.

璿 zien，821，G.4813.
A revolving gem.

瓊15 jong，421，G.2376.
Black jade.

瓈 li，515，G.6944.
Glass.

瓏16 long，568，G.7491.
Bright，cunning，smart.

瓚19 °tsan，946，G.316.
A kind of baton.

97 瓜

瓜 kwo，466，G.6281.
Melon.

爮見爬 bo.
To scratch.

瓞5 dih，891，G.11111.
A small melon.

瓠6 'oo，222，G.4990.
The calabash.

瓢11 biau，683，G.9126.
A gourd，cocoa-nut.

瓣14 °pan，652，G.8611.
A section，slip.

瓐16 loo，555，G.7406.
The calabash.

瓤17 naung，c. nyang，290，G.5571.
The pulp of a squash.

98 瓦

瓦 °wo，c. °ngau，1036，G.12420. A tile，pottery.

瓶6見甁 bing，702，G.9321.
A bottle，vase，jar.

瓷 dz，1033，G.12384.
A bottle，vase，jar.

瓿8 °boo，673，G.9455.
An earthen jar.

甁 bing，G.9321.
A bottle，vase，jar.

甄9 tsung，15，G.618.
To mould，fashion.

甌11 eu，625，G.8496.
A deep cup.

甎 tsen，117，G.2706.
Brick.

甏12 bung，c. bang，662，G.8889.
A large bellied jar.

甑 tsung°，951，G.2175.
A boiler.

甓13 bih，694，G.9022.
A glazed tile.

甕 ong°, 1046, G.12677. A wine jar.

99 甘

甘 ken, 310, G.5832. Sweet, pleasant.

甚4 sung°, 738, G.9839. What, very, extremely.

甜6 dien, 899, G.11218. Sweet.

甞8 見**嘗** dzang, c. zaung, 27, G.439. To taste, already.

100 生

生 sung, c. sang, 742, G.9865. Life, to produce, bring forth.

牲5 sung, 737, G.4591. Domestic animals.

產6 °ts'an, 14, G.360. Possessions, estate, to produce.

甥7 sung, c. sang, 742, G.9873. Child of a sister.

甦 soo, 816, G.10323. To revive, raise from the dead.

101 用

用 yong°, 1149, G.13449. To use, employ.

甩 hwah, 785. To cast away.

甫2 °foo, 146, G.3624. The first, to begin.

甬 °iong, 1148, G.13335. To burst forth, a central raised path.

甯 又見 **寧** nyung, 637, G.8325. Repose, a name.

102 田

田 dien, 898, G.11236. A field, land.

甲1 kyah, c. kah, k'ah, 355, G.1167. First, arms.

申 sung, 736, G.9816. 3—5 p.m., to state, extend.

由 yeu, 1111, G.13407. From, by, according, origin.

男2 nen, 614, G.8139. A male.

甸 dien°, 896, G.11180. A royal domain.

畀3 bi°, 675, G.8981. To give, distribute.

画 見 **畫** wo°, 241. A picture.

畊4 見 **耕** kung, c. kang, 322, G.2155. To cultivate, till, plow.

界 kya°, c. ka°, 361, G.1522. Boundary, limit, world.

畎 °choen, 453, G.3193. A drain in a field.

畆 見 **畝** °meu, c. °m, 588, G.8051. A mow (1/6 acre).

畋 dien, 898, G.11237. To prepare to cultivate, to hunt.

畏 we°, 1054, G.12548. Fear, awe.

畛 5 °tsung, 17, G.598. Raised path between fields.

畜 hyok, c. ts'ok, 98, G.2669. Cattle, to store.

留 lieu, 547, G.7254. Detain, leave, put by.

畝 °meu, c. °m, 588, G.8050. A mow(1/6 acre).

畔 ben°, 652, G.8606. A side, bank.

畚 °pung, c. pung, 655, G.8849. A basket for earth.

畦 6 yi, 179, G.1082. A parcel of ground.

異 yi°, 281, G.5505. Other, strange, heterodox.

略 liak, 547, G.7079. To seize, slightly, a little.

畧 見 略 liak, 547, G.7078. See above.

畢 pih, 692, G.8994. To end, close.

番 7 fan, 123, G.3383. Foreign, once.

畫 wo°, 241, G.3974. A picture, to paint.

| wah. A stroke.

畱 lieu, 547, G.7273. To detain, leave behind.

畯 tsing°, 1020, G.3282. A land officer.

畬 yui, 1121, G.13613. To till a field three years.

畸 8 kyi, 336, G.800. Bits, poor land.

當 taung, 857, G.10721. Aught, to bear, adequate to.

| taung°. To substitute, to pawn.

畷 見 域 yok, 1141, G.13666. Boundary.

畼 9 ts'ang°, 28, G.457. A barren country.

畿 10 kyi, 334, G.1066. Imperial domain, boundary.

疄 12 ling, 541, G.7177. Water furrows in field.

疇 14 dzeu, 51, G.2492. A hemp field, a class.

疆 kyang, 363, G.1230. Boundary.

疊 17 deh, 892, G.11138. To pile up.

疉 deh. See above.

103 疋

疋 soo, 695, G.9086. Sufficient.

| p'ih. A piece, a bale.

疎 7 soo, 775, G.10034. Distant, far.

疏 soo, 775, G.10026.
Open, wide apart, remiss.

| soo°.
To memorialize, discuss.

疑 [8] nyi, 275, G.5423.
To doubt, a doubt.

104 疒

疒 nyuh, c. dzih, 636, G.8225.
Disease.

疔 [2] ting, 904, G.11257.
An ulcer.

疚 [3] kyeu°, 416, G.2277. Chronic, long standing disease.

疙 kyi°, c. keh, 427, G.6050.
A pimple, boil, sore.

疘 kong, c. kaung, 460, G.6556.
Prolapsus of the rectum.

疝 san°, 734, G.9665.
Rupture, swelling.

疢 [4] °ts'ung, 21, G.670.
A fever.

疥 kya°, c. ka°, 361, G.1523.
The itch.

疤 po, 644, G.8516.
A scar.

疫 yok, 1095, G.5521.
Pestilence, epidemic.

痄 [5] tso°, 4, G.149. A sore under the ears, the mumps.

疹 °tsung, 17, G.600.
Measles.

症 tsung°, 76, G.691.
Illness.

痃 yien, 197, G.4482.
Indigestion.

痈 ken, 311, G.5835.
A sore in the mouth.

痂 kya, 351, G.140.
A scar.

痀 k'oo, 644, G.6083.
Fits, hump-back.

疲 bi, 680, G.9036.
Tired, weary.

病 bing°, 700, G.9300.
Sickness, to violate.

疸 同 癉 tan°, 852, G.10637.
Jaundice.

疼 dung, dong, 865, G.10894.
To ache, affected.

疾 dzih, 983, G.918.
Quick, sudden, illness.

疽 tsui, c. tsu, 1009, G.1436.
An ulcer, carbuncle.

疵 dz, t's, 1033, G.12393.
A blemish, flaw.

痔 [6] °dz, 60, G.1903.
Piles.

痕 'ung, 167, G.3905.
A scar, trace.

痐 we, 262, G.5170.
A tape-worm.

痍 yi, 277, G.5404.
A sore, a hurt.

痌 dong, 933, G.12276.
An ulcer, groaning.

痊 ts'ien, 1012, G.3180.
To cure.

痒 yang, 1073, G.12849.
A boil.

丨同癢 °yang.
To itch.

痣[7] ts°, 61, G.1919.
A mole, a spot.

痢 li°, 521, G.6890.
Dysentery, diarrhoea.

痗 me°, 587, G.7706.
Ill from anxiety.

痞 °p'i, 681, G.9074.
A pain, weak.

痧 so, 730, G.9628.
Cholera.

痠 soen, 833, G.10374.
Aching pain, rheumatism.

痘 deu°, 875, G.11414.
Small-pox.

痛 t'ong°, 936, G.12291.
To ache.

痮[8] tsang°, 24, G.412.
To expand, enlarge.

痴同癡 t's, 62, G.1932.
Insanity, foolish.

瘃 tsok, 97, G.2595. Sores arising from cold, chilblains.

痼 koo°, 435, G.6206. A chronic, incurable disease, gout.

痳 ling, 540, G.7161.
Gravel, disease of bladder.

痲 mo, 571, G.7592.
Numb, chicken-pox.

痭 pung, 659, G.8863.
Dropsy.

痺 bi°, 675, G.8985.
Dampness, rheumatism.

痰 dan, 855, G.10654.
Phlegm.

瘁 dzoe°, 1018, G.11929. Diseased, wearied, decrepit.

痿 soe, 'we, 1017, G.12560.
Paralysis, stiffness, impotent.

瘂同啞 °ia, c. °au, 1067,
G.12818. Dumb.

瘐 °yui, 1125, G.13600. Sick, weak, dying from cold.

瘀 iui, iui°, 1128, G. 13520.
Settled blood, bruise.

痦 p'e°, p'e.
Boil.

瘇[9] °tsong, 107, G.2885.
To swell.

瘋 fong, 156, G.3557.
Paralysis, leprosy.

瘓 °t'oen, 248, G.5084.
Incipient paralysis.

瘈 kyi°, 341, G.980.
Wild, agitated, mad.

瘕 ya, °kya, 352, G.1162. Disease of the bowels, a flaw.

瘝 kwan, 473, G.6370.
Infirm, incompetent.

瘌 lah, 498, G.6657. Severe pain, bald-head, scab-head.

瘏 doo, 918, G.12130.
Weary, worn out.

瘍 yang, 1071, G.12880.
A boil, sore.

瘖 iung, 1100, G.13212.
Dumb.

瘉 °yui, yui, 1126, G.13578.
To be cured, convalescent.

瘟見瘟 'wung.
Epidemic, plague.

瘡10 ts'aung, 115, G.2773.
A boil, sore.

瘋 kyien, lien, 197, G.4472.
Bronchitis.

瘞 i°, 282, G.5374.
To bury.

瘤 lieu, c. leu, 548, G.7262.
A tumor, wen.

瘧 nyak, ngauh, 638, G.8344.
Fever.

瘢 °pan, 653, G.8593.
Spot, blemish.

瘢見瘢 pan, 650, G.8596.
Spot, blemish.

瘦 seu°, 757, G.10021.
Thin, lean.

瘩 tah, 841, G.10486.
A sore, boil.

瘠 tsih, 986, G.895.
Thin, lean.

瘥 ts'oo, 1003, G.252.
Influenza, to get better.

瘟 'wung, 1040, G.12648.
Epidemic, plague.

瘵11 tsi°, 10, G.249.
A wasting disease.

瘴 tsang°, tsaung°, 24, G.401.
Malaria, miasma.

瘳 ts'eu, liau, 50, G.2488.
Cured, healed.

瘸 jo, 375, G.1560.
Lame.

瘻 leu°, 514, G.7345.
A wen.

瘰 °loo, °le, 552, G.7287.
A gland, swelling.

癇12 yien, c. jien, 198, G.4492.
Fits, convulsions.

癆 lau, 509, G.6797.
A chronic disease.

療 liau, 530, G.7050.
To heal, cure.

癉 tan°, 850, G.10607.
Wearied, visited.

癘13 li°, 523, G.6965.
Pestilence, plague.

癖 p'ih, 694, G.9023.
Indigestion, costiveness.

癡14 t's, 62, G.1966.
Insanity, mad.

癟 pih, 685, G.9012.
Shriveled, dried up.

癥15 tsung, 75, G.721.
Swelling of the abdomen.

癤 tsih, 975, G.1479.
Tumor.

癢 °yang, 1073, G.12859.
To itch.

癨16 hauh, 257, G.3981.
Asiatic cholera.

癩 le°, c. la°, 500, G.6701.
Leprosy, blotch.

癧 lih, 537, G.6929.
A mole, spot.

癬17 °sien, 801, G.4469.
Tetter, ring-worm.

癮 °iung, °yung, c. nyien°, 1103, G.13278. Eruption, craving, habit(as opium).

癯18 jui, 444, G.3684.
Lean, thin.

癰 iong, yong, 1145, G.13482.
Abscess, sore.

癱19 t'an, 854, G.10696.
Paralysis.

癲25 tien, 894, G.11197.
Fits, madness.

105 癶

癶 peh, 708, G.9403.
Back to back.

癸4 °kwe, 483, G.6453. Last of the ten stems, the menses.

登7 tung, 862, G.10858.
To rise, move, record.

發 fuh, 121, G.3376.
To issue forth, manifest.

𤼶見**發** fah.
See above.

106 白

白 buh, c. bak, 706, G.8556.
White.

百1 puh, c. pak, 707, G.8560.
One hundred.

皁2 zau°, 954, G.11604. Black, lictors, runners, manger.

皂見**皁** zau°, 954, G.11605.
See above.

的3 tih, 900, G.10978.
Sign of genitive, evident.

皇4 waung, 250, G.5106.
Imperial, great.

皆 kya, 358, G.1437.
All, whole.

皈見**歸** kwe, 481, G.6429.
To conform to law.

皋5 kau, 325, G.5943.
Eminent, river bank.

皎6 °kyau, 369, G.1305.
White, pure.

皓7 °'au, 172, G.3892.
Bright, white.

皖 °'wen, 247, G.5062.
Bright, Nganhwui.

晳8 sih, 802, G.4045. Clear, bright, to distinguish.

皜10 °'au, 326, G.5931.
White, pure.

皤12 boo, 704, G.9370.
White, silver hair.

皦18 °kyau, 369, G.1369.
White, brilliant.

皭18 dziak, ziak, 997, G.2222.
Pure, white, clean.

107 皮

皮 bi, 679, G.9032.
The skin, bark.

皅[4] po.
A seer.

皵[5] ts'iak, 960, G.255.
Wrinkles on the face.

皴[7] ts'ung, 1001, G.11970.
Chapped, shriveled.

皵[8] ts'iak, 998, G.2240.
To clip off.

皷[9] 見鼓 °koo, 434, G.6242.
A drum.

皺[10] tseu°, c. tsieu°, 962, G.2457.
Wrinkled.

皽[19] 見皽 °kyien.
Wrinkled face.

108 皿

皿 °ming, 601, G.7938.
A vessel.

盂[3] yui, 1120, G.13543.
A basin.

盅[4] tsong, 110, G.2878.
A wine cup.

盆 bung, 656, G.8850.
A plate, basin, tub.

盃 pe, 668, G.8782.
A cup, tumbler.

盈 yung, 1106, G.13292.
Full, overflowing.

盎[5] ngaung, 2, G.78.
A basin, dish, to fill.

盇 'eh, 218, G.3959.
Why not?

盌 °'wen, 1039, G.12463.
A bowl.

益 iuh, 1092, G.5485. Advantage, profit, increase.

盒[6] 'eh, c. 'ah, 218, G.3954.
A box with cover.

盖 見蓋 ke°, c. keh, 307, G.5786. So, then, thus.

盔 k'we, 487, G.6482.
A helmet.

盗 見盜 dau°, 868.
To rob, a thief.

盛[7] zung°, 772, G.767.
Abundant.

| zung.
To put in, deposit.

盖 同蓋 ke°, c. keh, 307, G.5785. To cover, so, then, thus.

盜 dau°, 868, G.10803.
To rob, a thief.

盞[8] °tsan, 12, G.300.
Lamp bowl, wine cup.

盟 mung, ming, 579, G.7791.
An oath, a covenant.

盐 見鹽 yien, 1086.
Salt.

監[9] kyan, c. kan, 387, G.1640.
Prison, to oversee.

| kyan°, c. kan°.
To examine.

盡 °dzing, 989, G.2055.
Extreme, ultimate, all.

盤[10] ben, 653, G.8620.
A tray, dish, expense.

盥[11] kwen°, 476, G.6376.
To wash.

盦 eh, °en, en, 621, G.69.
A cover, to cover.

盧 loo, 554, G.7396.
A vessel for rice.

盪[12] °daung, 859, G.10738.
To wash, wandering.

鹽[13] °koo, 433, G.6212.
A salt pond, temporary.

109 目

目 mok, 607, G.8080.
The eye, director, index.

直[3] dzuh, 70, G.1846.
Straight, only.

直見直 dzuh.
See above.

盱 hyui, 228, G.4730.
Side glance.

盲 mung, maung, mang, 609, G.7651. Blind.

盻[4] yi°, 181, G.4085.
Look at in anger.

看 k'oen°, 316, G.5852.
To see, to practice.

| k'oen.
To watch, to examine.

眊 mau°, 582, G.7681.
Dim-sighted.

眉 me, c. mi, 585, G.7714.
Eye-brow.

眇 °miau, 592, G.7862.
Look at with one eye.

盼 p'an°, 654, G.8644.
To hope, expect.

省 °sang, 743, G.4632.
A province, to save.

| °sing.
To examine.

相 siang, 790, G.4249.
Mutual, to help.

| siang°.
Appearance, to help.

眈 ten, 849, G.10613. Seeing but thinking of something else.

盾 °dung, 927, G.10152.
A shield.

盹 tsung, tsung°, 927, G.12218. To doze, nap.

眞[5] tsung, 15, G.589.
True, real.

真見眞 tsung, 15.
See above.

真見眞 tsung.
See above.

眩 yoen°, yoen, 232, G.4795.
Confused vision.

眛 me°, 587, G.7735.
Color-blind.

眠 mien, 594, G.7882.
Closed eyes.

眚 °sun, °sing, 743, G.9868.
A calamity, fault.

眎見視 z°, 763, G.9954.
To see, look.

眥 tsi°, 1028, G.963. Look angrily, corner of eye.

眦同眥 tsi°.
See above.

看見看 k'oen, 316.
To see.

眵 6 t's, 63, G.1939.
Diseased eyes.

眾 tsong°, 108, G.2901.
All, every.

眷 kyoen°, 450, G.3145. To care for, relative, family.

眶 k'waung, c. chaung, 480, G.6405. Corners of the eye.

眸 meu, 588, G.7964.
The pupil of the eye.

眯 mi, 590, G.7807.
Blinded with dust.

眺 t'iau°, 889, G.11078.
To look far away, gaze.

眼 °yan, c. °ngan, 1086, G.13129. The eye, a hole.

睏 7 k'wung°, 496, G.6546.
To sleep.

睊 kyoen°, 449, G.3133.
Looking awry.

睇 di°, 880, G.10954.
To gaze at, stare.

睃 tsing°, c. soo, 1020, G.3283.
To look carefully.

睚 8 ya, 2, G.25.
To stare at.

睁 °dzing, c. tsang, 29, G.710.
Open the eyes in anger.

睨 nyi°, 280, G.5431.
Looking sidewise.

睦 mok, 608, G.8086.
At peace, to make peace.

瞢見曾 mong, 610, G.7782.
Obscure, dim.

睥 bi°, 675, G.8986.
To look askance.

睒 °sen, °hyien, c. dan°, 752, G.9720. Lightning.

睡 dzoe°, zoe°, 782, G.10137.
To sleep, doze.

睢 hwe, 826, G.10385.
To gaze at.

睟 dzoe°, 828, G.11912.
To look straight at, clear.

督 tok, 921, G.12057.
To oversee, an overseer.

睬 °ts'e, 944, G.11511.
To notice.

睫 dzih, c. kyi°, 975, G.1486.
Eye-winkers.

睛 tsing, 993, G.2130.
To see, eye-ball.

睪 yuh, 1094, G.13177.
To spy, to lead.

睿 9 soe°, 301, G.5728.
Wise, able, to detect.

睽 k'we, kwe, 487, G.6489.
Strange, wonderful.

睹 °too, 916, G.12047.
To see.

瞋 10 ts'ung, 19, G.645.
To open the eye.

瞎 hyah, c. hah, 185, G.4210.
Blind, ignorant.

瞌 k‘eh，430，G.3961.
Sleepy.

瞑 ming，°ming，600，G.7905.
To close the eye.

瞍 °seu，729，G.10230. Blind
from having no pupil.

瞏 kwan°.
To see，sight.

瞠[11] ts‘ung，c. daung，29，G.722.
To fix the eyes on.

瞖 i°，282，G.5378.
A film on the eye.

瞞 men，575，G.7623.
To cover up.

瞘 eu，c. k‘eu，625，G.6172.
Deep sunken eye.

瞟 °p‘iau，683，G.9127.
To look askant.

瞢 mong，609.
Obscure，dim.

瞯[12] kyan°，200，G.4493.
To spy，watch.

瞶 kwe°，266，G.5207.
Dull-sighted.

瞰 k‘an°，315，G.5876.
Looking at secretly.

瞭 liau，529，G.7051.
Bright eyed.

瞥 p‘ih，686，G.9167.
To look at straight.

瞬 sung°，784，G.10157.
Wink.

瞪 dzung，c. dung°，864，G.725.
To stare at.

瞳 dong，935，G.12308.
A silly stare.

瞧 dziau，972，G.1408.
To glance at.

瞻[13] tsen，44，G.277.
To look at，reverence.

瞽 °koo，434，G.6244.
Blind.

瞿 jui，444，G.3081.
To stare at.

瞹 e°，620，G.19.
Dull，dim.

矇[14] mong，mang，609，G.7769.
Ignorant.

矆 hauh，hwauh.
Lightning.

矍[15] jak，492，G.2248.
To glance about.

矗[19] ts‘ok，99，G.2675.
Straight，lofty.

矙[20] k‘an°，315，G.5878.
Looking at secretly.

矚[21] tsok，96，G.2583.
To see clearly.

110 矛

矛 mieu，meu，c. miau，587，
G.7688. A dart，lance.

矜[4] kyung，405，G.2162.
To pity，boasting.

111 矢

矢 °s，760，G.9950.
A dart，swift，to arrange.

矣[9] °i, 279, G.5474. Final particle completing sense.

知[3] ts, 53, G.1783.
To know.

丨 ts°.
Wisdom.

矧[4] °sung, 738, G.9857.
Still, more, much, less.

矩[5] °kyui, 439, G.3009.
A square, a rule, custom.

短[7] °toen, 937, G.12135.
Short, dwarf.

矬 zoo, 1004, G.11780.
Short, stout.

矮[8] °ia, c. °a, 2, G.13.
Low, short, dwarf.

矲 joeh, 445, G.3233.
Short.

矯[12] kyau, 370, G.1340.
Proud, haughty.

矰 tsung, 951, G.11723.
A dart, javelin.

矱[14] 'wok, 257, G.5305.
A marking line.

112 石

石 zak, 766, G.9964.
A stone.

矼[3] chang, k'ong°, 363, G.1204.
Reliable.

丨 kaung.
A bridge with steps.

矻 kw'eh, 456, G.6264.
Laborious, diligent.

砆[4] foo, 142, G.3616.
Inferior gem.

砉 hyih, 259, G.3984. Sound of skinning an animal.

砍 °k'en, 315, G.5869.
To hack, chop.

砒 p'i, 679, G.9052.
Arsenic.

砂 so, 730, G.9620.
Sandstone.

砌 ts'i°, 967, G.1059.
A stone step, to pave.

砑 ya°, c. nga°, 1067, G.12803.
To grind, polish.

砧[5] tsung, 16, G.622.
Stone, block, anvil.

砥 °ti, 57, G.1886.
Polished stone.

砮 °noo, 641, G.8394.
Arrow-head flint.

砰 p'ung, 660, G.8894.
Crash of stones.

砲 p'au°, 667, G.8742.
Cannon, fire-works.

砭 pien, pien°, 687, G.9194.
A stone probe.

破 p'oo°, 705, G.9410.
Broken, ruined.

砣 doo, 912, G.11351.
Steelyard weight.

硃[6] tsu, 86, G.2550.
Vermilion stone.

硇 nau, 617, G.8163.
Camphor, a medicine.

研 nyien, nyien°, 1085, G.13102. To grind, rub.

硨[7] ts'o, 40, G.575. A stone from which 6th grade official buttons are made.

硜 k'ung, 323, G.6022. Sound of stones.

硫 lieu, 549, G.7245. Sulphur.

硭 maung, 579, G.7657. Crude salpetre.

硝 siau, 793, G.4301. Saltpetre, nitre.

硯 nyien°, 1090, G.13145. Ink stone, to rub.

硬 ngung°, c. ngang°, 1108, G.13341. Hard, stiff.

碁[8] 同 棋 ji, 343, G.1033. Chess.

碌 lok, 563, G.7277. Laborious.

碍 見 礙 nge°, 620, G.37. Obstruct, hinder.

硼 bung, c. bang, 661, G.8883. Borax.

碑 pe, 668, G.8764. Stone tablet, tomb stone.

碎 te°, 827, G.10416. Fragments, odds and ends.

碏 tsiak, 998, G.2237. A variegated stone.

碓 te°, 924, G. 12169. Foot pestle for hulling rice.

碗 見 盌 °'wen, 1039, G.12472. A bowl, dish.

碔 °voo, 1061, G.12746. A veined jasper.

碪[9] 同 砧 tsung, 16, G.626. A block, anvil.

碣 jih, 378, G.1457. A stone tablet.

碯 °nau, 617, G.8167. Camphor.

碰 見 掽 bung°, c. bang°, p'ang°, 662, G.8912. To run against.

碧 pih, 691, G.9009. Jasper stone.

碩 zuh, 766, G.9967. Great, eminent, ripe.

碟 zeh, c. dih, 891, G.11124. A plate, platter.

碫 同 鍛 toen°, 938, G.12143. A rough stone.

確[10] chak, 411, G.2243. Really, certainly.

磕 k'e°, c. k'eh, 430, G.6114. A knock, a bump.

磊 °le, 511, G.6849. Stones piled up.

碼 °mo, 572, G.7583. A yard, weight, numbers.

碾 °nyien, 634, G.8312. A stone roller.

磇 同 砒 p'i, 679, G.9065. Arsenic.

磐 ben, 654, G.8621.
A rock.

磅 baung, c. paung, 658, G.8679. Small stones, gravel.

磉 °saung, 725, G.9570.
Stone base for a post.

碭 t'ah, 843, G.10517.
To beat(as rice).

磓 te, dzoe, c. teh, 924, G.12177. Sound of stones, to collect stones for rock-work.

磋 ts'oo, 1003, G.11775.
To grind.

磁 dz, 1033, G.12407.
China-ware, a magnet.

磚[11] tsen, 117, G.2707.
A brick.

𥕢同罅 hya°, 184, G.4239.
Cleft in a rock.

硻同硜 k'ung°, 323, G.6019.
Sound of stones.

磬 chung°, 409, G.2208.
A musical stone, bells.

磠 °loo, 556, G.7427.
Fine stones.

磨 moo, 602, G.7974.
To grind, to rub.

| moo°.
Mill-stone.

䃙同碌 lok.
Green jade.

磺[12] waung, 253, G.5128.
Grindstone, sulphur.

磯 kyi, 334, G.789.
Steps.

磽 chau, 373, G.1390.
Poor soil.

磲 jui, 444, G.3115. Stone from which white sixth grade official buttons are made.

磷 ling, 541, G.7178.
Lofty, eminent.

磻 ben, 653, G.8630.
Arrow-head flints.

磰 °zen, 753, G.9713.
White porcelain clay.

礁 tsiau, 970, G.1321.
Rocks in a stream.

礎[13] °ts'oo, 94, G.2667.
A stone under a post.

礓[14] kyang, 363, G.1225.
Ore of metals.

礙 nye°, 620, G.38.
To hinder, objection.

礮見礟 p'au°, 667.
A cannon.

礬[15] van, 126, G.3409.
Alum.

礦 kw'aung°, c. k'aung°, 463, G.6588. A mine.

礪 li°, 523, G.6970.
To grind, whet.

礫 lih, 538, G.7000.
Gravel, small stones.

礤 ts'ah, 940, G.11479.
A coarse stone, grind.

礱[16] long, 568, G.7493.
A mill, to grind.

礮 p'au°, G.8755.
A cannon.

礵[17] saung, 787, G.10122.
Arsenic.

礶[18] 見罐 kwen°, 476, G.6362.
A jar, mug.

113 示

示 ji, 763, G.9953.
An omen.

丨 z°.
To reveal, make known.

礼[1] 見禮 °li, 520, G.6946.
Decorum, offering, etiquette.

礽[2] dzung, 291, G.769.
Blessing.

祁[3] ji, 345, G.1089.
Full, abundant, large.

社 ze°, c. zo°, 748, G.9803.
Tutelary gods, their altars.

祀 z°, 838, G.10286.
To sacrifice.

礿 同禴 yak, 1117, G.13348.
Vernal or summer sacrifice.

祉[4] °t's, 56, G.1840.
Happy, joyous.

祇 ji, 345, G.1086. Rest, the earth, as a divinity.

祈 ji, 345, G.1013.
To pray, supplicate.

祗[5] °ts, 55, G.1887.
Respect, only.

祝 tsok, 95, G.2597.
To bless.

祜 °'oo, 225, G.4970.
Blessing.

祛 chui, 443, G.3073.
To avert(as malaria).

祕 pi°, 676, G.8931.
A secret.

神 zung, 737, G.9819.
God, a spirit, a god.

祟 soe°, 828, G.10424.
Heaven sent calamity.

祖 °tsoo, 1007, G.11802.
Ancestors.

祚 dzo°, 1007, G.11851.
Emolument, felicity.

祠 dz, 1034, G.10253.
To sacrifice.

祐 yeu°, 1115, G.13438.
To protect.

票[6] p'iau°, 684, G.9118.
A bill.

祥 dziang, 792, G.4277.
Good fortune.

祧 t'iau, 888, G.11079.
An ancestral shrine.

祭 tsi°, 965, G.934.
To sacrifice, a sacrifice.

祺[8] ji, 343, G.1034.
Blessing.

禁 kyung°, 400, G.2033.
To prohibit, warn.

祼 kwen°, 476, G.6381. Pour out libations.

祿 lok, 563, G.7379. Happiness.

禀見**稟** °ping, 696, G.9257. To petition.

禎9 tsung, 73, G.609. Felicitous.

福 fok, 150, G.3707. Blessing.

禊 yi°, 181, G.4161. Harvest sacrifice for averting evil.

禍 °'oo, 256, G.3992. Calamity, evil, woe.

禘 ti°, 881, G.10944. Imperial spring and autumn sacrifice.

禋 iung, 1099, G.13234. A pure sacrifice.

禦11 nyui°, 1127, G.13646. To oppose, stop.

禧12 hyi, 178, G.4081. Good luck, blessing.

禪 zen, 751, G.348. To meditate(as Buddhist priest).

禫 °den, 856, G.1078. To strip for work.

禮13 °li, 520, G.6949. Propriety, worship, ceremony.

禱14 °tau, 866, G.10799. To pray.

禳17 zang, 290, G.5572. To pray and avert evil.

禴 yak, 1117, G.13361. Vernal or summer sacrifice.

114 禸

禸 °dzeu, 295, G.5664. A foot-print.

禹4 °yui, 1125, G.13618. Name of a king, free, loose.

禺 nyui°, 1119, G.13556. A monkey.

离6 同**魑離** li, 517, G.6895. To scatter, oppose.

禽8 jung, 402, G.2099. Birds.

115 禾

禾 'oo, 254, G.3943. Grain.

秀2 sieu°, 811, G.4675. Flowering, elegant, literary graduate.

私 s, 835, G.10308. Secret, private.

秃 t'ok, 923, G.12116. Bald, bare.

秉3 °ping, 699, G.9305. A handle, to hold.

秈 sien, 799, G.4450. Common rice.

杭4 同**粳** kung, c. kang, 322, G. 2181. Non-glutinous rice.

科 k'oo, 424, G.6089. A class.

秒 °miau，592，G.7860.
The beard on grain.

秕 °pi，674，G.8945.
Empty，withered grain.

秋 ts‘ieu，1000，G.2302.
Autumn.

秐同**耘** yuin，1142，G.13807.
To weed，root up.

秩[5] dzeh，69，G.1883.
A series，follow in order.

秤 ts‘ung°，80，G.782.
To weigh，steelyards.

秣 meh，me°，604，G. 8005.
Provender for horses.

秘同**祕** pi°，676，G.8932.
Mysterious，secret.

秦 dzing，991，G.2093.
Name.

租 tsoo，1007，G.11803.
To rent，lease.

秭 °tsi，1031，G.12361.
Great，numberless.

秧 iang，1070，G.12868.
Sprouts，rice plants.

移[6] yi，274，G.5417.
To remove，change.

程[7] dzung，79，G.757.
To travel，a journey.

稀 hyi，177，G.4058.
Sparse，thin.

稉 kung，c. kang，322，G.2160.
White rice(not glutinous).

稂 laung，505，G.6767.
Worthless grain，tares.

稍 sau°，c. sau，746，G.9761.
Slightly，gradually.

稅 soe°，782，G.10134.
Duties on goods.

稊 di，882，G.10993.
Cockles，tares.

稌 doo，920，G.12105.
Rice used in making wine.

稠[8] dzeu，51，G.2502.
Thick.

稚 dz°，60，G.1871.
Tender，delicate，young.

稔 °sung，288，G.5634.
Ripe.

稜見**棱** lung，506，G.6866.
A corner.

稟 °ping，542，G.7237.
Grain，to pay.

丨 °ling. Food，to nourish，to obtain.

稗 be°，c. ba°，648，G.8563.
Tares.

稱[9] ts‘ung，76，G.671. To style，praise，fitting，to weigh.

丨 ts‘ung°.
Steelyards.

種 tsong°，107，G.2886.
To plant.

丨 °tsong.
Seeds.

稺[10] dz°，60，G.1898.
Tender，delicate，young.

稾 °kau，325，G.5933.
Rough copy，grain stalk.

稿同槀 °kau, 325, G. 5932. Grain stalk, rough copy.

稽 kyi, 335, G.884.
To examine, study up.

丨 °chi.
To bow.

稼 kya°, 354, G.1143.
To sow, plant, harvest.

穀 kok, 453, G.6229.
All grains.

稻 °dau, 868, G.10800.
Grown rice.

稷 tsih, 987, G.904.
Panicled millet.

穉[11]同稚 dz°, 60, G. 1899. Tender, delicate, young.

穎 °iung, 1108, G.13338.
Beards on grain.

穅同糠 k'aung, 320, G.5911.
Chaff.

穆 mok, 608, G.8082.
Grand, respect.

穌 soo, 816, G.10315.
To collect, resuscitate.

穄 tsi°, 965, G.935.
A sorghum plant.

積 tsih, 986, G.831.
To store up, amass.

丨 ts°.
Grain stored out of doors.

穛 lih, c. seh, soeh. Heads of grain, course rice.

穗[12] dzoe°, c. seh, soeh, 827, G.10422. Ears of grain.

穠[13] nyong, 642, G.8412.
A thick decoction.

穡 suh, 728, G.9607.
To reap, gather.

穢 'we°, 1056, G.12610.
To defile.

穫[14] wok, 257, G.3927.
To reap, harvest.

穩 °'wung, 1042, G.12660.
Firm, secure, grain beards.

穰[17] zang, 290, G.5573.
Luxuriant, abundant.

116 穴

穴 yoeh, 230, G.4840.
A cave.

究[2] kyeu°, 415, G.2266.
To examine, finally.

穹[3] chong, 420, G.2359.
Lofty, vast, canopy.

空 k'ong, 464, G.6595.
Empty, hollow, insincere.

丨 k'ong°.
At leisure, to owe.

穸 dzih, 804, G.4112.
Night of death.

窆[4] dung, 103, G.2847.
Burial.

穿 ts'en, 119, C.2739.
To put through, or on.

突 deh, 921, G.12076.
Suddenly, to strike.

窃见竊 ts'ih，977，G.1554.
To steal，secretly.

穽 zing°，994，G.2153.
A pit.

窄[5] tsuh，c. tsah，959，G.243.
Narrow.

窈 °iau，1077，G.12949.
Deep，still.

窅 °iau，1077，G.12962.
Deep，still.

窒[6] tseh，69，G.1835.
To stop，close.

窓见窗 ts'aung，115，G.2777.
A window.

窕 °diau，886，G.11066.
Elegant，refined.

窗[7] ts'aung，115，G.2775.
A window.

窖 kyau°，872，G.1381.
A bin for grain.

窘 °kyuin，°chuin，419，G.2351.
Distress，affliction，to harass.

窠[8] k'oo，424，G.6093.
A bird's nest.

窟 kw'eh，455，G.6276.
A cave，a den.

窩[9] oo，1056，G.5314.
A bin for grain.

窨 iung°，1103，G.13213.
A cellar.

窬 yui，1123，G.13579.
A small door in a door.

窮[10] jong，420，G.2350.
Poor，exhausted.

窯 yau，1075，G.12919.
A kiln，pottery.

窳 °yui，1126，G.13694.
Dirty，sickly.

窶[11] °lui，441，G.3038.
Poor，poverty.

窺 k'we，487，G.6493.
To spy，peep.

窾 °k'wen，°k'en，477，G.6386.
Fissure in rocks，hollow.

邃 dzoe°，828，G.10409.
Deep，far in.

窵 tiau°，c. °tiau，887，G.11056.
Distant.

竅[13] chau°，375，G.1426.
A hole，a pore.

竄 ts'oen°，1027，G.3171.
To hide，secret，to flee.

竆[14]同窮 jong，420，G.2349.
Poor，exhausted.

竇[15] deu°，875，G.11435.
A duct，viaduct.

竉[16] °long，569，G.7483.
A hole，cave.

竈 tsau°，954，G.11625.
Chinese cook-range.

竊[17] ts'ih，977，G.1553.
To steal，secret.

117 立

立 lih，538，G.6954.
To stand.

竒[4] 見奇 ji，344，G.797. Odd，a single one.

丨 kyi. Wonderful，rare.

站[5] dzan°，13，G.270. A stage in a journey，to stand.

竝 同並 °bing，700，G.9281. Side，by side.

章[6] tsang，22，G.390. Chapter，section，essay，bright.

竟 kyung°，406，G.2166. Then，limit，to the end.

竦[7] °song，831，G.10460. To reverence，to fear.

童 dong，934，G.12299. A lad，a youth.

竣 tsing，1001，G.3284. Accomplished，finish.

竪[8] 見豎 °zu，777，G.10079. Erect，to stand up.

竭[9] jih，378，G.1459. Extreme.

端 toen，936，G.12138. Upright，decent，the origin，classifier of affairs.

競[14] jung°，407，G.2171. To quarrel，ambitious，violent.

118 竹

竹 tsok，95，G.2616. Bamboo.

竺[2] tsok，95，G.2574. A kind of bamboo.

竿[3] koen，310，G.5830. A pole，shaft.

竽 yui，1120，G.13544. Ancient reed organ.

笊[4] °tsau，c. °tsa，34，G.487. A ladle skimmer.

笏 hweh，267，G.4926. A tablet of ivory.

笄 見筓 kyi，335，G.889. An hair pin.

笈 kyih，394，G.845. A box，a satchel.

笆 po，644，G.8517. A fence.

笔 見筆 pih，693，G.8978. A pen，pencil.

笑 siau°，795，G.4343. To laugh，ridicule.

笋 見筍 °sung，813，G.4890. Bamboo sprouts.

笞[5] t'ṡ，63，G.1958. A stick，to beat.

符 voo，144，G.3687. Tally，charms.

笱 °keu，329，G.6143. A bamboo fish-trap.

笳 kya，ja，350，G.1148. A reed whistle.

笠 lih，538，G.6957. A rain hat made of bamboo leaves.

笨 bung°，655，G.8848. Awkward，stupid.

笙 sung，c. sang，742，G.9869. An organ.

笥 ṡ°，ṡ，838，G.10254. A bamboo trunk.

笪 °tan, 840, G.10492.
A name.

丨 tan°.
Basket.

第 di°, c. °di, 879, G.10955.
This, the, a house, a series.

笤 diau, 889, G.11089.
A broom, brush.

笛 dih, 902, G.10939.
A flute.

筏[6] vah, 122, G.3372.
A raft.

筓 kyi, 335, G.888. A hair-pin, to put up the hair, marriageable age.

筋 kyung, 397, G.2025.
Sinews, cords.

筇 jong, 421, G.2366.
A kind of bamboo.

筐 kw'aung, 479, G.6406.
A square basket.

筆 pih, 693, G.8979.
A pen, pencil.

筅 °sien, 801, G.4446.
Stockade of halberds.

筍 °sung, 813, G.4874.
Shoots.

答 teh, c. tah, 841, G.10479.
An answer.

等 °tung, 863, G.10877.
To wait, a sort.

筒 dong, 934, G.12278.
A tube, pipe.

策 ts'uh, c. ts'ak, 960, G.11691. Plan, stratagem, whip, book.

筌 ts'ien, 1013, G.3181.
A bamboo fishing trap.

筯[7] 同 箸 dzu°, 90, G.2601.
Chop-stick.

筥 °kyui, 439, G.3040.
A bamboo round basket.

筦 同 管 °kwen, 474, G.5714.
A tube, classifier.

筲 sau, 745, G.9764.
A basket.

筮 z°, 759, G.9948. To divine, a fortune-teller.

筭 同 算 soen°, 833, G.10380.
The abacus, to reckon.

筫 deu°, 875, G.11415.
A tray.

筩 dong, 934, G.12292.
A tube, pipe.

筴 ts'uh, 960, G.1567.
To divine by slips.

丨 kyah.
Bamboo chop-sticks.

筵 yien, 1085, G.13083.
A feast.

筠 yuin, 1143, G.13824.
New skin of bamboo.

筷 kw'an°.
Chop-sticks.

箚[8] tsah, 7, G.142.
A document, a letter.

箏 tsung, 29, G.711.
A virginal harpsichord.

箒 °tseu, 49, G.2471.
A broom.

箠 dzoe, 101, G.2810.
A kind of bamboo.

| °dzoe.
A whip, to whip and beat.

箕 kyi, 336, G.855.
A dust basket.

箝 jien, 389, G.1706.
Tweezers, nippers.

箇 koo°, c. kuh, 423, G.6075.
One, a.

箍 koo, 431, G.6233.
A hoop, fillet, garland.

管 °kwen, 474, G.6348.
To rule, govern, a tube.

箂 le, 499, G.6691.
A variety of bamboo.

箔 bok, 706, G.9351.
A bamboo screen.

箑 sah, 732, G.9651.
A fan.

算 soen°, 833, G.10378.
To reckon.

箋 tsien, 978, G.1584.
A tablet, slip for notes.

箴 9 tsung, 16, G.614.
To warn, maxims.

箸 dzu°, 90, G.2563.
Chop-sticks.

築 tsauh, 96, G.2576.
To build.

篆 °dzen, 118, G.2724.
Seal characters.

範 °van, 128, G.3429.
A law, rule, a mold.

篁 waung, 251, G.5116.
Old bamboo shoots.

箬 zak, c. nyak, 296, G.5647.
A kind of bamboo leaf.

篋 chah, 380, G.1569.
A box.

篇 p'ien, 690, G.9220.
A section.

箱 siang, 791, G.4253.
A box.

節 tsih, 974, G.1477.
A verse, a joint.

箭 tsien°, 978, G.1617.
An arrow, bamboo.

篪 10 dz, 65, G.1955.
A kind of flute.

篡 ts'oen°, 120, G.2749.
To snatch.

篚 °fi, 138, G.3481.
Square baskets.

篙 kau, 324, G.5934.
A pike-pole.

篝 keu, 329, G.6156.
Frame for lamp or clothes.

篦 bi, c. pien.
Fine comb.

篦見篦 bi, c. pien, 675, G.8953.
Fine comb.

篩 s, c. sa, 732, G.9652.
A sieve, to sift, strain.

篠 °siau, 795, G.4341.
A kind of bamboo.

篤 tok, 921, G.12071.
Firm, staple.

篔 yuin, 1143, G.13839.
A flute.

簆[11] k'eu°, 332, G.6181.
The reeds of a loom.

簆見簆 k'eu°.
The reeds of a loom.

簋 °kwe, 483, G.6455.
A round vessel.

簍 °leu, c. °lieu, 514, G.7346.
A basket.

篱 li, 517, G.6901.
A skimmer.

簏 lok, 562, G.7438.
A basket.

篾 mih, 593, G.7815.
Bamboo splints.

簰 be, c. ba, 649, G.8576.
A raft.

篷 bong, 661, G.8901.
A sale, awning.

篳 pih, 692, G.9000.
Wicker work.

篲 dzoe°, 828, G.10421.
A broom.

簀 tsuh, 958, G.11663.
A mat, luxuriant.

簉 ts'eu°, 963, G.2483.
Concubine, maid servant.

簎 ts'ok, 1006, G.11857.
To spear, hook up.

簇 ts'ok, 1015, G.11821.
A spike, a crowd.

䉬[12] fi°, 138, G.3489.
A rush, bed mat.

簧 waung, 252, G.5129. Reed of trombone or organ.

簡 °kyien, °kyan, c. kan°, 384, G.1604. A note, terse, rude.

簣 gwe°, 488, G.6510.
A basket.

簫 siau, 794, G.4321.
A flute.

簞 tan, 850, G.10608.
A basket for cooked rice.

簟 dien°, 897, G.10611.
Bamboo mat, mouth piece of a pipe.

簪 tsung, tsen, 945, G.627.
An hair pin.

簾[13] lien, 534, G.7129.
A curtain.

簸 °poo, poo°, 704, G.9338.
To winnow, a fan.

簿 °boo, 714, G.9467.
An account book.

簽 ts'ien, 981, G.1714.
To subscribe, a lot.

簷 yien, 1086, G.13096.
Eaves of a roof.

籌[14] dzeu, 51, G. 2493. To arrange, plan, a tally, a ticket.

籌見籌 dzeu.
See above.

籃 lan, 502, G.6731.
A basket.

籍 dzih, 985, G.899. Register of citizenship, to register.

籓15 van, 125, G.3396.
A dust basket.

籐 dung, 864, G.10888.
Rattan.

籙16 lok, 564, G.7387.
A map, chart.

籠 long, 568, G.7495.
A cage, to cover.

籜 t'auh, 915, G.11406. The fine leaves of bamboo.

籖17 ts'ien, 981, G.1698.
Bamboo slips, a lot.

籥 yak, 1117, G.13362.
A fife, flute, basket.

籩18 pien, 686, G.9193.
A basket for offering.

籬19 li, 517, G.6908.
A fence.

籮 loo, 551, G.7297.
A large basket.

籪 toen°, 938, G.12150. Bamboo network for fishing.

籯20 yung, 1107, G. 13332. A bamboo box.

籲26 yui°, yak, 1117, G.13365.
To implore, beseech.

119 米

米 °mi, 590, G.7802.
Rice.

籼3 同**秈** sien, 799, G.4451.
Common rice.

粉4 °fung, 131, G.3519.
Powder, meal, to plaster.

粃 見**秕** °pi, 674, G.8947.
Chaff.

粒5 lih, 539, G.6958.
A kernel.

粘 同**黏** nyien, 634, G.8298.
To paste, paste.

粕 p'ok, 711, G.9419.
Dregs.

粗 ts'oo, 1008, G.11863.
Coarse.

粥6 tsok, 97, G.2456.
Congee, mush.

粧 tsaung, 113, G.2754. Lady's dressing table, to adorn.

粞 si, 789, G.10304.
Broken rice.

粡 見**粞** si.
See above.

粟 sok, 823, G.4745.
Rice in the husk.

粢 ts, 1028, G.12341.
Rice in the husk.

粤 yoeh, 1130, G.13793.
Say, now, then, Canton.

粳7 見**稉** kung, c. kang, 322, G.2161. Hard rice, stiff, wilful.

粮 見**糧** liang, 524, G.7018.
Provisions, food.

粱 liang, 525, G.7023.
Sorghum, canary-seed.

粲 ts'an°, 948, G.11567.
White rice, bright, clear.

粿[8] °koo, 490, G.6631.
To clear rice.

粺 be°, c. ba°, 649, G.8564.
Good white rice or millet.

粹 dzoe°, 828, G.10117.
Clean, pure.

精 tsing, 992, G.2133.
Essence, best, skill, subtle, fine, semen.

粽同糉 tsong°, 1023, G.14979.
Dumplings.

糇[9]同餱 'eu, 174, G.4016.
Provision, food.

糊 'oo, 222, G.4936.
Paste, stupid.

糈 sui, 819, G.4708.
Food.

糉 tsong°, 1023, G.11999.
Dumplings.

縋[10] tsoe, c. teh, 100, G.2802.
Flour cakes, to stick.

糕同餻 kau, 325, G.5941.
Cake, pastry.

糗 °hyeu, 418, G.2338.
Dried grain.

穀見穀 kok, 453, G.6230.
The five grains.

糒 be°, bi°, 675, G.9014.
Dried grain.

糏 sih, 798, G.4645.
Fragments.

糖 daung, 861, G.10773.
Sugar.

糞[11] fung°, 132, G.3551.
Manure, dung.

糠 k'aung, 320, G.5912.
Chaff.

糜 mi, 590, G.7818.
Rice gruel.

糝 °sen, 723, G.9556.
White rice.

糰同糰 doen, 938, G.12154.
To mix together.

糟 tsau, 952, G.11608.
Dregs.

糙 ts'au°, 956, G.11650.
Dark rice.

漿 tsiang, 969, G.1279.
Starch.

糧[12] liang, 524, G.7016.
Provisions, food.

糤同饊 °san, 723, G.9560.
Flour cakes fried crisp.

糯[14] noo°, 639, G.8370.
Glutinous.

糰 doen, 938, G.12156.
To mix together.

糲[15] li°, 523, G.6661.
Coarse rice.

糴[16] dih, 902, G.10935.
To buy rice.

糵[17] nyih, 1081, G.8284. Leaven, grain for distilling.

糶[19] t'iau°, 890, G.11106.
To sell rice.

120 糸

糸 mih，596，G.7841.
Silk.

系[1] i°，yi°，181，G.4061.
To connect，connection.

糾[2] °kyeu，414，G.2270.
To examine，twist.

紂[3] ° dzeu， 49， G. 2472. A trace，crupper of a saddle.

紇 ‘eh，220，G.3986.
Fringe，tassels.

紅 ‘ong，235，G.5270.
Red.

丨 kong.
Needle work.

紈 wen，247，G.5067.
White，plain.

紉 zung，c. ling，289，G.5601.
To sew.

紀 °kyi，337，G.922.
To record，a record.

約 iok，1117，G.12899.
About，a covenant，agree.

紆 iui，1118，G.4731.
Crooked.

紙[4] °ts，56，G.1889.
Paper.

紛 fung，129，G.3520.
Confused，disordered.

紡 °faung，135，G.3445.
To spin.

級 kyih，c. kyuh，394，G.846.
Steps，series.

紟 kyung，398，G.2029.
A tape，sash.

納 neh，611，G.8106.
To receive，give.

紐 °nyeu，639，G.8353.
A button，knot.

紗 se，730，G.9622.
A thread.

紓 su，775，G.10044.
Slowly，little by little.

純 zung，783，G.2868.
Pure，simple，silk.

索 sauk，815，G.9601. A cord，search，scattered，demand.

素 soo°，816，G.10188.
White，formerly，now.

紋 vung，1011，G.12636.
Veins，seams.

紊 ’vung°，vung，1043，G.12637.
Confused，tangled.

紜 yuin，1142，G.13808.
Confused，tangled.

紮[5] tsah，7，G.128.
To bind，tie.

紾 °tsung，17，G.602.
Single，one thickness.

紬 dzeu，51，G.2485.
Woven silk.

紵 °zu，91，G.2606.
Coarse hemp.

絀 tseh，98，G.2621.
To blame，degrade.

終 tsong，106，G.2894.
At the last，wholly.

紱 feh, 154, G.3699.
A ribbon, tape.

紼 feh, 154, G.3662.
Tassels, cords.

絃 yien, 197, G.4483.
Strings of a harp.

紺 ken°, 313, G.5836.
A violet color.

絅 kyong, 422, G.2379.
An outer garment.

累 le°, le, 511, G.6820.
To implicate, stain, often.

絆 pen°, c. pan°, 652, G.8607.
To hamper, entangle.

紳 sung, 736, G.9821.
Gentry, a sash.

紹 °zau, 746, G.9775.
To connect, succeed.

細 si°, 790, G.4163.
Fine, minute.

紲 sih, 799, G.4413.
To bind.

紿 °de, 848, G.10587.
Tangled, to doubt, jeer.

紽 doo, 912, G.11352.
A skein of silk, a seam.

組 °tsoo, 1007, G.11828.
A band, a tape.

紫 °ts, 1031, G.12329.
Purple.

絢 6 hyoen°, yoen°, 232, G.4824.
Adorned, colored, variegated.

絨 nyong, 303, G.5751.
Felt cloth.

絳 kyang°, c. kaung°, 364, G.1251. A deop red color.

絞 °kyau, c. °kau, 369, G.1307.
To bind around.

結 kyih, 376, G.1470.
To contract, form, a knot.

絜 kyih, 377, G.1493.
To rule, repress.

丨 yih.
To measure.

給 kyih, 393, G.927.
To give.

絝 k'oo°, 437, G.6270.
Pants, trousers.

絖 kw'aung°, 478, G.6417.
Fine floss.

絡 lauh, 553, G.3260.
To bind, to continue.

絥 be°, 678, G.9008.
To harness, saddle.

丨 vok.
A rest in a carriage.

絏同紲 sih, 799, G.4384.
Bonds, to tie up.

絮 sui°, c. si°, 819, G.4774.
Refuse of silk, or cotton.

絲 s, 835, G.10259.
Silk.

絛 t'au, 868, G.10837.
A band, silk edging, cord.

絰 dih, 890, G.11135.
Hemp mourning clothes.

統 °t'ong, 936, G.12316.
A cue, hint, the whole.

絕 dzih，1010，G.3213.
To sever.

絶見**絕** dzih.
To sever.

絺7 t‘s，63，G.1969.
Fine grass cloth.

綌 hyih，396，G.1002.
Coarse grass cloth.

經 kyung，404，G.2122. Classics，pass through，already.

絹 kyoen°，451，G.3139.
Gauze silk，handkerchief.

綑 °k‘wung，496，G.6548.
To bind，tie.

綁 °paung，657，G.8653.
To tie，bind.

綃 siau，794，G.4299.
Raw silk.

綉見**繡** sieu°，811，G.4677.
To embroider.

綏 soe，826，G.10392. A cord，regular，quiet，steady.

綈 di，882，G.10994.
Heavy and thick silk.

綻8 °dzan，12，G.311.
To rend open.

綢 dzeu，51，G.2503.
Woven silk.

綽 ts‘ak，84，G.517.
Liberal，generous.

綴 tsoe°，tseh，101，G.2425.
Adorned，to unite.

緋 fi，136，G.3469.
Dark red color.

緌 soe，301，G.10426.
The fringe of a cap.

綱 kaung，319，G.5900.
A law，a principle.

綦 kyi，343，G.1049.
The utmost of.

綮 °chi，348，G.1113.
Embroidered banner.

綺 °chi，348，G.998.
Variegated silk.

緊 °kyung，399，G.2067.
Tight stringent，important.

綣 °choen，choen°，453，G.3166.
Connected，friendship.

綾 ling，544，G.7232.
Thin silk，satin.

綹 °lieu，549，G.7275.
A strand，a tress.

綠 lok，563，G.7380.
Green color.

綸 lung，566，G.6372.
A silk thread.

綿同**緜** mien，593，G.7884.
Soft down，cotton.

綳見**繃** pung，c. pang，659，G.8864. A frame for embroidering.

綬 °zeu，zeu°，756，G.10018.
A band.

綫 sien°，801，G.4559.
A thread.

綯 dau，869，G.10826.
To wind，twist，braid.

綵 °ts'e, 944, G.11512.
Variegated.

緅 tseu, 961, G.11794.
Purple color.

綜 tsong°, 1023, G.11734. Patten of a loom, to collect.

緇 ts, 1030, G.1806.
Black, dark silk.

綰 °'wan, 1039, G.12483.
The harness of a loom.

網 °vaung, c. °maung, 1045, G.12515. A net, web.

維 vi, 1049, G.12598.
To tie, help, only.

緢 °mang.
Close, compact.

緩 9 °'wen, 247, G.5071.
Slowly.

緘 kyan, 383, G.1612.
To tie up close.

緙 k'uh, 431, G.6133. To seam, to form the woof.

練 lien°, 536, G.7151.
To practice, drill.

緲 °'miau, 592, G.7864.
Small, minute.

緜 mien, 593, G.7885.
Cotton, silk.

緬 °mien, 595, G.7891.
To think of, reflect.

緡 ming, 597, G.7924.
A cord, fishing-line.

編 pien, 687, G.9178.
To braid, records, book.

緶 °bien, c. pien, 688, G.9189.
Braid, a queue.

緗 siang, 791, G.4254.
Bright yellow color.

線見綫 sien°, 801, G.4532.
A thread, a line.

緒 °zui, 819, G.4772. A clue, patrimony, to connect.

緦 s, 834, G.10274.
Fine hemp thread.

締 di°, 881, G.10945.
Inseparable, joined.

緞 doen°, 937, G.12144.
Satin, silk.

緝 ts'ih, 988, G.1091.
To tie, connect.

緯 me°, c. yui°, 1056, G.12535.
Meridian line, woof.

緣 yoen, 1136, G.13104.
Cause, reason.

緼 °'wung, 1144, G.13832.
Confused, disordered.

緻 10 ts°, 59, G.1834.
Picturesque, fine view.

縋 dzoe°, 101, G.2803.
To suspend.

縛 vok, 141, G.3634.
To bind, to tie.

縣 yoen, yoen°, 201, G.4545.
District, to suspend.

緜見縣 yoen, yoen°.
See above.

縊 i°, 284, G.5487.
To hang one's self.

縟 zok, 300, G.5687.
Pretty, elegant.

縞 °kau, kau°, 326, G.5935.
Unornamented, simple.

縚同絛 t'au, 868, G.10817.
Sash, fringe, cord.

縐 tseu°, c. tsieu°, 962, G.2458.
A kind of silk.

縗 ts'oe, 1017, G.11936.
White mourning clothes.

縈 yong, 1146, G.5743.
To bind, reel, wind.

縶[11] tseh, 67, G.1798.
To bind.

繁 van, 125, G.3404.
Numerous, splendour.

縫 vong, 158, G.3572.
A tailor.

| vong°.
A seam.

繄 i, 272, G.5379.
Alas! black, or blue color.

繈 °chang, 364, G.1237. A cloth for carrying children on the back.

縴 c. chien°, 388, G.1704.
To connect, a tow-rope.

縲 le, 510, G.6823.
To bind, a chain.

縭 li, 516, G.6902. To sew shoes, a bridal cord.

縷 °lui, 559, G.7347.
Silk thread.

縵 man°, 575, G.7634.
Plain, simple.

縻 mi, 590, G.7820.
Bind.

繆 meu, mieu, 601, G.7965.
An error.

| mieu°, miau°.
Error, mistake, surname.

|同穆 mok.

繃 pung, c. pang, 659, G.8866.
Embroidering frame.

縹 °p'iau, 683, G.9128.
Blue greenish silk.

繅 sau, 726, G.9587.
To wind silk.

縮 sok, c. sauh, 780, G.10081.
To turn back.

績 tsih, 986, G.832.
To wind, twist, business.

縱 tsong°, 1022, G.11991.
To loose, liberate.

總 °tsong, 1023, G.12010.
All, whole.

繇同由 yeu, 1111, G.13424.
To resemble, be like.

織[12] tsuh, 70, G.1812.
To weave.

繙 fan, 124, G.3388.
To translate.

繞 °zau, c. °nyau, 292, G.5580.
To surround, wind around.

繚 liau, 529, G.7053.
To wrap, wind, to manage.

繖同傘 san°, °san, 724, G.9561. An umbrella.

繕 zen°, 752, G.9714. To write, to mend.

繡 sieu°, 811, G.4680. To embroider.

繒 tsung, 951, G.11726. Silk fabrics.

繫13 i°, yi°, 181, G.870. To bind, gird.

繪 we°, 265, G.5185. To paint, sketch, color, adorn.

繳 °kyau, 370, G.1370. To bind, a thread.

繮 kyang, 363, G.1226. Bride, reins.

繭 °kyien, 383, G.1665. Wild silk cocoons.

繩 zung, 772, G.9886. A rope.

繹 yuh, 1094, G.5494. To translate, connected.

繼14 kyi°, 338, G.966. Connect, continue, hereditary.

繾 °chien, 391, G.1747. Joined, attached.

辮 °bien, c. bien°, 689, G.9208. A queue, to braid, plait.

繽 ping, 696, G.9240. Confused, mixed color.

纂 °tsoen, 1026, G.11889. To connect.

纜見纜 lan°, 507. A rope, to bind.

纏15 dzen, dzen°, 46, G.339. To bind, hamper.

纊 k'waung°, 478, G.6416. Fine unsorted floss.

纍 le, 510, G.6843. To join, bind, involve.

續 zok, 823, G.4773. To connect, continue.

纖17 sien. 800, G.4476. Minute.

纔 dzan, c. k'an, k'ak, 943, G.11503. Just now, then, before.

纓 iung, 1106, G.13325. Lapels to a cap.

纛19 dok. 922, G.10804. Banners.

纘 °tsoen, 1026, G.11884. To succeed.

纜21 lan°, G.6739. A rope, a hawser, to drag.

121 缶

缶 °feu, 141, G.3604. Pottery.

缸3 kaung, 319, G.5888. A kong for water.

缺4 choeh, 448, G.3250. Lack, want.

缾6同瓶 bing, 702, G.9322. A bottle.

鋼8 kaung, 319, G.5901. A water kong.

罅 11 hya°, 184, G.4241.
A minute hole, pore.

罄 chung°, 408, G.2209.
Exhausted, a jar.

罈 12 den, 855, G.10679.
A wine bottle.

罇 tsung, 1019, G.11953.
A bottle, wine cup.

罋 13 ong°, 1046, G.12678.
A water jar.

罌 14 iung, c. ang, 1105, G.13316.
A jar, the poppy.

罍 15 le, 510, G.6838.
A wine jar.

罏 16 loo, 555, G.7411.
A wine jar.

罐 18 kwen°, 476, G.6361.
A jar, a pitcher.

122 网

网 °vaung, 1044, G.12511.
A net.

罕 3 °hoen, 164, G.3787.
Rare, strange.

罔 °vaung, 1044, G.12512.
Not, a net.

罘 4 veu, 140, G.3598.
A net, a screen.

罡 5 kaung, 319, G.5906. Four stars of the Dipper, four guardians of Buddhists' temples.

罛 koo, 431, G.6217.
A fish net.

罟 °koo, 433, G.6194.
A fish net.

罝 tsie, 973, G.3247.
A rabbit net.

罣 6 kwo°, 467, G.6309. To think of, to keep in mind.

罩 8 tsau°, 34.
A cover, a shade.

罩 同 罩 tsau°, G.495.
A cover, a shade.

置 ts°, 60, G.1852.
To bury, release, arrange.

置 見 置 ts°.
See above.

罪 dzoe°, °dzoe, 1016, G.11910.
Sin.

罰 9 vah, 122, G.3382.
To punish.

罱 °lan, c. °nyien, 503, G.6754.
A two-leaved net.

署 dzui°, 778, G.10066.
A public office.

罵 10 mo°, 572, G.7585.
To revile.

罷 °bo, c. °ba, 645, G.8537.
To cease, finish.

罸 見 罰 vah.
To punish.

罹 11 li, 516, G.6940.
To encounter, happen.

罽 12 kyi°, 340, G.978.
Wings, a rug.

罾 tsung, 951, G.11727.
A square lifting net.

羅[14] loo, 550, G.7291. A net, to arrange, to meet with.

羆 bi, 680, G.8784. A spotted bear.

羈[17] kyi, 336, G.808. An inn, to lodge.

羈[19] kyi, 335, G.875. A halter, to arrest.

123 羊

羊 yang, 1072, G.12842. A sheep.

羋[1] mi, 591, G.7829. To bleat.

羌[2] chang, 365, G.1265. Western shepherds.

美[3] °'me, °me, 586, G.7727. Beautiful.

羒[4] vung, 130, G.3521. A ram, a ewe.

羔 kau, 325, G.5940. A lamb.

羗見羌 chang, 365, G.1264. Western shepherds.

羖 °koo, 433, G.6226. A ram.

羓 po, 644, G.8518. A hog, jerked meat.

羚[5]同麢 ling, 545, G. 7208. A stag, deer like a sheep.

羞 sieu, 810, G.4658. Savory food, shame, to be abashed.

羝 ti, 877, G.10909. A he-goat, a ram.

着[6]見著 dzak, tsak, 80, G.480. Just hit, to put on, to cause.

義[7] nyi°, 280, G.5454. Righteous.

羣 juin, 420, G.3304. Flock, group.

群見羣 juin, 420, G.3305. Flock, group.

羨 zien°, 802, G.4546. To admire, overplus.

羮[9]見羹 kung, c. kang, 322. Broth, soup.

羱[10] nyoen, 1133, G.13706. A species of sheep.

羲[11] kyi, 177, G.4092. Vapor.

羵[12] vung, 130, G.3542. A sheep with large head.

羸[13] le, 511, G.6846. Lean, poor.

羶 sen, 751, G.9680. The smell of mutton.

羹 kung, c. kang, G.6008. Broth, soup.

124 羽

羽 °yui, 1124, G.13617. Feathers.

羿[3] nyi°, 283, G.5501. Name of a prince.

翅[4] t'sº, 66, G.1994.
Wings, fins.

翀 ts'ong, 109, G.2911.
To fly high.

翁 ong, 1046, G.12667.
An old man.

翎[5] ling, c. lih, 545, G.7209.
Feathers, wings.

習 dzih, 805, G.4087.
To practice, study.

翌 yuh, 1093, G.5502.
Tomorrow.

翕[6] kyih, 264, G.4132.
To gather together.

翔 dziang, 792, G.4278.
To fly, soar, high.

翛[7] siau, 795, G.4342.
A rapid flight.

翡[8] fiº, 140, G.3470.
King-fisher, chrysoprase.

翣 sah, 732, G.9649. Feathers for adorning coffins.

翟 dih, 902, G.241.
A Tartar pheasant.

翠 ts'oeº, 1018, G.11933. A king-fisher, humming bird.

翥[9] tsuº, 90, G.2564.
To fly.

翬 hwe, 260, G.5153.
Noise of swift flight.

翩 p'ien, 690, G.9221.
Rapid flight.

翦 ºtsien, 978, G.1619.
Shears.

翫 wanº, 1039, G.12462.
To study till weary.

翰[10] 'oenº, 166, G.3828.
A pencil, writing.

翯 ngauh, 210, G.4649.
Crane's feathers.

翮 kuk, 220, G.4002.
The quill of a feather.

翳[11] iº, 271, G.5382.
To cover, hide.

翼 yuh, 1093, G.5507.
Wings.

翻[12] fan, 124, G.3390.
To fly, upset.

翹 jau, 374, G.1392.
To erect, long tail-feathers.

翺 ngau, 624, G.108.
To fly high.

翽[13] kweº, 266, G.5211.
Noise of flying.

耀[14] yauº, 1078, G.12956.
Brightness, glory.

125 老

老 ºlau, 508, G.6783.
Old.

考[3] ºk'au, 327, G.5966. To examine, test, aged, ancestors.

者[4] ºtse, 38, G.542.
This, he, who, sign of completed action.

耆 ji, 346, G.1099.
A man of sixty.

耄 mau°, 582, G.7682. A man of ninety.

耇 5 °keu, 329, G.6144. Old, decrepit.

耋 6 dih, 890, G.11136. A man of eighty.

126 而

而 r, 719, G.3345. And, yet, also, nevertheless.

耎 3 同 輭 °nyoen, 305, G.5697. Weak, mild.

耐 ne°, 613, G.8123. To bear, patience.

耍 4 °sa, 731, G.9640. To play, trifle.

耑 見 專 tsen. 116, G.2713. Singly.

丨 toen, 936. Spring or cause of anything.

127 耒

耒 le°, 512, G.6847. To plow.

耔 3 °ts, 1029, G.12323. To plant.

耖 4 ts'au°, 36, G.511. To harrow, a harrow.

耗 hau°, 173, G.3883. To spoil, to consume.

耕 kung, c. kang, 322, G.2156. To plow.

耙 bo, 645, G.8519. To harrow, a harrow.

耘 yuin, 1142, G.13809. To hoe, to thin out.

耞 5 kya, c. ka, kan, 350, G.1149. A flail.

耜 °z, 837, G.10287. A spade, a hoe.

耦 9 °ngeu, 626, G.8502. A pair, a mate.

耨 10 neu°, 618, G.8381. To weed out, hoe.

耰 15 ieu, 1110, G.13385. To cover (as grain).

128 耳

耳 °r, c. °nyi, 720, G.3336. The ear, final particle.

耶 3 ya, 1078, G.12832. Final particle.

耻 4 見 恥 °t's, 65, G.1961. Shame.

耿 °kung, c. °kang, 323, G.2164. Bright.

耽 ten, c. tan, 849, G.10615. To delay, ear-lobe.

聊 5 liau, 528, G.7071. Carelessly.

聆 ling, 545, G.7210. To hear.

聒 6 kwah, 469, G.6292. Angry look, dim sight.

聘 7 p'ing°, 702, G.9326. To invite, betroth.

聖 sung°, 773, G.9892. Holy, sacred, sage.

聚[8] °dzui, c. zu°, 1610, G.3061.
To collect, congregate.

聞 vung, c. mung, 1041, G.12651.
Hear, smell.

丨 vung°.
To state to, fame.

聧[9] gwe, 487, G.6490.
Deaf.

聯[11] lien, 533, G.7135.
Connected.

聲 sung, c. sang, 771, G.9883.
Sound, voice, fame.

聳 °song, 832, G.10461.
Born deaf, ambitions.

聰 ts'ong, 1024, G.12036.
Astute, wise.

職[12] tsuh, 70, G.1813.
Duties of office.

聶 nyik, 632, G.8269.
To whisper.

聵 kw'e°, 1037, G.12449.
Deaf.

聱 c. bang°.
Deaf.

聾[16] long, 568, G.7496.
Deaf.

聽 t'ing, 906, G.11299.
To hear.

丨 t'ing°.
To comply with.

129 聿

聿 ioeh, yoeh, 1138, G.13644.
A style, pencil.

肄[7] yi°, 284, G.5540.
To practice, learn.

肅[8] sok, 822, G.10343.
Dread, respectful.

肆 s°, 837, G.10300.
Four, reckless, a mart.

肇 °dzau, 35, G.499.
To commence, at first.

130 肉

肉 zok, c. nyok, 300, G.5665.
Flesh, meat.

月 同 肉 zok, c. nyok, 300, G.5663. Flesh, meat.

肌[2] kyi, 334, G.839.
The body, flesh.

肋 luk, 509, G.6851.
The ribs.

肘[3] °tseu, 49, G.2474.
The elbow, a cubit.

肐 iuk, 204, G.4148.
Sternum, breast bone.

肓 hwaung, 250, G.5095.
The thorax.

肝 koen, 310, G.5822.
The liver.

肛 kaung, 319, G.5889.
The anus.

肖 siau°, 795, G.4295.
To imitate, resemble, like.

肚 °doo, 917, G.12044.
The belly, mind.

肢[4] ts, 55, G.1877.
The limbs.

肫 tsung, 103, G.621.
Truly, earnestly, offal.

肥 vi, c. bi, 137, G.8484.
Fat, rich.

肺 fi°, 139, G.3497.
The lungs.

肴 yau, 192, G.4332.
Savory food.

肸 hyih, 204, G.4086.
A buzzing sound.

肯 °k'ung, 324, G.5979.
Willing, to consent.

肩 kyien, 380, G.1625.
The shoulder, to bear.

股 °koo, 433, G.6227.
The thigh, a peninsula.

肱 kong, kwung, 460, G.6583.
The arm.

育 yok, c. nyok, 1140, G.18659.
To being up, nourish.

胄[5] dzeu°, 49, G.2468.
A descendant.

胡 woo, 'oo, 221, G.4930.
The dewlap of an ox, how, what, why.

胛 kyah, c. ka, kah, 356, G.1169. Shoulders.

脉見脈 muh, c. mak, 584, G.7615. The pulse, veins.

胖 ben, c. p'aung°, 659, G.8689. Stout, fat.

胞 pau, 663, G. 8701. The womb, bladder, a blister.

背 pe°, 669, G.8774.
The back.

丨 be°.
To oppose.

胚 p'e, 671, G.8825.
Embryo.

胥 sui, 818, G.4704.
As inferior clerk.

胎 t'e, 847, G.10588.
The womb.

胆見膽 °tan, 851, G.10638.
Gall, courage.

胙 dzo°, 1007, G.11852.
Sacrificial flesh.

胃 we°, 1053, G.12574.
The stomach.

胤 yung°, 1104, G.13287.
Generations, to inherit.

胕 voo°.
The intestines.

胷見胸 hyong.
The breast.

脂[6] ts, 55, G.1792.
Fat, lard.

脇同脅 hyih, 195, G. 1510.
The ribs, sides, to coerce.

脅 hyih, 195, G.1509.
The ribs, sides, to coerce.

胷 hyong, 214, G.4695.
The breast.

胸見胷 hyong, 214, G.4696.
The breast.

胰 yi, 276, G.5405. Fat over the stomach or spleen.

胳 kauh, c. keh, 427, G.6031. The armpit.

胯 k'oo°, 468, G.6321. The legs, hips.

胱 kwaung, 478, G.6392. The bladder.

脈 muh, c. mak, 584, G.7614. The pulse, veins.

能 nung, 616, G.8184. Able, can.

胼見**胼** bien, 687, G.9199. Hard, callous skin.

脊 tsih, 986, G.893. Back-bone, a ridge.

脆見**脃** ts'oe°, 1018, G.11938. Cartilage, gristle, brittle.

脃 ts'oe°, 1018, G.11939. Gristle, brittle.

胭 ien, 1082, G.13030. The throat, a cosmetic.

脯7 °foo, 146, G.3626. Dried meat.

脛 yung°, 209, G.2182. Shin bones, bones below knee.

脚 kyak, 410, G.1362. The foot.

脘 °kwen, 475, G.12461. Aesophagus.

脬 p'au, 666, G.8757. Bladder.

脣 zung, 783, G.2871. The lips.

脩 sieu, 811, G.4662. Dried meat, salary, to cultivate.

脫 t'eh, t'oeh, 914, G.11375. To cast off, undress.

脗 ° vung, c. ° ming, 1042, G.12658. To join, blend.

脹8 同**痮** tsang°, 24, G. 413. To swell.

腁 bien. See No.5440. Hard, callous skin.

腓 fi, 137, G.3471. Calf of the leg.

腐 voo°, 145, G.3686. Rotten.

腑 °foo, 145, G.3685. The viscera.

腔 chang, 365, G.1272. Vain, puffed up, hollow.

脾 bi, 680, G.9078. The spleen.

腎 °zung, 738, G.9860. The kidney, testicles.

腊 sih, 802, G.3734. Dried meat.

腆 °t'ien, 899, G.11227. Thick, good.

腕 °'wen, 1039, G.12473. The fore-arm.

腋 yuh, 1095, G.5510. The wrist, ankle.

腴 yui, 1121, G.13601. Fat, flabby.

腸 9 dzang，27，G.458.
Bowels，affections.

腫 °tsong，107，G.2887.
Inflated.

腹 fok，151，G.3715.
The belly.

腬 dzeu，295，G.5658.
Juicy，excellent meat.

腳通脚 kyak，410，G.1363.
The foot.

腦 °nau，617，G.8168.
Brains，soft.

腭同齶 ngauh，c. hauh，k‘auh，628，G.8457. Roof of the mouth.

腮見顋 se，722，G.9547.
The jaws.

腥 sing，809，G.4607.
Measly flesh，noisome.

腠 ts‘eu°，963，G.11819.
Flesh next the skin.

腰 iau，1074，G.12893.
The waist.

賭 c. °too. Stomach(especially of animals)，tripe.

膏 10 kau，324，G.5936.
Lard，ointment.

丨 kau°.
To anoint，enrich.

膈 kuh，c. kak，428，G.6066.
The breast，chest.

膂 °lui，559，G.7542. The backbone，seat of strength.

膀 baung，658，G.8680. Region of the groin and false ribs.

丨 c. °p‘ang.
A joint of the leg or arm.

膊 pok，c. pauh，706，G.9375.
The arm，dried meat，naked.

腿 °t‘e，926，G.12184.
The leg，thighs.

膚 11 foo，143，G.3651.
The skin，superficial，great.

膠 kyau，c. kau，368，G.1346.
Glue，adherence.

膜 mok，603，G.7993.
Filmy skin.

膘 p‘iau，683，G.9129.
Flank of an animal.

膝 sih，c. ts‘ih，804，G.4140.
The knee，lap.

膛 daung，861，G.10761.
Plump，breast.

膩 12 nyi°，631，G.8228.
Fat，smooth.

膨 bung，c. bang，662，G.8891.
Swollen.

膳 °zen，752，G.9715.
Savory food.

臌 13 °koo，433，G.6245.
Swollen，enlarged.

膾 kwe°，485，G.6475.
Minced meat.

臈見臘 lah，497，G.6676.
Sacrificed offered in the 12th month.

臁 lien，534，G.7125.
The leg above the ankle.

臉 °lien，535，G.1664.
The face.

膿 nong，643，G.8189.
Matter，pus.

臂 pi°，678，G.8790.
The fore-arm.

臊 sau，726，G.9592.
Rank，rancid.

膽 °tan，851，G.10629.
Gall，courage.

臀 dung，929，G.12242.
The seat，stern.

臆 iuh，1093，G.5371.
Bosom，heart，full.

膺 iung，1106，G.13295.
The breast.

朦 14 mong，609，G.7772.
Corpulent，fat.

臍 dzi，966，G.1076.
The navel.

臘 15 lah，497，G.6667.
To bind，winter sacrifice.

臕 piau，682，G.9108.
Fat，grass.

臚 16 loo，555，G.7412.
Skin，arrange.

臙 ien，1082，G.13050.
Throat，a cosmetic.

臞 18 jui，444，G.3085.
Thin，ghostly.

臟 zaung°，949，G.11584.
The bowels.

臠 19 °len，561，G.7561.
Jerked meat，sliced meat.

131 臣

臣 dzung，20，G.648.
A statesman，minister.

臥 2 ngoo°，1057，G.12691.
Sleep，rest.

臧 8 tsaung，949，G.11582.
Good，virtuous.

臨 11 ling，540，G.7165.
To descend to.

132 自

自 z°，1031，G.12365.
Self.

臬 4 nyih，1080，G.8278.
A target，judge.

臭 ts'eu°，52，G.2521.
Stink，bad odor.

丨 hyeu°.
To smell，fragrance.

臯 6 同皋 kau，325，G.5944.
Dry ground.

133 至

至 ts°，60，G.1817.
To reach to.

致 3 ts°，58，G.1832.
To cause，occasion，result.

臶 6 tsien°，979，G.1688.
To double，come again.

臺 8 de，847，G.10577.
A terrace，stage，title.

臻10 tsung, 16, G.612.
To reach.

134 臼

臼 °jeu, 414, G.2286.
A mortar.

臾2 yui, 1121, G.13594.
A moment.

臿3 同插 ts'ah, 9, G.203.
To hull wheat, to insert, pierce.

舁 yui, 1121, G.13616.
To raise, easy.

舀4 同舀 °yau, 1076, G.12447.
To bail out water.

舀 °yau.
To bail out water.

舂5 song, 115, G.2920.
To beat in a mortar.

舃6 sih, 803, G.4188.
Shoes.

舅7 °jeu, 414, G.2288.
An uncle.

與8 °iui, 1125, G.13522.
With, together, by, give.

| yui°. Have part in, connected with.

興9 hyung, 205, G.4611.
Prosperity, to increase.

| hyung°. Increased, to desire, elated.

舉11 °kyui, 439, G.3034.
To raise, elevate.

舊12 jeu°, 414, G.2289.
Old.

135 舌

舌 zeh, 749, G.9788.
The tongue.

舍2 se°, c. so°, 748, G.9789.
A cottage, shed, neighbor.

| °se, c. °so.
To put away.

舐4 °z, 761, G.9980.
To lick.

舒6 su, 774, G.10045.
Open, stretch out, leisure.

辞7 見辭 dz, 1033, G.10277.
To answer, reply.

舔8 °t'ien, 899, G.11214.
To lick.

舖9 見鋪 p'oo, 716, G.9503.
To open up.

| p'oo°.
A shop, store,

舘10 見館 °kwen, 475, G.6354.
Inn, public hall.

136 舛

舛 °ts'en, 120, G.2746.
To oppose.

舜6 sung°, 784, G.10155.
Benevolent.

舞8 °voo, 1062, G.12760.
To dance.

137 舟

舟 tseu, 48, G.2446.
A boat.

舢3 san.
A small boat.

舫4 °faung, 135, G.3447.
A boat.

航 ‘aung, 168, G.3852. Passenger boat, navigate, sail.

般 pen, 650, G.8591.
A class, sort.

船5 zen, 120, G.2742.
A boat, ship.

舶 buh, 708, G.9344.
A sea going boat.

舵 °doo, 910, G.11331.
The rudder, helm.

艄7 sau, 745, G.9751.
The rear of a boat.

艇 °t‘ing, 908, G.11291.
A small boat.

艕8 lung, 566, G.7473.
The bow of a vessel.

艋 °mung, 580, G.7798.
A small boat.

艘10 siau, seu, 726, G.9584.
A ship.

艙 ts‘aung, 950, G.11595.
The hulk of a boat.

艟12 dong, 934, G.2918.
A long boat.

艣13 °loo.
An oar.

艦14 °chan, 201, G.1643.
A war-junk.

艨 mong, 609, G.7773.
A war-junk.

艫16 loo, 555, G.7413.
A square boat, the stern.

138 艮

艮 kung°, 317, G.5972.
To preserve.

良1 liang, 524, G.7017.
Good, virtue.

艱11 kyien, c. kan, 382, G.1639.
Difficult.

139 色

色 suh, 727, G.9602.
Color, lust.

艴5 feh, 154, G.3590. The countenance becoming angry.

艶13 見豔 yan°, 1091, G.13143.
Beautiful.

艷18 見豔 yan°. Beautiful, captivating.

140 艸

艸 °ts‘au, 956, G.11631.
Grass.

艿2 c. na°, 612, G.8116.
Small tubers, taro.

艾 nge°, 620, G.32.
A kind of grass.

芄3 wen, 247, G.5068.
A sedge plant.

芑 °chi, 347, G.1069.
A grass.

芎 chong, kong, 461, G.4698.
A medical plant.

芒 maung, 578, G.7655.
The beard of grass.

芃 bong, 661, G.8906.
Luxuriant, bushy.

芍 zak, 773, G.9770.
The peony.

芊 ts'ien, 981, G.1729.
Profuse.

芋 °yui, 1128, G.13546.
Potatoes, taro.

芝 4 ts, 53, G.1788.
A variety of flowers.

芷 °ts, 56, G.1841.
A fragrant plant.

芻 ts'oo, 91, G.2643.
Fodder.

芬 fung, 129, G.3529.
Fragrance.

芳 faung, 133, G.3448.
Excellent.

芾 °fi, 139, G.3498.
To overshadow.

芣 veu, 141, G.3599.
A plantain, rib-wort.

芙 voo, 144, G.3617.
Beautiful flower.

花 hwo, 239, G.5002.
Flowers, to spend.

芰 ji°, 341, G.863.
Water caltrop.

芪 ji, 346, G.1087.
Medicinal plant, lungwort.

芥 kya°, c. ka°, 360, G.1525.
The mustard plant.

芡 °jien, c. °chien, 391, G.1753.
A kind of water lily.

芨 jih, 394, G.847.
A medicinal plant.

芩 jung, 403, G.2106.
A salt marsh plant.

芹 jung, 403, G.2092.
Celery.

芭 po, 644, G.8520.
A banana.

芟 san, 734, G.9722.
To hoe up.

苧 同 苎 °zu, c. °dz, 820, G.4770.
A kind of sedge.

芽 ya, c. nga, 1067, G.12804.
A short sprout.

芫 yoen, 1135, G.13747.
Coriander, caraway.

芸 yuin, 1142, G.13810.
Fragrant plant.

茁 5 tsah, 8, G.141.
A sprout, to sprout.

苧 °zu, c. °dz, 94, G.2658.
Hemp, China grass.

范 °van, 128, G.3426.
Herbage.

苛 'oo, c. k'oo, 215, G.3937.
Petty, trifling, to annoy.

苢 見 苡 °i, 278, G.5468.
Pearl-barley.

苡 °i，278，G.5463.
Pearl-barley.

苒 °zen，286，G.5557.
Fender，herbs，gradually.

若 zuk，296，G.5589.
If，as，same as.

苟 °keu，329，G.6145. If，if so，but，illicit，careless.

茄 kya，c. ga，376，G.1150.
Eggplant，tomatoes，mandrakes.

苽 koo，432，G.6219.
A grain resembling rice.

苦 °k‘oo，436，G.6258.
Bitter，sorrow.

苣 °jui，441，G.3012.
Lettuce，chicory.

苙 lih，538，G.6959.
A pig pen，pig basket.

苓 ling，545，G.7212.
A tuber，fungus.

茅 mau，581，G.7689.
Reeds.

茂 meu°，589，G.7698.
Thrifty，luxuriant.

苗 miau，591，G.7851.
Sprouts，prosperity.

茉 meh，604，G.8006.
The jasmine.

苜 mok，607，G.8081.
A grass.

苞 pau，663，G.8702.
The husk，luxuriant.

苾 pih，692，G.8933.
Fragrant.

苹 bing，702，G.9314.
A species of cress.

苫 tsen，751，G.271.
Coarse grass.

苔 de，848，G.10589.
Moss.

苐見第 di°，882，G.10997.
This，the，a grass.

苕 diau，889，G.11090.
A broom grass.

苳 tong，931，G.12247.
A snow-thistle.

苴 tsui，1009，G.138.
Hemp，coarse，rustic.

英 iung，1104，G.13308.
Brave，excellent，England.

苑 °yoen，1137，G.13718.
A park for animals.

茶[6] dzo，5，G.208.
Tea.

茱 tsu，86，G.2553.
A flower.

茯 vok，152，G.3695.
China root.

荇 °yung，209，G.3911.
Aquatic plant.

荒 hwaung，250，G.5098.
Wild，barren，distant.

茴 we，262，G.5171.
Fennel.

荏 °zung，288，G.5619.
A large bean，gentle.

茹 °zu, 297, G.5672.
To eat.

丨 zu.
Roots of plants.

茸 dzong, zong, 304, G.5736.
Luxuriant.

茭 kyau, c. kau, 367, G.1308.
Water grass.

荆 kyung, 403, G.2040.
Thorns, brambles.

茁 chok, 458, G.3064.
A tray for silk-worms.

荔 li°, 522, G.6985.
Water chestnut.

茫 maung, 578, G.7654.
Doubt, vast, vague.

茗 °ming, 601, G.7942.
Leaves of tea.

荀 sing, 812, G.4875.
A plant.

荅同答 teh, c. tah, 841, G. 10481. To reply, answer.

草 °ts'au, 956, G.11634.
Plants, a rough copy.

荐見薦 tsien°, 979, G.1761.
To continue, repeat.

茜 ts'ien°, 983, G.1762.
A plant.

荃 ts'ien, 1013, G.3182.
Spicy plants, polite.

兹 ts, 1029, G.12346. Thick grass, this, now, here.

茨 t's, 1033, G.12385.
A thorn plant.

茵 iung, 1098, G.13219.
Cushion, worm wood.

莊[7] tsaung, 112, G.2760.
Suckers, sincere, correct.

莖 'ung, 170, G.2123.
Stalk, stem.

莧 hyien°, 202, G.4541.
Spinach, coarse grass.

荷 'oo, 216, G.3942.
The lotus.

丨 °'oo.
To carry.

莢 kyah, c. kyih, 356, G.1135.
Bean pods.

莒 °kyui, 439, G.3041.
A kind of turnip.

莞 wen, 473, G.5063.
A smile, the cat-tail.

莉 li°, 516, G.6891.
A flower.

莅 li°, 522, G.6962.
Water rushes, attend to.

莓 me, 584, G.7709.
A moss.

莫 mok, 603, G.7977.
Do not, a plant.

莽 °'maung, °maung, 579, G.7667. Thick grass, confused, rustic.

莪 ngoo, 627, G.8433.
A species of mugwort.

莩 foo, 143, G.3649.
A rush, related, friendly.

荸 beh，710，G.8920.
An edible tuber.

莘 sing，734，G.4565.
A marsh plant.

荽 soe，826，G.10393.
The coriander.

荳見**豆** deu°，875，G.11417.
Beans.

荻 dih，901，G.10931.
Water grass，a rush.

荼 doo，919，G.12114.
A weed.

莠 °yeu，1114，G.4678.
Tears.

菖 8 ts'ang，c. ts'aung，26，
G.434. Sweet flag，calamus.

菲 °fi，138，G.3472. A marsh plant，coarse，shabby.

菔 bok，vok，153，G.3729.
Turnips.

菡 °'en，164，G.3811.
Buds.

華 wo，239，G.5005.
Flowery，splendor.

| wo°.
A surname.

| hwo.
A flower.

萁 ji，336，G.856.
Stalks，tendrils.

菅 kyan，382，G.1626.
A coarse grass for mats.

菌 °ckuin，c. °zing，419，G.3298.
The mushroom.

菰 koo，431，G.6224. Tender stalk of water grass.

菇 koo，432，G.6210.
A kind of tuber.

菊 kyok，457，G.2964.
Marigold.

菓 °koo，489，G.6633.
Fruit.

萊 le，499，G.6691.
Turnips.

菱 ling，544，G.7233.
Arrowroot.

菉 lok，563，G.7381.
A kind of beans.

萌 mung，579，G.7792.
Sprouts.

菴 en，621，G.51.
A nunnery.

萆 bi，pe，668，G.8766.
A medical plant.

萍 bing，701，G.9318.
A water plant.

菠 poo，703，G.9337.
Spinach.

菩 boo，716，G.8581.
An image，idol.

菽 sok，780，G.10042.
Beans.

萄 dau，869，G.10827.
A vine，the grape.

菟 t'oo°，919，G.12124.
A medical plant.

菜 ts'e°，944，G.11513.
Vegetable food.

萋 ts'i, 966, G.988.
Thick growing grass.

菁 tsing, 993, G.2135.
Flower of the leek.

菹 tsui, 1009, G.2984.
Pickles, sour-krout.

萃 dzoe°, 1018, G.11931.
To collect, congregate.

莿 t's°, 1035, G.12413.
A thorn, thistle.

菑 ts, 1029, G.1804.
Overgrown, uncultivated.

萎 'we, 1047, G.12561.
Blasted, rotten plant.

菸同烟 yui, ien, 1082, G.13065. Smoke, mist.

菀 °'wen, 1137, G.12474.
Luxuriant, tender, fresh.

著[9] tsu°, 90, G.483. To arrange, write, renowned.

丨 tsak.
To dress, to put on.

丨 dzak.
To obtain, yet.

葑 fong, 157, G.3585.
Poor, cheap vegetables.

葫 'oo, 222, G.4937.
A gourd.

萱 hyoen, 231, G.4811.
Day-lily, mother.

葷 hwung, 268, G.4861.
Meat diet.

葭 kya, 351, G.1163.
A bulrush.

葛 koeh, 428, G.6069.
A creeper, a relative.

葵 gwe, 487, G.6454.
Sun-flower.

落 lauh, 553, G.6672.
To fall, drop, a place.

萼 ngauh, 628, G.8458.
A flower.

葩 p'o, 646, G.8553.
A flower.

葆 °pau, 664, G.8715.
Luxuriant.

萹見篇 p'ien, 687, G.9180.
A section.

葡 boo, c. beh, 715, G.9497.
Grape vine.

葠 sung, 735, G.9829.
Ginseng-root.

葚 °zung, c. °tung, 737, G.5632. Mulberry berries.

葸 °si, 790, G.4145.
To reverence.

蒂 ti°, 881, G.10946.
The flower end of fruit.

董 °tong, 931, G.12259.
To rule, an office.

葬 tsaung°, 949, G.11580.
To bury.

葺 ts'ih, 988, G.1092.
Repair, put in order.

葱 ts'ong, 1024, G.12021.
Onions, garlic.

萬 van°, c. man°, 1040, G.12486. A myriad, all.

葦 °we, 1051, G.12536. A reed.

萵 oo, 1057, G.12689. All salads, as lettuce, succory, etc.

葉 yih, 1081, G.9798. A leaf, hinge, posterity.

葯見藥 yak, 1116, G.12900. Medicine.

萸 yui, 1121, G.13602. A medical plant.

蓁10 tsung, 16, G.613. Luxuriant, good.

蒸 tsung, 74, G.718. To steam, vapor, all.

蒭見芻 ts'oo, 91, G.2646. Grass, hay.

蓄 hyok, 99, G.4744. To store up, collect.

蒿 hau, 170, G.3871. Tansy, wormwood.

蓐 zok, c. nyok, 300, G.5688. Suckers, sprouts.

蓋 ke°, kuh, keh, 307, G.5784. A cover, to cover, build.

蒹 kyien, 382, G.1635. A marsh plant.

蒯 kw'e°, 471, G.6335. A kind of rush.

蒞同莅 li°, 522, G.6964. To enter, as an office, seat of office.

蓏 °loo, 552, G.6644. Fruits that ripen on the ground—melons, pine-apples.

蓂 'ming, 600, G. 7957. A lucky plant which grew in Yao's palace.

蒙 mong, 608, G.7763. Dull of perception, to cover, receive.

蒲 boo, 715, G.9502. A vine.

蒐 seu, 755, G.10237. A dye plant, to search.

蓍 s, 758, G.9958. Plant resembling mayweed.

蒔 z°, 760, G.9925. To plant.

蒓同蓴 dzung, zung, 783, G.10150. A vegetable.

蓆 zih, dzih, 804, G.4131. Matting.

蓑 soo, 814, G.10200. A cloke made of leaves, or grass.

蓀 sung, 829, G.10435. Rock sweet flag.

蒜 soen°, 833, G.10381. Garlic.

蒼 ts'aung, 950, G.11596. Azure, green, old.

蒺 dzih, 984, G.920. Thorns, a medical plant.

蓊 ong, 1046, G.12672. Stalk of a flower.

蓉 yong, 1047, G.5759. A flower.

蔯11 dzung, 19, G.659. A medical plant.

蔗 tso°, 39, G.534.
Sugar-cane.

蔛 ‘ok, 233, G.4951.
A medical plant.

蔲 k‘eu°, 332, G.6182.
Nutmegs, flowers.

蔻見蔲 k‘eu°.
See above.

蓼 °liau, 529, G.7067.
Smart weed.

蓮 lien, 533, G.7115.
A water-lily.

蔞 leu, 558, G.7517.
Parsley, celery.

蔴 mo, 571, G.7595.
Hemp.

蔑 mih, 593, G.7876.
Not, minute, to pare.

蔦 °’nyau, 632, G.8247.
Cypress vine.

蓬 bong, 661, G.8902.
Flag, confused.

蓽 pih, 692, G.9002.
A wicker hedge.

蔢 boo, 705, G.9413.
Luxuriant.

蔔同菔 bok, vok, 711, G.8805. Turnips.

蔀 °boo, 716, G.9518.
Luxuriant plant.

蔘 sung, 735, G.9827. Wide branches, medical plant.

蔬 soo, 775, G.10027.
Vegetable food.

蓴 dzung, 783, G.10148.
A water vegetable.

蓰 °si, 789, G.4122.
A measure, five-fold.

蓿 sok, 825, G.10339.
A kind of clover.

蓨 diau°, 890, G.11097.
A basket.

蓪 t‘ong, 933, G.12295.
A plant from the pith of which “rice-paper” is made.

蔡 ts‘e°, c. ts‘a°, 944, G.11519.
A kingdom, tortoise.

蔣 °tsiang, 968, G.1218.
A water plant.

蔟同簇 ts‘ok, 1015, G.11876.
To collect, a crowd.

蔓 man°, 1040, G.7635.
A creeping vine.

蔚 we°, 1055, G.12625.
Luxuriant, elegant.

蔫 yien, 1083, G.13046.
Faded.

蔭 iung°, 1103, G.13229.
Shade, shady.

蔥同葱 ts‘ong.
Onions, garlic.

蕃12 van, 125, G.3392.
Thick growing grass.

蕙 we°, 264, G.5201.
A spicy orchid.

蕘 zau, 292, G.5581.
Grass, stubble.

蕊 °dzoe, c. °nyui, 301, G.5723.
A stem, head.

蘂見蕊 °dzoe, c. °nyui, 301, G.5722. See above.

蔾見藜 li.
A thistle.

蕎 jau, 374, G.1399.
Buckwheat.

蕤 jui, 444, G.3116.
Water-lily.

蕨 kyoeh, 446, G.3207.
A fern with edible root.

蕢 gwe°, 488, G.6512.
Straw shoes.

蔽 pi°, 677, G.8975.
Brush wood, to hide.

蕭 siau, 794, G.4324.
Very fragrant.

蕈 °zing, 808, G.4580.
Mushroom.

蕩 °daung, 859, G.10740.
Vast, splendor, heedless.

蕉 tsiau, 970, G.1324.
Planting.

蕞 tsoe°, 1017, G.11909.
Small.

蕪 voo, 1059, G.12759.
Jungle, neglected.

蕕 yeu, 1113, G.13406.
Bad stinking grass.

薤13 ye°, 188, G.4430.
Leeks, scallions.

薢 °kya, 188, G.4426.
A woody plant.

薌又通香 hyang, 189, G.4261.
Odor of mown grass.

薨 hwung, hong, 234, G.5290.
Death of an official, buzzing sound.

薏 i°, 283, G.5372.
Seeds of a water-lily.

薊 kyi°, 338, G.958.
A thistle, name.

薑 kyang, 363, G.1228.
Ginger.

薟 lien, c. hyien, 535, G.7141.
Medical plant.

薜 bi°, 675, G.8960.
An herb, celery.

薄 bok, 705, G.8719.
Thin, stingy, a reed screen.

丨 pok.
Near at hand.

薩 sah, 721, G.9530.
An idol, image.

薛 sih, 798, G.4371.
A name.

薪 sing, 806, G.4575.
Fuel, wood.

薙 t'i°, 885, G.11028.
To shave, weed.

薔 ziang, 969, G.1290.
A flower.

薦 tsien°, 979, G.1680.
Grass, to recommend.

薇 vi, 1050, G.12587.
An herb.

薈 we°, 1056, G.12632.
Flowers of plants.

蕹 'wung, 1144, G.13831.
Aquatio plant.

薰 14 hyuin, 212, G.4859.
Perfume, to embalm.

藁 見 稾 °kau, 325, G.5939.
A rough copy.

藍 lan, 502, G.6732.
Blue.

薶 同 埋 me, c. ma, 573, G.7604.
To bury, hoard.

藐 °'miau, 592, G.7866.
Petty, to despise.

薸 biau, piau, 683, G.9139.
Water plants.

藊 °pien, 687, G.9186.
Flat beans.

藷 見 薯 zu°, 776, G.10068.
Potatoes.

薹 de, 847, G.10582.
A vegetable.

藏 dzaung, 950, G.11583.
Conceal, hide.

| dzaung°,
A storehouse.

薺 °zi, 965, G.821.
A kind of greens.

藉 dzie°, 973, G.900. A means of, through, to help, to rely on.

| dzih. In confusion, to offer as tribute.

藎 tsing°, 989, G.2061.
To promote.

藩 15 van, 125, G.3397.
To protect, defend.

藝 nyi°, 283, G.5517.
A trade, skill.

藜 li, 515, G.6945.
A kind of bramble.

藕 °ngeu, 626, G.8503.
Lotus root.

藪 °seu, 729, G.7357.
A marsh root.

藤 dung, 864, G.10889.
Rattan.

藥 yak, 1116, G.12958.
Drugs, medicine.

藹 16 e°, 1, G.30.
Mild, gentle.

藿 hauh, 257, G.3983.
An herb for tea.

蘂 °dzoe, 301, G.5724. Stamens, pistils, a leaf-bud.

蘆 loo, 555, G.7414.
Rushes, reeds.

蘋 bing, 697, G.9252.
Water grass, apples.

蘇 soo, 816, G.10320.
A species of thyme, to cheer, Soochow.

蘀 t'auh, 915, G.11407.
Fallen leaves.

藻 °tsau, 953, G.11622.
A water plant.

蘊 °'wung, 1144, G.12649.
To gather, pile up.

虆[17] van, 125, G.3406.
A kind of celery.

蘭 lan, 501, G.6721.
The epidendrum.

蘚 °sien, 801, G.4470.
Moss.

蘖 nyih, 1081, G. 8283. The stump of a tree, sprouts.

蘸[19] tsan°, 12, G.317.
To dip into.

蘹同茴 we, 243, G.5033.
A medical plant.

蘿 loo, c. lau, 551, G.7298.
The turnip, a vine.

虀[21] tsi, 964, G.822.
A leek, to blend.

齏見虀 tsi.
See above.

141 虍

虍 hoo, 221, G.4919.
A tiger.

虎[2] °hoo, 224, G.4920.
A tiger.

虐[3] nyak, 638, G.8343.
Fierce.

虓[4] hyau, 192, G.4353.
Tiger's growl.

虔 jien, 390, G.1744. To kill, act with reverence.

處[5] ts'u°, 94, G.2660.
A place.

| °ts'u.
To dwell, to judge.

處見處 ts'u°, 94, G.2661.
A place.

| °ts'u.
To dwell, to judge.

虛[6] hyui, 227, G.3048.
False, unreal.

虜[7] °'loo, 557, G.7392.
A captive, to capture.

號 'au°, 173, G.3884.
A mark, sign.

| 'au.
To cry aloud.

虞 nyui, 1122, G.13608.
Anxious.

虢[9] kweh, 493, G.6626.
A place.

虧[11] kw'e, c. chui, 486, G.6484.
To lose, fail.

142 虫

虫 °hwe, 110, G.2932.
An insect.

| 又見蟲 dzong.
An insect.

虬[1]同虯 jeu, 417, G.2347.
To wriggle, squirm.

虱[2]同蝨 seh, 728, G.9929.
A louse, flea.

虯 jeu, 417, G.2346.
To wriggle, squirm.

虹[3] 'ong, 235, G.1206.
The rainbow.

虺 °hwe, 263, G.5182.
A viper.

蝱見蝱 mung, c. maung, 609, G.7788. Horse fly.

蚩4 t'ṡ, 63, G.1950.
A worm, stupid.

蚨 voo, 144, G.3618.
Cash, a beetle.

蚘 we, 262, G.5181.
A worm in the bowels.

蚋見蜹 dzoe°, 301, G.5718.
A mosquito, gnat.

蚧 kya°, ka°, 361, G. 1526.
Red spotted lizard used for medicine exciting sexual desire, chameleon.

蚣 kong, 460, G.6569.
Centipede.

蚌 °baung, c. °bang, 657, G.8647. A clam, mussel.

蚪 °teu, 874, G.11430.
A tadpole, porwigle.

蚕見蠶 zen, 947, G. 11575.
Silk-worm.

蚤 °tsau, 953, G.11629.
Fleas(used also with 早).

蚊 vung, c. mung, 1041, G.12638.
Mosquito, gnat.

蚓 °yung, 1102, G.13266.
An earth-worm.

蛀5 tsu°, 89, G. 2536. Insect which destroys books.

蚶 hen, 162, G.3779.
A scolloped shell.

蚯 cheu, 416, G.2312.
An earth-worm.

蛄 koo, 431, G.6197.
A caterpillar.

蛉 ling, 545, G.7213.
A venomous fly.

蛇 zo, 747, G.9786.
A snake.

蛋 dan°, 851, G.10648.
An egg.

蚱 tsuh, c. keh, 959, G.151.
A kind of locust.

蛆 tsui, c. ts'i, 1010, G.3067.
Maggots.

蚰 yeu, 1111, G.13410.
A harmless insect.

蛭6 tseh, dih, 68, G.1827.
A blood-sucker.

蛛 tsu, 86, G.2554.
A spider.

蛔 we, 262, G.5172.
A worm in the bowels.

蛟 kyau, 367, G.1309. Dragon of thickets and morasses.

蛣 kyih, 397, G.1097.
Beetles.

蛩 jong, 421, G.2368.
Cricket, cicada.

蛤 keh, 428, G.3755.
Clam, oyster.

蛐 chok, 458, G.3065.
Earth-worm.

蛑 meu, 588, G.8047.
An enormous crab.

蛓 t'sº, 1035, G.12419. Caterpillar.

蛙 'wo, 1036, G.12425. A frog.

蜇[7] dzeh, 41, G.555. To sting, a sting.

蛰 tseh, dzeh, 41, G.556. See above.

蜍 dzu, 93, G.2637. A toad.

蜉 veu, 140, G.3602. A grub, gnat.

蜂同䗬 fong, 156, G.3567. A bee, wasp.

蜆 ºhyien, 200, G.4542. A smooth bivalve.

蛺 kyah, c. ih, 379, G.1450. A butterfly.

蜋同螂 laung, 504, G.7019. The common mantis.

| liang. An insect used for medicines.

蜊 li, 515, G.6892. A kind of clam.

蛾 ngoo, 627, G.3316. A miller, moth.

蜃 ºzung, 739, G.656. A huge crab.

蜀 zok, 780, G.10057. An ancient western tribe.

蛸 siau, 794, G.4300. Chrysalis, egg-cocoon.

蜓 ding, 907, G.11241. The dragon fly.

蛻 soeº, t'ooº, c. t'oenº, t'eº, 913, G.11377. To slough off the skin.

蜈 'oo, 1060, G.12750. A centipede.

蜒 yien, 1085, G.13085. Insect allied to the centipede.

蛹 ºiong, 1148, G.13454. Chrysalis of the silk-worm.

蜜見蜜 mih. Honey, sweet.

蜡[8] dzoº, 4, G.178. Imperial offering, at end of the year.

蜘 ts, c. tsih, 53, G.1786. A spider.

蜚 fiº, 136, G.3473. A cockroach.

蜞 ji, 343, G.1038. A small crab.

蜣 chang, 365, G.1267. Insects that lay eggs in dung.

蜷 joen, 452, G.3167. Coiled around(as a snake).

蜾 ºkoo, 490, G.6634. A wasp.

蜢 ºmung, c. ºmang, 580, G.7799. Small grasshopper, small frog.

蜜 mih, 596, G.7834. Honey, sweet.

蜩 diau, 888, G.11101. A katydid.

蜨 sih, dih, 890, G.1487. A butterfly.

蝀 tong, 931, G.12254.
The rainbow.

蜻 tsing, c. sing, 993, G.2136.
Dragon fly.

蜴 yuh, 1095, G.5500.
A chamelion.

蜿 'wen, 1132, G.13727.
A squirming motion.

蜮 yok, 1144, G.13669. A marine animal, underhanded.

蝠 9 fok, 150, G.3709.
A bat.

蝮 fok, 151, G.3716.
A viper.

蝦 hya, ya, c. hoen, 182, G.3756. A shrimp.

蝎 oeh, 217, G.4360.
A tree grub.

蝴 ‘oo, 223, G.4938.
A butterfly.

蝗 waung, 251, G.5118.
The locust.

蝌 k‘oo, 424, G.6090.
A tadpole.

蝸 kwo, koo, 466, G.6304.
A snail, a hovel.

蝥 meu, 581, G.7690.
A grub that eats grain.

蝱 mung, c. mang, 609, G.7789. A mosquito.

蝻 nen, 615, G.53.
Immature locust.

蝙 pien, 687, G.9181.
A bat.

蝨 seh, 728, G.9930.
A louse.

蝕 zuh, 767, G.9972.
To eat, an eclipse.

蝶 dih, 890, G.11125.
A butterfly.

蝍 tsih, 984, G.882.
A centipede.

蝤 dzieu, 999, G.4669.
A caterpillar.

蝟 we°, 1053, G.12578.
A hedge-hog.

蝣 yeu, 1112, G.13422.
A species of fly.

⿰虫耑 toen.
A small frog.

螘 10 同蟻 °nyi, 280, G.5471.
An ant.

螂 laung, 504, G.6781.
The mantis.

螞 °mo, 572, G.7586.
The ant, blood-sucker.

螟 'ming, 600, G.7958. An insect, an adopted child.

螃 baung, 659, G.8682.
A small crab.

螄 s, 758, G.9913.
A crenulated shell, a snail.

螣 dung, 864, G.10883.
A flying serpent.

丨 duh.
Grain insect.

螗 daung, 861, G.10774.
The beetle.

蟾 ts'aung, 956, G.11597.
A fly.

蝨同蚤 °tsau, 953, G.11630.
Flea.

螈 nyoen, 1135, G.13707.
A species of silk-worm.

螢 yong, yung, c. yeu, 1146, G.13303. The firefly.

融 yong, 1147, G.5762.
To blend, to fuse metal.

螭 11 t's, 63, G.1973.
A dragon with no horns.

蟄 dzeh, dzuh, 67, G. 560.
Burrowing animals.

螽 tsong, 106, G.2895. A long headed green grasshopper.

蟈 kok, 492, G.6614.
A green frog.

螻 leu, 513, G.7350.
The mole cricket.

蟒 °maung, 579, G.7671.
A serpent.

螺 loo, 551, G.7289.
A crenulated shell, snail.

蟆 mo, 571, G.7590.
A frog.

蟊 meu, 581, G.7691.
A grain insect.

螯 ngau, c. gau, 624, G.95.
The arms of a crab.

螵 p'iau, 683, G.9130.
A chrysalis.

蟋 sih, 804, G.4139.
A cricket.

蜁 zien, 821, G.4784.
A land snail.

螫 seh, 769, G.545.
To sting, venomous.

蟀 soeh, 774, G.10210.
A cricket.

螮 ti°, 880, G.10970.
The rainbow.

螳 daung, 861, G.10762.
The mantis, a locust.

螬 zau, 955, G.11643.
A grub.

螿 tsiang, 967, G.1219.
A large locust.

蟁見蚊 vung, c. mung, 1041, G. 12664. A mosquito, gnat.

蟲 12 dzong, 110, G.2933.
Worms, insects.

蟢 °hyi, 180, G.4082.
A flat-bodied spider.

蟥 waung, 253, G.5131.
A green beetle, leech.

蟣 °kyi, 337, G.791.
Eggs of insects.

蟧 lau, 507, G.6799.
Shell-fish, cicada, spider.

蟠 ben, 653, G.8632.
Coiled up.

蟚 bung, c. bang, 662, G.8892. A small crab.

蟬 zen, 751, G.349.
A locust.

蟮 °zen, 753, G.9716.
The earth-worm.

蠆[13] ts'en°, 11, G.263.
The sting in the tail.

蟶 ts'ung, 77, G.746.
A bivalve.

蟹 °hye, c. °ha, 187, G.4427.
A crab.

蠍 hyih, 195, G.4362.
A scorpion.

蟻 °nyi, 279, G.5459.
An ant.

蠁 kyang, 363, G.1229.
A dead silk-worm.

蠃 °loo, 552, G.7304.
A wasp.

蟾 zen, 751, G.342. A striped toad, said to be in the moon.

蠈 zuh, 957, G.11672.
A grain insect.

蠅 iung, 1107, G.13313.
A fly.

蠕[14] °nyoen, 305, G.5711.
Crawling.

蠐 dzi, 966, G.1079.
A fruit insect.

蠖 wauh, 1057, G.5307. Geometrical worms, loopers.

蠢[15] °ts'ung, 105, G.2858.
Stupid.

蠟 lah, 497, G.6668.
Wax.

蠡 °li, 521, G.6953.
A wood-borer.

蠣 li°, 523, G.6972.
Oyster.

蠹[16] too°, 918, G.12085.
A book-worm.

蠭[17] fong, 156, G.3573.
Hornets, wasps.

蠱 °koo, 434, G.6251. Dropsy, worms in the belly.

蠲 kyoen, 450, G.3141. Glow-worm, bright, to excuse.

蠶[18] zen, 947, G.11574.
Silk-worm.

蠻[19] man, 574, G.7644.
Barbarian, noisy, slowly.

丨 'man.
Very.

143 血

血 hyoeh, 230, G.4408.
Blood.

衄[4] nyok, 640, G.8354.
To bleed at the nose.

衅[5] 同 釁 hyung°, 205, G.4588.
Consecrate with blood.

衇 見 脈 muh, c. mak, 584, G.8013. The pulse.

衆[6] 見 眾 tsong°, 108, G.2900.
A multitude, all, whole.

衊[15] mih, 593, G.7880.
To defile (as by smearing).

144 行

行 yung, c. 'ang, 207, G.3858.
Act, do.

| 'aung.
A row, class, a firm.

| yung°.
To travel.

衍[3] °ien, 1087, G.13113. To flow, enlarge, abundant.

衒[5] yoen°, 232, G.4797.
To display, brag.

術 dzeh, 778, G.10053.
To deceive, artifice.

衖[6] 同巷 yang°, c. long°, 238, G.5254. An alley-way.

街 kya, c. ka, 359, G.1434.
Street, thoroughfare.

衕 dong, 932, G.12268.
A side street, alley.

衙[7] ya, c. nga, 1067, G.12831.
A public office.

衝[9] ts'ong, 109, G.2916.
To rush against.

衚 'oo, 222, G.4939.
A side street.

衛[10] 見衞 we°, 1054, G.12542.
To guard, protect.

衡 yung, 'ung, 169, G.3912.
To weigh, adjust.

衞 we°, 1054, G.12547.
To guard, protect.

衢[18] jui, 444, G.3086.
A highway.

145 衣

衣 i, 270, G.5385.
Clothes.

| i°.
To dress.

衩[3] ts'e°, c. ts'o°, 5, G.191.
The skirt, flap.

表 °piau, 682, G.9114.
Manifest, index, watch.

衫 san, 733, G.9688.
Clothing of one thickness.

衷[4] tsong, 106, G.2879.
Goodness, equity, just.

| tsong°.
Ought, should be.

衽 zung°, 289, G.5613.
A lapel.

衿 kyung, 398, G.2031. A collar, garment of one thickness.

衾 chung, 402, G.2107.
A quilt.

衮 °kwung, 494, G.6532.
Court robes.

袂 me°, 586, G.7742.
A sleeve.

衲 neh, 612, G.8101.
A priest's robe.

衰 se, 785, G.10104.
To destroy, vanquish.

衺 zie, 796, G.4394.
A buskin, uncouth.

袁 yoen, 1133, G.13739.
A robe.

袗[5] °tsung, 17, G.604. A garment of one thickness.

袈 kya, c. ka, 350, G.1151.
Buddhist robes.

祛 chui，443，G.3071.
The opening in sleeves.

衮見袞 °kwung，494，G.6529.
Court robes.

袜 meh，573，G.8007.
Napkin，stomacher.

丨同襪 meh，mah.
Socks，stockings.

袤 meu°，588，G.8037.
A waist.

袍 bau，667，G.8744.
A gown，robe.

被 °be，c. °bi，669. A quilt，
to suffer，sign of passive.

丨 be°.
To cover.

袖 zieu°，812，G.4683.
A sleeve.

袋 de°，845，G.10550.
A satchel，bag.

袒 °t'an，856，G.10704.
To strip bare.

袱 6 vok，152，G.3694.
To embrace，opened.

衽同袵 zung°，289，G.5620.
A lapel.

袷 kyah，c. kah，357，G.1177.
Lining.

袴 k'oo°，437，G.6271.
Pants，trousers.

裂 lih，531，G.7088.
To split，crack.

裒 beu，673，G.9453.
To collect，to diminish.

裁 dze，ze，943，G.11502.
A tailor，to cut.

裎 7 dzung，79，G.756.
To disrobe，naked.

裝 tsaung，113，G.2759.
To fill up，to load.

裔 i°，284，G.5392.
Descendants，posterity.

裘 jeu，416，G.2325.
Fur clothes.

裙 juin，420，G.3306.
Lady's skirt，apron.

裡見裏 °li，519，G.6880.
Within，a lining.

裏 °li，519，G.6881.
Within，a lining.

裊見褭 °nyau，632，G.8248.
To tie a horse.

補 °poo，712，G.9463.
To repair，mend.

裟 so，730，G.9629.
A Buddhist robe.

裕 yui°，1128，G.13639.
Wealthy，abundant.

裌同袷 kyah.
c. kah. Lining.

裯 8 dzeu，51，G.2504.
A quilt.

製 ts°，59，G.1911. To construct，make，compound.

裾 kyui，c. ke，438，G.2995.
The tail of a coat.

褂 kwo°，468，G.6313.
An outer jacket or robe.

裹 °koo, 490, G.6638.
To wrap up, bind.

裸 °loo, 551, G.7308.
Naked.

裴 be, 672, G.8831.
A beautiful long robe.

裨 pe, 680, G.8767.
To assist.

裱 °piau, 682, G.9117.
To paste, line, a wrapper.

裳 zang, c. zaung, 740, G.9734.
Clothes.

裼 sih, 803, G.4156.
A thin garment.

褚 9 °t's, °ts'u, 93, G.2650.
A satchel, bag.

複 fok, 152, G.3717.
Double, to reiterate.

褉 hyih, 196, G.1494.
A short garment.

褐 oeh, 217, G.3932.
Coarse clothes, poor.

褒見襃 pau, peu, 663, G.8717.
To praise, a long robe.

褓 °pau, 664, G.8716.
Swaddling clothes.

褙 pe°, 669, G.8777.
To paste.

褆 °z, di, 762, G.9944.
Handsomely dressed.

| yeu°.
Embroidered clothes.

褫 10 °dz, °t's, 65, G.1956.
To undress, put off.

褥 zok, c. nyok, 300, G.5689.
Cushion.

褰 chien, 389, G.1693.
Pants, trousers.

褧 °kyong, 422, G.2388. Clothes of a single thickness.

褲見袴 k'oo°, 437, G.6280.
Pants, trousers.

褡 tah, 841, G.10487.
A pouch, pocket.

褪 t'ung°, c. t'oen°, t'en°, 930, G.12243. To expose.

襁 11 °chang, 364, G.1240.
Swaddling clothes.

褵 li, 516, G.6903.
A girdle, to sew shoes.

褳 lien, 533, G.7117.
A pocket, pouch.

褸 leu, 559, G.7518.
Spoiled.

| °lui.
Coat lapel.

襃 pau, peu, 663, G.8718.
To praise, a long robe.

襄 siang, 791, G.4266.
To assist.

褻 sih, 798.
To profane, blaspheme.

亵見褻 sih, G.4434.
See above.

褶 dih, tseh, 890, G.964.
Double garment, overalls.

﨨 men°.
A man's long garment.

襉12 kyien°, c. °kan, 384, G.1605.
A flounce, plait.

襏 peh, 709, G.9366.
A rain garment.

襌同單 tan, 850, G. 10609.
Clothes of one thickness.

襍同雜 zeh, 939, G. 11474.
Mixed, variegated.

襟13 kyung, 398, G.2039.
The lapel or fold of a coat.

襖 °au, 624, G.116.
A wadded coat.

襞 pih, 691, G.8961.
To fold clothes.

襠 taung, 858, G.10727.
Trousers.

襦14 zu, 298, G.5681.
A short coat.

襤 lan, 502, G.6733.
Ragged, shabby garments.

襫15 seh, 769, G.2018.
A raincoat made of leaves.

襪 mah, 1037, G.12434.
Stockings, hose.

襯16 ts'ung°, 22, G.676.
Inner garment.

襲 dzih, zih, 805, G.7499.
Hereditary.

襴17 lan, 501, G.6722.
Ancient literary dress.

襻19 p'an°, 654, G.8635.
A loop, a belt, to tie.

146 襾

襾 ia°, 184, G.4244.
A cover.

西 si, 788, G.4031.
West.

要3 iau°, 1077, G.12889.
Want, necessity.

| iau. Make an agreement, seek, diligent.

覃6 den, 855, G.4579.
Great, vast.

覆12 fok, 151, G.3610.
To go to and fro.

| feu°.
To cover, to hatch.

覈13 'eh, 220, G.1371.
To investigate.

覇見霸 po°.
Tyrant, fierce.

147 見

見 kyien°, 385, G.1671.
To see.

| yien°.
Manifest, show.

观2見觀 kwen, 474. To look at, to observe, an evidence.

| kwen°.
Taoist temples.

規4 kwe, 482, G.6423.
A rule, a custom.

覓 mih, 596, G.7830.
To seek, search.

覔見覓 mih, 596, G.7831.
To seek, search.

覘 5 ts'en, 46, G.384.
To spy, glance.

視 z°, 763, G.9955.
To look at, regard.

覡 7 yuh, 203, G.968.
A wizard.

覩 9 見睹 °too, 916, G.12048.
To see, observe.

親 ts'ing, 991, G.2081.
To love, kindred.

覦 yui, 1124, G.13584.
To desire, long for.

覬 10 kyi°, 339, G.957.
To covet, long for.

覯 keu°, 330, G.6158. To see suddenly, accidentally.

覲 11 jung°, 400, G. 2052. To have an audience with the Emperor.

覰同覻 ts'i°, 1011, G.3050.
To spy, watch for.

覼 12 loo, c. 'loo, 551, G.7311.
To look about.

覻見覰 ts'i°, 1011, G.3049.
To spy, watch for.

覺 13 hyauk, kyak, c. kauh, 410, G.1373. Perception, intelligence.

| kyau°, c. kau°. To awaken from a dream or from sleep.

覷見覰 ts'i°.
To spy, watch for.

覽 14 °lan, 502, G.6735.
To inspect.

覿 15 dih, 902, G.10936.
To see face to face.

觀 18 kwen, kwen°, 474, G.6363.
To observe, look at.

148 角

角 kyak, c. kauh, 409, G.1354.
A horn, corner, ten cents.

觔 2 同斤 kyung, 397, G.2026.
An ax, a catty.

觖 4 kyoeh, 447, G.3224.
Expect impatiently.

觕見粗 ts'oo, 1008, G.11877.
To loose, explain.

觚 5 koo, 431, G.6221.
A wine vase, a corner.

觝 °ti, 877, G.10910.
To gore, butt.

觜 tsoe, ts, 1029, G.2806. 21st Zodiacal constellation.

| tsoe.
To look incensed, a beak.

解 6 °kya, c. °ka, 359, G.1515.
To open, extricate.

| ka°.
To transmit.

| ye°.
Proper name.

觧見解 °kya, c. °ka, 359, G.1517. See above.

觥 kwung, kong, 478, G.6393. A wine jar.

觫[7] sok, 823, G.10329. To start, tremble.

觱[9] pih, 693, G.9013. Sound of north wind, a musical horn.

觳[10] 'ok, 233, G.4953. A sort of quiver.

觴[11] saung, 740, G.9744. A wine cup.

觶[12] ts°, 62, G.1925. A wine cup.

觸[13] ts'ok, 99, G.2677. To gore, offend.

觿[18] yi, 179, G.4171. A bone or ivory bodkin.

149 言

言 yien, 1083, G.13025. To say, words.

訃[2] foo°, 149, G.3741. A letter telling one's death.

訇 hong, 235, G.5291. A roaring sound.

計 kyi°, 338, G.940. A plan, to calculate.

訂 ting°, 905, G.11261. To arrange, settle.

訏[3] hyui, 228, G.4732. Deceptive words.

訓 hyuin°, 212, G.4881. To teach, instruct.

訌 'ong, 238, G. 5267. To make confusion, litigate.

訒 zung°, 289, G.5603. Cautious, slow of speech.

記 kyi°, 340, G.923. To record, remember.

訐 kyih, 379, G.1514. To reveal another's sins.

訖 chih, c. chuh, 392, G.874. To finish.

訕 san°, 734, G.9666. To slander.

訊 sing°, 808, G.4585. To judge, examine.

討 °t'au, 871, G.10838. To ask, beg.

託 t'auh, 915, G.11368. To entrust, commit to.

訪[4] faung°, °faung, 134, G.3449. To enquire.

許 °hyui, c. °he, 228, G.4761. To promise, excess.

訣 kyoeh, 447, G.3225. Farewell words.

訛 ngoo, 626, G.3320. Error.

訥 neh, 640, G.8373. Slow of speech, stammer.

設 seh, 750, G.9800. To establish, supposing.

訟 dzong°, 832, G.10447. To contend, wrangle.

訝 ya°, 1067, G.12805. To express surprise at.

訢 同 欣 hyung, 1102, G.4570. Pleasant, gracious.

詐 5 tso°, 4, G.152.
To deceive, impose.

診 °tsung, 17, G.605.
To examine, as disease.

詔 tsau°, 35, G.470.
To proclaim.

詋同呪 tseu°, 49, G.2477.
Revile, swear.

証又見證 tsung°, 76, G.694.
To inform, testify, proof.

詛 tsoo°, 88, G.2598.
To curse.

註 tsu°, 90, G.2537.
To explain, a comment.

訶 hoo, 215, G.3940.
To blame, ridicule.

詒 yi, 275, G.5409.
To ridicule, to displease.

詁 °koo, 434, G.6198.
To explain.

詎 °jui, 440, G.3013.
How, in what manner.

詈 li°, 522, G.7003.
To revile.

詖 bi°, 678, G.8968.
To gainsay.

評 bing, 701, G.9315.
To judge.

訴 soo°, 817, G.10357.
To tell.

詞 dz, 1034, G.10256.
A tale, to accuse.

詠 iong°, 1149, G.13508.
To sing.

詫 6 ts'o°, 6, G.222. To lie, deceive, vaunt, amazed.

詹 tsen, 44, G.276.
Verbose.

誅 tsu, 86, G.2556.
To reprove, kill, destroy.

詡 °hyui, 228, G.4753.
Boasting talk.

話 wo°, 240, G.5017.
To speak.

詣 nyi°, 284, G.5537.
To go to.

該 ke, 306, G.5776.
Ought, to belong to.

詬 heu°, 330, G.6166.
To reproach, revile.

詰 kyih, 396, G.1098.
To judge, prohibit.

誇 k'wo, 468, G.6323.
Boasting talk.

誆 gwaung°, 480, G.6407.
Lying, deceptive talk.

詭 °kwe, 483, G.6459.
Strange, blame.

詼 hwe, 487, G.6483.
Levity, light talk.

誄 °le, 511, G.6848. To eulogize the dead, an obituary.

诜 sing, 735, G.9831.
To begin, enquire.

詩 s, 759, G.9918.
A hymn.

試 s°, 765, G.9987.
To try, test.

詳 dziang, 792, G.4279.
Clearly, minutely.

詢 sing, 812, G.4876.
To enquire about.

詮 ts'ien, 1012, G.3183.
To explain.

誌[7] ts°, 61, G.1922.
Records, a note.

誠 dzung, 78, G.766.
Sincerely, truly.

誨 hwe°, 264, G.5180.
To instruct, teach.

認 zung°, c. nyung°, 289, G.5609.
To recognize, know.

誥 kau°, 326, G.5953.
To command.

誡 kya°, c. ka°, 360, G.1533.
Commandment, law.

誑 kw'aung°, c. hwaung°, 479, G.6395. False talk.

誓 z°, 765, G.9994.
An oath.

說 soeh, c. seh, 788, G.9598.
To speak.

丨同悅 yoeh.
Happy.

丨 soe°.
Urge, persuade.

誦 dzong°, 832, G.10456.
To study, read.

誕 °tan, 852, G.10644.
Boastful talk.

丨 tan°.
Birthday, to bear children.

誚 dziau°, c. ts'iau°, siau°, 972, G.1423. To revile.

誣 voo, 1059, G.12736.
To slander, malign.

誤同悞 ngoo°, 1063, G.12751.
Faults, sins.

誘 °yeu, 1114, G.13435.
To lead, induce.

語 °nyui, 1126, G.5539.
A discourse, expression.

丨 nyui°.
To tell, speak.

諍[8] tsung°, 30, G.713.
Reprove, remonstrate.

諂 °ts'en, 47, G.355.
Flattery.

諂見諂 °ts'en.
Flattery.

諑 tsauh, 83, G.2405.
Accuse, vilify.

諄 tsung, 103, G.2843.
Teach carefully.

誹 °fi, 138, G.3475.
To backbite, slander.

誼 nyi°, 281, G.5354.
Suitable, right, fit.

課 k'oo°, 425, G.6094.
A lesson.

諒 liang°, 527, G.7032.
To guess, consider.

論 lung. 566, G. 7475. 丨語
Confucian Analects.

| lung°.
To discuss, consider.
誰 dzoe, 781, G.10130.
Who, which.
誶 soe°, 828, G.10418.
Vilify, rail at.
談 dan, 855, G.10656.
To converse.
調 diau, 888, G.11053.
To mix, stir, transfer.
| diau°.
A tune.
諏 tsui, tseu, 961, G.11796.
To enquire.
請 °ts' ing, 996, G.2138.
To invite, please.
誾 nyung, 1101, G.13264.
Speak kindly, gentle.
諛 yui, yui°, 1121, G.13604.
To flatter, flattery.
諸[9] tsu, 86, G.2571.
Many, all.
諷 fong°, 159, G.3558.
To ridicule.
諧 ye, 187, G.4398.
To agree, speak.
諴 yan, 199, G.4503.
Cordial, hearty.
諠同喧 hyoen, 231, G.4812.
Clamor, noise.
諼 hyoen, 231, G.4818.
To impose on, deceitful.
諱 hwe°, 266, G.5217.
To shun, avoid.
諫 kyan°, 386, G.1670.
To point out the right.
謀 meu, 587, G.8032.
To plan, devise.
諳 en, 621, G.59.
Skilled in.
諤 ngauh, 628, G.3323.
To speak plainly, blunt.
諾 nauh, 640, G.8366.
To respond.
諞 bien, 690, G.9923.
Artful, plausible words.
諶 zung, 737, G.9844.
Sincere, true.
諟 °z, 761, G.9945.
Right, proper.
諡同謚 z°, 764, G.10002.
Posthumous title, a memoir.
諦 ti°, 881, G.10947.
To judge, examine, decide.
諜 dih, 891, G.11126.
A spy.
諮 ts, 1028, G.12345.
To cnquirc, ask.
謂 we°, 1054, G.12580.
To designate.
謁 ih, 1080, G.13007.
To state, to intimate.
諺 nyien°, 1090, G.65.
A proverb, saying.
諭 yui°, 1129, G.13585.
To proclaim, an edict.

諭 見 諭 yui°.
To proclaim, an edict.

謔[10] hyak, 210, G.4647.
Pleasantry.

謊 °hwaung, 253, G.5105.
To talk wildly.

講 °kyang, c. °kaung, 363, G.1244. To preach, herald.

謙 chien, 389, G.1722.
Humble.

謌 同 歌 koo, 423, G.6047.
To sing, a song.

謎 mi°, c. me°, 591, G.7811.
A riddle, puzzle.

謗 paung°, 657, G.8666.
To revile.

謝 zie°, c. zia°, 797, G.4432.
To thank, fall off.

謄 dung, 865, G.10884.
To copy, transcribe.

謟 t'au, 868, G.10818.
To doubt, suspect.

謠 yau, 1076, G.12920.
Slander, lies.

謹[11] °kyung, 399, G.2053. Respectful, attentive, careful.

謾 men, 575, G.7637.
To deceive, insult.

謬 mieu°, 601, G.7447.
Error, wrong.

謨 moo, 605, G.7994.
Consult, imitate.

謳 eu, 625, G.8498.
A song, to sing.

讁 同 謫 tsuh, 959, G.229.
To blame, scold.

證[12] tsung°, 76, G.726.
Evidence.

譖 tsung°, 947, G.628.
To slander.

譁 hwo, 240, G.5008.
Clamor, noise.

譏 kyi, 334, G.792.
Ridicule.

譎 kyoeh, 446, G.3217.
To impose, wily.

譊 nyau, 616, G.8156.
Wrangling, noisy.

譌 ngoo, 626, G.3329.
To lie, erroneous.

譒 poo°, 704, G.9371.
To spread abroad.

識 suh, 770, G.1816.
To know, recognize.

| ts°.
Keep in mind.

譚 den, 855, G.10681.
To boast, contend.

| 同 談 dan.
To converse.

譙 dziau°, c. ts'iau°, 972, G.1409. To revile.

譭[13] 見 毀 °hwe, 262, G.5198.
To revile.

議 nyi°, 280, G.5460.
To deliberate, discuss.

警 °kyung, 405, G.2146.
To warn, caution.

譬 p'i°, 681, G.9025.
Similar, compare.

譜 °poo, 712, G.9478.
Register, genealogy.

譯 yuh, 1094, G.5495.
To translate.

譸 14 tseu, 49, G.2494.
To revile.

護 'oo°, 226, G.4979.
To protect.

譴 chien°, 391, G.1748.
To scold, blame.

譽 yui°, 1122, G.13529.
To praise.

譾 15 °tsien, G.1621. Stupid, superficial, unskilled.

讀 dok, 923, G.11436.
To read, study.

丨 deu°.
Half-stop, comma.

讁同謫 tsuh, 959, G.230. To blame, collate, compare.

讎 16 dzeu, 52, G.2516.
An enemy, to revenge.

讐同讎 dzeu, 52, G.2515.
See above.

變 pien°, 689, G.9210.
To change.

讓 17 zang°, c. nyang°, 291, G.5575.
Waive one's rights.

讕 lan, 501, G.6723.
To defame.

讖 ts'an°, 948, G.373.
Prognostic, omen.

讙 18 hwen, 244, G.5053.
Clamor.

讒 dzan, 13, G.331.
Misrepresent.

讚 19 tsan°, 945, G.11532.
To praise, bless.

讜 20 °taung, 858, G.10735. Right words, proper advice.

讞 nyih, 1091, G.8318.
To sentence, judge.

讟 22 dok, 923, G.12070.
To slander.

150 谷

谷 kok, 453, G.6239.
A valley.

豁 10 hwah, 258, G.3956.
To enlarge.

谿 chi, 341, G.1007. Mountain gorge and rivulet.

151 豆

豆 deu°, 874, G.11412.
Beans, pulse.

豈 3 °chi, 346, G.1083.
How?

豇 kaung, 319, G.1207.
Beans.

豉 4 z°, 764, G.1996.
Rotted beans, etc.

豊 6 見豐 fong.
Rich, opulent.

豋 tung, 862, G.10857.
Sacrificial platter.

豎 8 °zu, 777, G.10080.
To establish.

豌 'wen, c. ‘oen, 1038, G.12475. A kind of pea.

豐 11 fong, 157, G.3578.
Rich, opulent.

豓 20 yan°, 1091, G.13142.
Fresh.

豔 21 同**豓** yan°, 1091, G.13141.
Fresh.

152 豕

豕 °s, 760, G.9981.
A hog.

豝 4 po, 644, G.8522.
A sow.

豚 dung, 929, G.12240.
A pig.

象 5 °ziang, 792, G.4287.
An elephant, image, star.

豢 6 wan°, 248, G.5089.
To feed pigs.

豪 7 ‘au, 171, G.3874.
Martial, eminent.

豨 hyi, 177, G.4057.
To call swine, a hog.

豬 9 tsu, c. ts, 87, G.2568.
A hog.

豫見**預** yui°, 1128, G.13678.
Prepared, beforehand.

豳 10 ping, 696, G.9259.
A kingdom.

153 豸

豸 °dz, °dza, 10, G.245.
A reptile.

豺 3 ze, c. za, 11, G.265.
A wolf.

豻 ngoen°, ‘oen°, 166, G.3789.
A feline beast, a prison.

豹 pau°, 665, G.8697.
A panther, leopard.

貂 5 tiau, 885, G.11045.
A sable.

貅 6 hyeu, 211, G.4655.
A ferocious beast.

貉 ngauh, hauh, 220, G.3973.
A badger.

丨 muh.
A wild tribe.

貊 muh, 583, G.7611.
Barbarian.

貍 7 li, 518, G.6882.
Fox.

貌 mau°, 582, G.7675.
Appearance, manner.

貋見**豻** ngoen°, ‘oen°.
A ferocious dog.

貓 9 mau, 581, G.7677.
A cat.

貔 10 bi, 680, G.9068.
A leopard.

貛 18 hwen, c. hoen, 244, G.5054.
A badger.

154 貝

貝 pe°, 670, G.8793.
A pearl, precious.

貞[2] tsung, 73, G.607.
Choice, pure.

負 °voo, c. veu°, 149, G.3743.
To bear.

貢[3] kong°, 464, G.6560.
To present.

財 dze, 943, G.11500.
Wealth.

质[4] 見質 tseh, 68, G. 1893.
Substance, a pawn-shop.

販 fan°, 127, G.3418.
To trade, barter.

貨 hoo°, 256, G.3993.
Goods, produce.

貫 kwen°, 475, G.6378.
To connect, to string.

貧 bing, 697, G.9264.
Poor, destitute.

貪 t'en, 853, G.10689.
To covet.

責 tsuh, c. tsak, 957, G.231.
To upbraid, a duty.

貯[5] °dzui, 91, G.2609.
To store up.

費 fi°, 139, G.3494.
Vast, extensive.

丨 vi°.
A name.

賀 'oo°, 216, G.3994.
To congratulate, to present.

貺 hwaung°, 254, G.5148.
To give, contribute.

貽 yi, 275, G.5410.
Bequest.

貴 kwe°, c. kyui°, 484, G.6461.
Honorable.

買 °me, °ma, 573, G.7606.
To buy.

貿 meu°, 589, G.7697.
To trade, barter.

賁 pi°, 677, G.8843.
To adorn.

丨 vung.
Great, big.

貶 °pien, 688, G.9196.
To wound.

貳 r°, c. nyi°, 721, G.3365.
Two, a second, substitute.

貰 s°, 764, G.9795.
To borrow, get on credit.

貸 t'e°, de°, 845, G.10552.
To lend, forgive.

貼 t'ih, 893, G. 11151. To stick up, to make up, just.

賄[6] hwe°, 263, G.5188.
A bribe.

賅 ke, 306, G.5777.
Sufficient.

賈 °koo, 434, G.1181.
A trader.

丨同價 kya°, c. ka°.
Price.

丨 °kya.
A surname.

賂 loo°, 557, G.7363.
A bribe.

賃 nyung°, 636, G.7197.
To rent, charter.

賊 zuh, 957, G.11671.
A thief, to rob, injure.

資 ts, 1027, G.12342.
Goods, help.

賍見贓 tsaung, 949.
Stolen goods.

賑[7] °tsung, 18, G.641.
Wealthy, rich.

丨 tsung°.
Alms.

賔見賓 ping, 695, G.9233.
A guest.

賓 ping, 695, G.9246.
A guest.

賖 se, c. so, 747, G.9781.
To trust, owe.

賬[8]見帳 tsang°, 24, G.414.
An account, debt, to reckon.

賙 tseu, 48. G.2453.
To bestow alms.

質 tseh, 68, G.1892. Original elements, to perfect.

丨 ts°.
To pawn.

賦 foo°, 149, G.3748.
Poetry, to give.

賢 yien, 197, G.4513.
Virtuous, good, worthy.

賡 kung, 321, G.6002. To encore, to join in harmony.

賚 le°, 500, G.6692.
To give money.

賣 me°, c. ma°, 574, G.7608.
To sell.

賠 be, 672, G.8809.
To restore, refund.

賞 °saung, 740, G.9735.
A gift.

賜 s°, 838, G.10303.
To give.

賛見贊 tsan°, 945, G.11523.
To assist.

賤 dzien°, 979, G.1589.
Mean, cheap, depreciate.

賴[9] le°, c. la°, 500, G.6696.
To rely on.

賭 °too, 916, G.12049.
To gamble.

賺[10] dzan°, 13, G.318.
To increase in riches.

賻 voo°, 149, G.3635. To give money for funeral expenses.

購 keu°, 330, G.6159.
To buy.

賽 se°, 723, G.9544.
Emulate, race.

賾 tsuh, 958, G.11664.
Deep, occult.

賸 dzung°, c. dzang°, 772, G.9878. An overplus, to

keep back.

賩11 見**賺** dzan°, 13, G.2720. Profit, gain.

贄 ts°, 61, G.1800. Presents for weddings, teachers, etc.

贅 tsoe°, 101, G.2813. Repetition.

贊12 tsan°, 945, G.11521. To assist.

贈 dzung°, 951, G.11730. To give.

賺13 同**賺** dzan°, 13, G.354. To increase in wealth.

贍 tsen°, 753, G.9685. To aid, abundant.

贏 yung, 1107, G.13331. To win in a game.

贒14 見**賢** yien, 197, G.4515. Virtuous, good, worth.

贐 tsing°, 989, G.2062. Parting gifts.

贓 tsaung, G.11585. Booty, plunder.

贖15 zok, 781, G.10063. To redeem.

贜18 見**贓** tsaung, 949, G.11585. Booty, plunder.

155 赤

赤 ts'uh, c. ts'ak, 72, G.1967. Flesh color, bare, pure.

赦4 se°, c. so°, 748, G.9802. To pardon.

赧 °nen, c. °ne, 615, G.8144. To blush, a blush.

赫7 huh, 219, G.3969. Bright, red-hot.

赭9 °tse, c. °tso, 39, G.546. Ochre color.

156 走

走 °tseu, 961, G.11791. To walk.

赴2 foo°, 149, G.3742. To go to.

赳 °kyeu, 414, G.2269. To carry a high head.

赶3 見**趕** °koen, 313, G.5823. To expel, pursue.

起 °chi, 347, G.1070. To arise, begin.

趁5 ts'ung°, 21, G.662. To take advantage of.

趂 見**趁** ts'ung°, 21, G.663. To take advantage of.

超 ts'au, 36, G.506. To expel, to save.

越 yoeh, 1130, G.13781. To pass over, much more.

趋 見**趨** ts'ui, 1010. To walk fast.

趙7 °dzau, °zau, 34, G.498. To hasten to, a long time.

趕 °koen, 313, G.5829. To expel, save.

趣8 ts'ui°, 1011, G.3120. Beautiful.

趨10 ts'ui, 1010, G.3077.
To walk fast.

趫12 jau, chau, 374, G.1400.
Nimble, robust.

157 足

足 tsok, 1014, G.3025.
The foot, enough, can be.
tsui°,
Treat with respect.

趴2 bo, 646, G.8542.
To pull on, to burrow.

趵3 pau°, 708, G.9402. Noise made by walking on stones.

趾4 °ts, 56, G.1843.
Foot-steps, tracks.

趺 foo, 143, G.3620.
To sit in state.

距5 °jui, 441, G.3014.
Removed, at a distance.

跇 °moo, °meu, c. °m, 588, G.8034. The thumb, great toe.

跑 bau, 667, G.8745.
To walk.

跛 °poo, 703, G.9335.
To walk, to halt, limp.

跋 bah, c. beh, 709, G.9386.
To trudge, draggle.

跚 san, 733, G.9698.
To hobble, limp.

跌 tih, 891, G.11114.
To fall.

跎 doo, 911, G.11355.
To slip, miss.

跟6 kung, 317, G.5977.
To follow, the heel.

跨 k'wo°, 468, G.6324.
To straddle.

跪 °gwe, c. °jui, 484, G.6460.
To kneel.

跬 yi, 488, G.6503.
To step, a stride.

路 loo°, 557, G.7365.
A road.

跣 °sien, 801, G.4447.
Barefoot.

跳 t'iau°, 889, G.11083.
To jump.

跡 tsih, 985, G.890.
Foot-prints.

踦7 chi°, c. zeh, 66, G.2001.
Lame.

踶見踦 chi°, c. zeh.
Lame.

跽 °ji, c. °jui, °gwe, 341, G.926.
To kneel.

跼 jok, 456, G.2959.
To bow the head, bent.

踉 liang°, 524, G.6771.
To jump.

踊 °iong, 1148, G.13456.
To leap, jump.

踟8 dz, 65, G.1933.
Undecided, embarrassed.

踝 °k'wo, c. °koo, 240, G.5018.
The ankle.

踞 kyui°, 441, G.2997.
To crouch, squat.

踡 joen，452，G.3168.
Legs contracted.

踘 kyok，457，G.2966.
A football.

踛 lok，563，G.7382. To move about. Shanghai，—to turn a somersault.

踏 dah，842，G.10502.
To trample.

踧 ts'ok，902，G.10981.
To travel a smooth road.

踢 t'ih，903，G.10985.
To kick，a kick.

踐 dzien°，979，G.1587.
To tread，walk.

踖 tsih，986，G.901.
To stride，a measured step.

踪見蹤 tsong，1023，G.11983.
A foot-print.

踵[9] °tsong，107，G.2889.
The heel，to follow.

蹂 dzeu，295，G.5659.
To tread，calamity.

踽 °kyui，439，G.3033.
To walk alone.

蹁 pien，690，G.9224.
To walk lamely.

踶 di°，883，G.11007.
To tread on，to kick.

蹄 di，883，G.11016.
A hoof(solid or cleft).

蹀 dih，890，G.11127.
To step.

踱 dauh，914，G.11309.
To walk，tread.

踰 yui，1124，G.13588.
To pass over.

⿱並疋 ban.
To creep，crawl.

⿱足亚 t'an°.
To crawl(unable to walk).

蹊[10] yi，c. chi，178，G. 4070.
To tread，step.

蹇 °kyien，384，G.1653.
Lame，halt.

蹋 t'ah，842，G.10496.
To tread.

蹈 dau°，868，G.10801.
To tread on，violate.

蹏同蹄 di，883，G.11034.
A hoof.

蹌 ts'iang，969，G.1260.
To walk rapidly，skip.

蹉 ts'oo，1003，G.11776.
A misstep，to err.

蹠[11] tsuh，70，G.1915.
To tread on，to stamp.

蹣 ben，575，G.7624.
To leap.

| men.
To leap over a wall.

蹕 pih，692，G.9003.
To press off，warn.

蹜 sok，780，G.10082.
To walk with short steps.

蹝 °si，789，G.4123.
Straw sandals.

蹔同暫 dzan°, G.307.
Briefly, meanwhile.

蹧 tsau, 952, G.11610.
To tread on.

蹡 ts'iang, 969, G.1281.
To walk quickly.

蹟同迹 tsih, 985, G.834.
Foot-prints, marks.

蹙 ts'ok, 1014, G.11843.
To urge, press.

蹤 tsong, 1023, G.11994.
Trace, foot-print.

蹻12 同蹺 chau, 373, G.1401.
To march, prance.

蹺 chau, 373, G.1393.
See above.

蹶 kyoeh, 446, G.3210.
To jump, leap, tall.

蹩 bih, p'ih, pih, 686, G.9169.
To limp, lean on one foot.

蹼 p'ok, 718, G.9406.
Web-footed.

躚 sien, 800, G.4462.
To pace around.

蹅 dah, c. sa, 842, G.10538.
To walk proudly.

蹬 dung°, c. tung°, 864, G.10869.
To hurry but not get on.

蹴 ts'ok, 1015, G.11855.
To tread on, press.

蹲 dzung, zung, 1021, G.11974.
To squat.

躇13 dzu, 93, G.2651.
Uncertain, at a loss.

躅 dzok, 96, G.2580.
To limp, halt.

躄 pih, 691, G.8962.
Lame.

躉 °tung, 928, G.12222.
A whole number.

躁 tsau°, c. ts'au°, 954, G.11619.
Hasty, rash, to haste.

躊14 dzeu, 51, G.2495.
Wavering, uncertain.

躋 tsi, 964, G.824.
To ascend, rise.

躍 yak, iak, 1118, G.13371.
Leap, skip.

躔15 dzen, 46, G.338.
Revolve, orbit.

躓 ts°, tseh, 62, G.1896.
To stumble.

躑 dzak, 71, G.1862.
Embarrassed, bewildered.

躕 dzu, 93, G.2636.
Puzzled, uncertain.

躐 lih, 532, G.7105.
To tread, to leap over.

躚16 同躚 sien, 800, G.4463.
To walk around.

躝17 lan, 502, G.6724.
To leap over.

躠同躃 sah, sih.
To walk lame.

躃 sah, sih, 798, G.4850.
See above.

躞 sih, 799, G.4401.
To walk.

蹑[18] nyih，632，G.8274.
To tread on，step on.

躩[20] jak，492，G.2229.
A quick step，to leap.

躝 ling°，542，G.7193.
To tread on.

158 身

身 sung，735，G.9813.
The body.

躬[3] kong，461，G.6567.
Personally，body.

躭[4] 見 **耽** ten，c. tan，849，G.10616. To prevent，stop，to look but think of other things.

躲[6] °too，910，G.11324.
The body，to hide.

躷[8] 同 **矮** °ia，c. °a，2，G.14.
Low，short.

躺 °t'aung，862，G.10758.
To lie down，to sprawl.

軀[11] chui，443，G.3090.
Body，person.

軄[12] 見 **職** tsuh，70，G.1814. To govern，office，duty.

159 車

車 kyui，c. ts'o，39，G.574.
A wheel.

軋[1] tsah，c. gah，1068，G.12823. Creaking of wheels，to press.

軍[2] kyuin，419，G.3276.
An army，a troop.

軌 °kwe，483，G.6451.
A rut，path，orbit.

軒[3] hyien，196，G.4474.
A projection，a porch.

軔 zung°，288，G. 5604. To chock，a catch，to embarrass.

軏 yoeh，1131，G.13794. A bar，tongue of a carriage.

軟[4] 見 **輭** °nyoen，305，G.5712.
Soft，weak，limp.

軛 uh，c. ak，629，G.8473.
A yoke，collar.

軫[5] °tsung，17，G.606.
To turn，revolve.

軸 jok，96，G.2468.
A roller，axle.

軻 k'oo，424，G.6085. Wheels on axles，infant name of Mencius.

軺 yau，zau，1076，G.12963.
An open carriage.

軼 jih，1097，G.11115.
To rush on.

輊[6] ts°，61，G.1829.
A carriage，cart.

較 kyau°，372，G.1311.
To compare，to test.

輅 loo°，557，G.7371.
A state carriage.

軾 suh，768，G.9988. Leaning board of a cart or sedan.

載 tse°, 941, G.11485.
A load, to contain.

丨 °tse.
A year.

輒7 ts'eh, 41, G.567. Side of a carriage, suddenly.

輔 °voo, °foo, 146, G.3627.
To help.

輕 chung, 407, G.2183.
Light, slightly.

輓 °'wan, 1039, G.12482.
To pull.

輙8 見輒 ts'eh, 41, G.566. Side of a carriage, abruptly.

輟 tseh, 81, G.2426.
To rest, stop.

輝 hwe, 260, G.5154.
Brightness, glory, shining.

輗 nyi, 273, G.5433.
A yoke, whipple-tree.

輛 °liang, 526, G.7013.
A cart.

輦 °nyien, 535, G.7138.
A sovereign's carriage.

輪 lung, c. ling, 566, G.7476.
To wheel.

輩 pe°, 670, G.8780.
A clan, a kind.

輞 daung, c. t'aung°, 862, G.10759. Once, a row.

輜 ts, 1030, G.1808.
Baggage wagon.

輞 °vaung, 1045, G.12517.
The tire of a wheel.

輻9 fok, 151, G.3710.
Spoke of a wheel.

輭 °nyoen, 305, G.5707.
Soft, delicate, limpid.

輸 su, 775, G.10029. To pay a tribute, lose, rotate.

輳 ts'eu°, 963, G.11820.
Near, collect.

輯 dzih, 985, G.943.
To arrange, collect.

輶 yeu, 1113, G.13404. A light carriage, light, trifling.

輾10 °tsen, 44, G.295.
To turn half over.

丨 °nyien.
To crush.

轄 hah, 185, G.4211.
To govern, the linch-pin.

轂 kok, 454, G.6232.
A wheel hub.

輿 yui, 1122, G.13533.
Carriage box, to hold.

轅 yoen, 1134, G.13742.
The thills of a carriage.

轉11 °tsen, 117, G.2694.
To revolve.

轇 kyau, c. au, 369, G.1348.
Indistinct, confused.

轆 lok, 562, G.744, G.7441.
A rut, a wheel.

轍12 ts'eh, 42, G.549.
A track, rut.

轎 jau°, 371, G.1341.
A sedan-chair.

轗[13] °k'en, 315, G.5881.
Impeded, always losing.

轕 koeh, 429, G.6071.
A kind of chariot.

轟[14] hong, 234, G.5289.
A rumbling noise.

轡[15] p'i°, c. p'e°, 673, G.8837.
The reins.

轣[16] lih, 537, G.6932.
A carriage rut.

轤 loo, 555, G.7415.
A pulley.

韀[24] c. hya. Expensive beyond expectation.

160 辛

辛 sing, 806, G.4564.
Distress, bitter, grief.

辜[5] koo, 432, G.6200.
Faults, crimc.

辟[6] pih, 694, G.8955.
A prince, to punish.

丨同僻闢 p'ih. Mean, low, secluded, to split open.

丨同避 bi°.
To escape.

丨同譬 p'i°.
To compare, like as.

辞見辭 dz, 1033, G. 10277. Words, evidence, to excuse.

辣[7] lak, 498, G.6659.
Bitter, pungent.

辤[8]見辭 dz, 1033, G.10278. To excuse, take leave of.

辦[9] bien°, c. ban°, 652, G.8610.
To manage.

辨 bien°, 688, G.9207.
To cut, divide, distinguish.

辭[12] dz, 1033, G.10279.
To resign, take leave of.

辯[14]同辨 bien°, 688, G.8612.
To dispute, argue.

161 辰

辰 zung, 20, G.652.
Time, early morning.

辱[3] zok, 299, G.5684.
Shame, contempt.

農[6] nong, 642, G.8186. To cultivate the soil, farmer.

162 辵

辵 ts'iak, 82, G.2434.
Walking.

边[2]見邊 pien, 686.
A side.

迄[3] chih, 204, G.4149.
To reach, even, till.

迆 °i, 279, G.5447.
To walk crooked.

迅 sing°, 808, G.4586.
Quick, swift.

巡 dzing, 813, G.4884.
To search, police.

迁見遷 ts'ien, 980, G.1730.
To remove.

迂 iui, 1118, G.13547.
Vague, not clear.

过見過 koo°, 490.
To pass over.

返[4] °fan, 127, G.3420.
To go and return.

近 °jung, 401, G.2021.
Near, recent.

丨 jung°.
To come near.

迕 'oo°, 1063, G.12773.
Obstinate, perverse.

迓 ya°, 1067, G.12806.
To go out to greet one.

迎 nyung, 1108, G.13291.
To meet, to receive.

丨 nyung°.
To invite.

还見還 wan, 244. To return, repay, now, still.

迤[5]同迆 °i, 274, G.5450.
To walk awkwardly.

迦 ja, kya, c. ga, ka, 351, G.1153. Used in names.

迥 °kyong, 422, G.2380.
Remote, waste, void.

迫 puh, c. p'uh, 708, G.9345.
To persecute.

述 dzeh, 779, G.10054.
To narrate, tell.

迨同逮 de°, 846, G. 10564.
Till, to, unto.

迯見逃 dau, 870, G. 10841.
To escape.

迢 diau, 889, G.11091.
Remote.

迭 dih, 891, G.11116.
To change, exchange.

迪 dih, 902, G.10940.
To follow, direct.

追[6] tsoe, 100, G.2801.
To follow, pursue.

逅 'eu°, 175, G.4029.
Unexpected meeting.

迴 we, 262, G.5173.
To return.

迷 mi, 580, G.7809.
To deceive, delude.

迺同乃 °'ne, 612, G.8120.
It may be, and, but.

逆 nyuh, 636, G.5535.
To disobey, rebel.

迸同进 pung°, c. pang°, 660, G.8860. Dispel, separate.

送 song°, 832, G.10463.
To escort, give.

逃 dau, 870, G.10809.
To flee, escape.

退 t'e°, 926, G.12183.
To recede, draw back.

迹 tsih, 985, G.891.
Foot-print, step.

這[7] nyien°，tse°，39，G.244.
This，here.

逞 °ts'ung，80，G.758. To presume，hasty，careless.

逐 jok，dzok，97，G.2591. To drive out，expel，each，successively.

逢 vong，158，G.3569.
To meet with，to accuse.

逕 kyung°，407，G.2124.
To pass by.

連 lien，532，G.7109.
To connect，bind.

逋 poo，712，G.9465.
To flee，a defaulter.

逝 z°，764，G.9995.
To depart，pass away，die.

逍 siau，794，G.4303.
To ramble，saunter.

速 sok，823，G.10330.
Hurry，hasty.

逗 deu°，875，G.11418.
To delay，loiter.

透 t'eu°，877，G.11448.
To penetrate，leap over.

逖 t'ih，903，G.11032.
To remove，remote.

途 doo，918，G.12106.
Path，way.

通 t'ong，932，G.12294.
Through，universal，all.

造 °zau，954，G.11624.
To make，build，create.

| ts'au°.
To，unto，so that.

遞見遞 di°，881.
To transmit，change.

週[8] tseu，48，G.2455.
To circulate.

逭 wan°，248，G.5087.
To flee，escape.

逵 gwe，488，G.6505. The place where four roads meet.

逮 de°，846，G.10562.
Till，to，even to.

迸 ping°，pung°，c. pang°，G.8860. Dispel，separate.

進 tsing°，990，G.2075.
To enter，advance.

逸 yih，c. yuh，1097，G.5536.
Ease，idle，to escape.

遄[9] ts'oen，120，G.2735.
To hurry，go on to.

遐 ya，182，G.4204.
Distant，remote.

遑 waung，251，G.5119.
At leisure.

過 koo°，490，G.6622.
Passed，error，fault.

| koo.
To pass.

遏 oeh，629，G.8488.
To stop，out，off.

遍同徧 pien°，689，G. 9183.
Everywhere，the whole.

逼 pih，692，G.8918. To crowd upon，to press，impetuous.

遂 dzoe°, 828, G.10402. Thereupon, then, as you like.
達 dah, 840, G.10473.
To make known, pervade.
道 °dau, 867, G.10780. A road, doctrine, principle, reason.
| dau°.
To speak, to instruct.
遁 dung°, 928, G.12225.
To hide, escape, remove.
遒 yeu, 999, G.2342. To urge, to collect, fern, a throng.
違 we, 1049, G.12539.
To disobey, oppose.
遊 yeu, 1112, G.13423.
To ramble, saunter.
逾同踰 yui, 1124, G.13587. To pass over, to extend.
遇 nyui°, 1128, G.13562.
To meet, unexpected.
運 yuin°, 1144, G.13817.
To revolve, move about.
遘10 keu°, 330, G.6160.
To meet with, accidental.
遣 °chien, 390, G.1746.
To send, drive away.
遛 lieu, c. 'lieu, 548, G.7264.
To lead, to saunter.
遡同泝 soo°, 817, G. 10367.
To trace to its source.
遜 sung°, 829, G. 4903. To respect, humble, to yield.
遝 deh, 842, G.10507. To repeat, mix.
遢 tah, 843, G.10521.
To spoil, hurried.
遞 °di, di°, 881, G.10964.
To transmit, change.
遙 yau, 1076, G.12923.
Distant.
遠 °yoen, 1137, G.13743.
Distant, afar off.
| yoen°.
To go away.
遮11 tso, 38, G.539.
To cover, secret.
遲 dz, 64, G.1988.
To delay, late, slow.
遨 ngau, 624, G.97.
To ramble, saunter.
適 suh, 768, G.10000. To satisfy, accord, just now.
| tih.
To clarify.
遯同遁 dung°, 930, G.12241.
To hide, obscure.
遭 tsau, 952, G.11611.
To meet, happen, occur.
遴12 ling°, 542, G.7181.
Covetous.
| ling.
To select.
遺 yi, 277, G.5440. To leave behind, forget, a will.
| yi°.
To give, to present.
遶同繞 °zau, c. nyau°, 292, G.5584. To wind about,

compare.

遼 liau, 527, G.7058.
A dynasty.

選 °sien, 821, G.4822.
Select, choose.

遷 ts'ien, 980, G.1711.
To remove.

遵 tsung, 1019, G.11955.
To follow orders, obey.

邂 13 ye°, 188, G.4425.
To meet unexpectedly.

還 wan, 244, G.3763.
To return, still, now.

| zien.
To revolve.

遽 jui°, 442, G.3047.
Rapid, agitated.

邁 me°, 574, G.7620.
To wax old, to depart.

避 bi°, c. ben°, 675, G.8791.
To avoid, escape, hide.

邀 iau, 1075, G.12898.
To invite, induce.

邈 14 mok, 604, G.7998.
To disregard, remote.

邃 dzoe°, G.10409.
Deep, remote.

邇 °r, 721, G.3355.
Near to.

邋 15 lih, 497, G.6670.
To exceed, to pass by.

| lah.
Sloven, filthy.

邊 pien, 686, G.9192.
A side, border, edge.

163 邑

邑 ih, 1096, G.5481.
A city, a parlor.

邢 4 yung, 206, G.4618.
An ancient principality.

那 noo, 610, G.8090.
Where.

| °na, na°, c. °'a.
That, then, what, which.

邦 paung, 656, G.8648.
State, country.

邠 ping, 696, G.9261.
A place in Shensi.

邪 zie, c. zia, 796, G.4395.
Heterodox, vicious, evil.

| 同耶 ya.
Final particle.

邨 同村 ts'ung, 1020, G.11969.
A hamlet, town.

邯 5 'oen, 162, G.3781. Name of a district and river.

邱 cheu, 416, G.2313. A place, to affect, a mound.

邳 p'e, 672, G.8827.
A place, district.

邵 zau°, 746, G.9777.
A city in Shansi.

郅 6 tseh, 68, G.1831.
Flourishing, very.

郊 kyau, 367, G.1312.
Frontier, open common.

郇 zing, sing, 812, G.4878.
A feudal state.

郁 iok, 1140, G.13689.
Elegant, adorned.

郗 7 t's, hyi, 177, G.4059.
Ancient city.

郝 hauh, c. huh, 220, G.3968.
Name of a city.

郤 hyih, 396, G.1003.
Intimate relative, a city.

郡 juin°, 419, G.3273.
A district.

郎 laung, 504, G.6777.
A gentleman, literati.

郢 °yung, 1108, G.13334.
City in Hupeh.

郭 8 kwauh, 492, G.6617. Suburb, second wall of a city.

部 °boo, 714, G.9484. Official board, class, division.

郵 9 yeu, 1112, G.13426.
A lodge, post office.

鄂 ngauh, 628, G.122.
Ancient place in Hupeh.

都 too, 916, G.11423.
All, the whole, capital.

鄉 10 hyang, 189, G.4258.
A village, country.

鄒 tseu, 961, G.11811.
Name of a state.

鄔 °oo, oo, 1058, G.12730.
District in Chehkiang.

鄙 11 °pi, 674, G.8965.
Vulgar, a boundary.

鄢 ien, 1087, G.13047.
A place in Honan.

鄞 nyung, 1102, G.13284.
The district of Ningpo.

鄭 12 dzung°, 76, G.724.
A feudal state, a plane.

鄰 ling, 541, G.7182.
Near to, a neighbor.

鄱 boo, c. bok, 704, G.9432.
Poyang in Kiangsi.

鄲 tan, 850, G.10610.
Place in Chihli.

鄧 dung°, 863, G.10870.
A feudal state.

酆 18 fong, 158, G.3581.
Old capital of Shensi, hell.

164 酉

酉 °yeu, 1114, G.13398.
Evening, 5—7 p.m.

酊 2 °ting, 905, G.11262.
Drunk, stupid.

酋 yeu, 999, G.2257.
Spirit, cooked, herdsman.

酌 3 tsak, 81, G.475. To pour out wine, an executive body.

配 p'e°, 672, G.8836.
Worthy, fit.

酒 °tsieu
999, G.2260. Wine.

酗 4 hyui°, 229, G.4775.
Mad with drink.

酣 5 hen, 164, G.3780.
Jolly.

酥 soo，816，G.10314.
Butter，crisp.

酬[6] dzeu，51，G.2508.
To thank，recompense.

酧見酬 dzeu，51，G.2509.
See above.

酪 lauh，553，G.6810.
Cream.

酩 °ming，601，G.7944.
A kind of whisky.

酵[7] kyau°，c. kau°，372，G.1353.
Leaven，yeast.

酷 kw‘auh，456，G.6267.
Superior，extreme.

酸 soen，833，G.10376.
Sour.

醅[8] p‘e，be，671，G.8810.
Unstrained liquor，surfeited.

醇 zung，783，G.2865.
Generous，liberal，clear.

醋 ts‘oo°，1008，G.11873.
Vinegar.

醉 tsoe°，1016，G.11913.
Drunk.

醃 ion，1083，G.13062.
To salt，pickle.

醒[9] °sing，809，G.4608.
To awaken.

醎見鹹 yan，c. ‘an.
Salty.

醡[10] tso°，4，G.155.
A press，to squeeze.

醜 °ts‘eu，52，G.2511.
Ill-looking，deformed.

醢 °he，161，G.3766.
Minced pickled sauce.

醞 ’wung°，1144，G.13829.
Spirits made from fruit.

醫[11] i，272，G.5380.
To heal，cure，a doctor.

醪 lau，507，G.6801.
Spirits having sediment.

醬 tsiang°，968，G.1220.
Pickle，relish，sauce.

醯[12] hyi，177，G.4113.
Sour condiments.

醮 tsiau°，971，G.1325.
To pray.

醵[13] jak，jui°，412，G.3095.
To contribute to a picnic.

醴 °li，520，G.6950.
Newly distilled wine.

醺[14] hyuin，212，G.4860.
Intoxicated.

釀[17] nyang°，631，G.5576.
To brew，ferment，excite.

釁[18] hyung°，205，G.4589.
Consecrate with blood.

釃[19] s，c. sa，759，G.9656.
To warm，putrify.

165 釆

釆 bien°，689，G.9212.
To discriminate.

采 °ts‘e，943，G.11504.
To pluck，a color.

釋[13] suh，seh，767，G.9983. To release，explain，Buddhist.

166 里

里 °li, 518, G.6870.
A mile, an alley.

重 dzong, 108, G.2880.
Double, repeated, again.

丨 °dzong. Thick, good, careful, to respect.

丨 dzong°. Heavy, important, difficult.

野[4] °ye, °ian, c. °ya, 1079, G.12989. A wild, wilderness.

量[5] liang, 526, G.7015.
To measure, deliberate.

丨 liang°.
A measure.

釐[11] li, 516, G.6939. 1/1000 of a tael, small, least.

167 金

金 kyung, 398, G.2032.
Metal, gold.

針[2] tsung, 15, G.616.
A needle, pin.

釜 °foo, 147, G.3739.
A caldron.

釘 ting, 904, G.11263.
A nail.

丨 ting°.
To nail.

釵[3] ts'e, c. ts'a, 11, G.256.
A large hair-pin.

釧 ts'oen°, ts'en.121, G.2730.
Armlet, bracelet.

釬 'oen°, 165, G.3791.
To solder metals.

釭 kaung, 319, G.5892.
Globular jar.

釦 °k'eu, c. k'eu°, 332, G.6179.
A button.

釣 tiau°, 886, G.9771.
A hook to fish with.

鈔[4] ts'au°, 37, G.514.
A voucher, receipt, copy.

丨 ts'au.
To take up, pinch.

鈎見鉤 keu, 328, G.6138. A hook, bearded claw.

鈐 jien, 390, G.1700.
A seal, a lock.

鈞 kyuin, 418, G.3294. Harmonious, thirty catties.

鈕 °nyeu, 638, G.8355.
Button, knob.

鈀 bo, 645, G.8523.
A drag, harrow, clamp.

鈍 dung°, 928, G.12220.
Blunt, obtuse.

鉦[5] tsung, 74, G.695.
A small gong.

鉏同鋤 dzoo, c. dz, 93, G.2630.
A hoe, a mattock.

鉤 keu, 328, G.6148.
A hook, a barb, to hook.

鉗 jien, 389, G.1707.
A pair of tongs.

鉅 °jui, 441, G.3015.
Great, hard, fierce.

鈴 ling, 545, G.7215.
A round small bell.

鉋 bau°, 665, G.8703.
To plane.

鉑 bak, 706, G. 9346. Thin sheet of metal, tinsel.

鉢 peh, 709, G.9354.
A basin.

鈸 beh, 709, G.9387.
A cymbal.

鉄見鐵 t'ih, 893, G.11161.
Iron, firm, decided.

鈿 dien, 898, G.11179.
A metallic head-dress.

鉞 yoeh, c. nyoeh, 1131, G.13780. A battle axe, lictor's axe.

鉛 yien, c. k'an, 1136, G.1732.
Lead.

鈺 nyok, 1138, G.13631.
Pure, hard gold.

銃 6 ts'ong°, 111, G.2929.
A mortar, gun, pistol.

銜 yan, 'en, 'an, ngen, 199, G.4506. Brevet rank, position.

鉸 °kyau, c. °kau, 372, G.1313.
A hinge, pivot.

銘 ming, 599, G.7945.
To engrave, crave.

銖 tsu, 776, G.10038.
A small coin, blunt, dull.

銕見鐵 t'ih, 893, G.11162.
Iron, firm, decided.

銅 dong, 934, G.12285.
Brass, copper.

銓 ts'ien, 1012, G.3186.
To weigh, estimate.

銀 nyung, 1101, G.13253.
Silver.

銬 c. k'au°.
Hand-cuffs.

鋤 7 dzoo, zoo, c. dz, 93, G.2632. A hoe, to hoe.

鋒 fong, 157, G.3568.
A sharp point.

銲同釬 'oen°, 165, G.3802.
To solder metals.

銳 soe°, 302, G.5727. Sharp weapon, acute, zealous.

鋏 kyih, 356, G.1137. A pair of tongs, to take up.

鋩 vaung, maung, 579, G.7658.
A sharp point.

鋪 p'oo, 715, G.9493.
To spread out.

| p'oo°.
A shop.

銷 siau, 793, G.4304.
To melt, fuse.

銹見鏽 sieu°, 811, G.4679.
To rust, corrode.

銼 ts'oo°, 1004, G.11785.
A file, rasp.

錚 8 tsung, ts'ung, 29, G.714.
A small cymbal.

錐 tsoe, c. ts, 100, G.2797.
An awl, point.

錘 dzoe, dzoe°, c. dz, doo, 102, G. 2811. A weight, hammer.

錡 °ji, 279, G.5361. A boiler, spider, a chisel.

鋼 kaung, 319, G.5903. Steel.

錦 °kyung, 399, G.2068. Flowered.

錮 koo°, 435, G.6207. To stop, securely.

鋸 kyui°, c. ke°, 441, G.2998. A saw.

錄 lok, 564, G.7386. To record, records.

錫 sih, 803, G.4157. Tin, to give.

錠 ding°, 905, G.11252. A silver ingot.

錢 dzien, c. dien, 982, G.1736. Money, copper coin.

錯 ts'ok, ts'auk, c. ts'o, 1004, G.11770. Wrong, error, to polish.

丨 ts'oo°. To hide, to place.

錙 ts, 1030, G.1807. 1/4 tael, an ancient weight.

錗見**錘** dzoe°. A steelyard, weight.

錶 c. °piau. A watch.

鍤9 ts'ah, 9, G.207. A peck, crowbar.

鍼同**針** tsung, 15, G.615. A needle, pin.

鍾 tsong, 106, G.2891. A cup, to like.

鍵 °jien, 386, G.1599. The bolt of a Chinese lock.

鍋 koo, 489, G.6621. Pot, boiler.

鍊 lien°, 536, G.7152. To smelt, refine.

鍪 meu, 588, G.8041. An iron pan, helmet case.

鍍 doo°, 917, G.12092. To guild, to plate.

鍛 toen°, °toen, 937, G.12147. To forge metal, perfect.

鍫 ts'iau, 971, G.1417. To dig, shovel.

鍬同**鍫** ts'iau. See above.

錨 mau. 581, G.7678. An anchor.

鍚 yang, 172, G.10748. Bridal head ornaments.

鎮10 tsung°, 17, G.593. To repress, rule.

鎚 dzoe, c. dz, 102, G.2805. A hammer.

鎬 °'au, 172, G.3870. A warming stove.

鎧 °k'e, 308, G.5798. Armor, mail.

鎌 lien, c. kyien, 534, G.7127. A hook, sickle.

鎊 baung，658，G.8685.
To pare off.

| c. paung.
A pound.

鎩 sa°，sak，732，G.9634.
A spear with a guard.

鎖 °soo，815，G.10204.
A lock，to lock.

鎻見鎖 °soo.
See above.

鎗 ts'iang，968，G.1263.
A gun，musket.

鎡 ts，1029，G.12351.
A narrow-bladed hoe.

鎰 yih，1092，G.5489.
A large piece of gold.

鎔 yong，1147，G.5760.
To mould，cast metal.

鎑 yih.
Iron implement.

鎳 nyih.
Nickle.

鎝 tah.
A farming hook.

鏟11 °ts'an，14，G.368.
A shovel，to shave off.

鏗 k'ung，323，G.6020.
Ringing of metal.

鏡 kyung°.
406，G.2170. A mirror.

鏤 leu°.
514，G.7354. To engrave.

鎪見鏤 leu°.
To engrave.

鏈 lien，533，G.7118.
A chain，crude ore.

鏝同槾墁 men，576，G.7638.
Mason's trowel.

鏖 iau，623，G.105.
To slaughter.

鏊 ngau°，625，G.98.
A griddle.

鏢 piau，683，G.9132. A scabbard，a sword point.

鏑 tih，901，G.10855.
Head of a javelin.

鏇 zien°，822，G.4785.
To turn on a lathe.

鏜 t'aung，c. t'ang，860，G.10763. The noise of gongs.

鏨 dzan，c. zen°，dzan°，946，G.11544. A chisel，to chisel.

鏘 ts'iang，968，G.1282.
Jingling sound.

鏃 ts'ok，1015，G.11847.
The point of a dart.

鏞 yong，1148，G.13466.
A large bell.

鐘12 tsong，106，G.2893.
A bell，a clock.

鏹 °chang，364，G.1241.
Money，coin，cash string.

鐧 kyien°，c. kan°，387，G.1607.
The iron inside a hub.

鐐 liau，528，G.7059.
Manacles.

鐃 nau，616，G.8157.
Cymbals.

鏽 sieu°, 811, G.4681.
To roast, corrode.

鐙 tung°, 864, G.10871.
A stirrup.

鐲 13 dzauh, 83, G.2410.
Bracelets.

鐶 gwan, 245, G.5048.
A ring, link.

鐮同鎌 lien, c. kyien, 534, G. 7130. A hook, a sickle.

鐮見鎌 lien, c. kyien.
A hook, a sickle.

鐺 taung, 858, G.741.
A clasp, peddler's gong.

| t'aung.
Sound of a gong.

| ts'ung.
A pan for cooking rice.

鐵 t'ih, 893, G.11156.
Iron, firm, decided.

鐸 dauh, 914, G.11319.
A square-mouthed bell.

鐫 tsien, 1012, G.1649.
To engrave.

鑄 14 tsu°, 90, G.2613.
To cast, melt.

鑊 wauh, c. 'ok, 258, G.3928.
A caldron, to bore, cut.

鑑 kyan°, c. kan°, 387, G.1644.
A metal mirror.

鑒同鑑 kyan°, c. kan°, 387, G.1645. Mirror, examine.

鑛 15 °k'waung, 463, G.6590.
The ore of metals, a mine.

鑞 lah, 498, G.6671.
Tin, copper, pewter.

鑠 sak, 773, G.10175.
To melt, fuse metal.

鐕見鑽 tsoen, 1026, G.11886.
A gimlet, to bore.

鑭 16 zah, 8, G.185.
Heavy shears, to cut, slice.

鑪 loo, 554, G.7416.
A brazier, a stove.

鑲 17 siang, 791, G.4272.
Border, inlaid.

鑰 yak, 1117, G.12961.
A key.

鑱 18 dzan, 13, G.332.
A chisel, cut into.

| ts'an°.

鑵 kwen°, 476, G.6364.
A water jar.

鑷 nyih, c. 'nyien, 632, G.8275.
Forceps, pincers.

鑼 19 loo, 551, G.7301.
A gong.

鑾 loen, 570, G.6745. Little bells, royal, term of respect.

鑿 zauh, 1006, G.11614.
A chisel, to chisel.

鑿見鑿 zayh.
A chisel, to chisel.

鑽 tsoen, 945, G.11534.
A gimlet.

丨 tsoen°.
To bore.

鬡[21] c. tsa.
Smart, bright.

168 長

長 dzang, 27, G.408.
Long.

丨 °tsang.
Elder, to grow up.

169 門

門 mung, 576, G.7751.
Door.

閂[1] sen, 786, G.10115.
Bolt.

閃[2] °sen, 752, G.9707.
A flash, to evade.

閈[3] ‘oen°, 165, G.3792.
A village, a wall.

閉 pi°, 676, G.8990.
To close, stop up.

閆同閻 nyien, 1084, G.13105.
A hamlet, hamlet gate.

閑[4] yan, c. ‘an, 198, G.4494.
To restrain, leisure.

閒 kyien, c. kan, 198, G.4487.
Space, a limit, a room.

丨 yan, c. ‘an.
Leisure, idleness.

丨 kyien°.
To cause to separate.

閏 zung°, c. nyung°, 302, G.5731.
Intercalary, extra.

開 k‘e, 308, G.5794.
To open, explain.

間同閒 kyien, c. kan, 381, G. 1601. A room, a limit, space.

閔 °ming, 597, G.7929.
To mourn with, grieve.

閘[5] iah, c. zah, 8, G.143.
A gate, a pass.

閙見鬧 nau°, 617, G.8170.
Noisy, tumult.

閥[6] vah, 122, G.3373.
The left side of a gateway.

閧同衖 hong°, 238, G.5255.
A narrow street.

閣 kauh, 426, G.6037. A door, screen, vestibule, balcony.

閤 keh, 426, G.6059.
A small courtyard gate.

閨 kwe, 481, G.6440.
Women's private room.

閩 'ming, 597, G.7932.
A snake, Fuhkien.

閡 nge°, ‘e°, 620, G.43.
To shut off, hinder.

関見關 kwan.
To shut, bolt.

閭[7] lui, 558, G.7523.
A village, hamlet.

閱 yoeh, 1131, G.13777.
To examine, to look at.

閶[8] ts ‘ang, c. ts ‘aung, 26, G.436. Palace gate, gate of heaven.

閽 hwung，268，G.5228.
To close，a porter.

閼 oeh，629，G.8447.
To shut，stop，to hoodwink.

閹 ien，1083，G.13063.
To castrate.

閻 nyien，1084，G.13153.
The gate of a village.

閾 yok，1141，G.13670.
Sill，threshold.

闋 9 choeh，449，G. 3254. To shut the door，to prohibit.

闃 chih，459，G.3124.
To live alone，quiet，still.

闊 kw‘eh，493，G.6125.
To open，brood.

闌 lan，501，G.6710.
A door screen，to seclude.

闇 en°，622，G.60.
A recess，retired.

闈 we，1049，G.12540. The door of a harem，to examine.

闖 10 ts‘ung°，c. ts‘aung°，21，G.672. To bolt out，suddenly.

闔 ‘eh，218，G.3962.
To shut doors，all.

闕 choeh，448，G.3252. Imperial gate，deficiency，fault.

闗 見 關 kwan，472，G.6369.
To shut，bolt.

闐 dien，899，G.11190.
To fill up，full，ample.

關 11 kwan，472，G.6368.
To shut，bolt.

闡 12 °ts‘en，46，G.351.
To open，expand.

闠 gwe°，265，G.5208.
Market gate，a street.

闞 chan°，315，G. 3806. To look toward，to come to.

闤 13 wan，gwan，245，G.5049.
A wall around，a market，or its gate.

闢 p‘ih，694，G.9026. To burst forth，disclose，to retire.

丨 bih.
To split open.

闥 t‘ah，c. dah，844，G.10535.
Inner door of a palace.

170 阜

阜 °veu，141，G.3607.
A mound，fertile.

阡 3 ts‘ien，981，G.1731.
A north and south road.

阪 4 °fan，127，G.3421.
A bank，a dike.

防 baung，134，G.3452.
To guard against.

阨 uh，629，G.8475.
A dangerous defile.

阱 °dzing，994，G.2154.
A pit-fall，a hole.

阮 °nyoen，1136，G.5713.
A mountain，feudal state.

阻 5 °tsoo，88，G.2599.
Hinder.

附 voo°，147，G.3690. Near to，to enclose，possessed by.

阿 oo，643，G.1.A high ridge，much used in names.

丨 ak，ah. Exclamation，brother，final particle.

陂 pe，704，G.8770. A bank，a side.

陀 doo，911，G.11358. Rugged paths.

阽 nyien，1086，G.13147. Dangerous，ready to fall.

限 6 °yien，c. °yan，°‘an，202，G.4553.A boundary，limit.

降 kyang°，c. kaung°，364，G.1255. To descend，come down.

丨 ‘aung. To submit，return to loyalty.

陋 leu°，514，G.7359. Ugly，low，base.

陌 muh，c. mak，pak，583，G.7612.East and west road，a stranger.

陣 7 dzung°，19，G.643. To array，an army.

陟 tseh，70，G.1855. To ascend，advance，promoted.

除 dzu，92，G.2638. To divide，take away，expect.

陜 yah，186，G.4221. A narrow defile.

陛 °be，677，G.8952. Steps，sides.

陝 °sen，752，G.9709. Province of Shansi.

陞 sung，771，G.9881. To ascend.

陡 °teu，874，G.11434. Suddenly，perpendicular.

院 yoen°，1137，G.13752. A court.

陳 8 dzung，19，G.658.To spread out，to state to a superior.

陷見陥 yan°，c. ‘an°. To sink.

陷 yan°，c. ‘an°，202，G.4528. To sink.

陵 ling，543，G.7235. A tomb，to insult.

陸 lok，562，G.7432. Dry land，six.

陪 be，672，G.8811. To add，accompany.

陶 dau，869，G.10831. A furnace.

陬 tseu，961，G.11798. A nook，corner，abashed.

陰 lung，1099，G.13224.Shade，the female principle.

隊 9 de°，925，G.2817. Army，group. Used also for 墜 dzoe°.

隍 waung，251，G.5121. City moat.

階 kya，c. ka，358，G.1440. Steps，elementary.

隆 long, 567, G.7504. Grand, eminent.

隋 dzoe, 826, G.10394. Name of a dynasty.

隄 di, 877, G.10917. An embankment.

隈同渨 'we, 1047, G.12556. A bend or cove.

陽 yang, 1071, G.12883. The male principle, the sun, heaven.

隂見陰 iung, 1099, G.13226. Shadow, shade, female principle.

隅 nyui, 1119, G. 13564. A corner, cave, lowest term in cube root.

隘[10] °ie, iuh, 2, G.39. A pass, defile, distressed.

隙 hyih, 396. A crack, a fissure in a wall.

隔 kuh, c. kak, 427, G.1476. To separate.

隕 °yuin, 1143, G.13842. To fall, roll down.

障[11] tsang°, 25, G.404. Separate so as to protect, where.

際 tsi°, 965, G.936. Border, region, then, time.

隟見隙 hyih, G.1119. A crack, a fissure.

隣[12]見鄰 ling, 541, G.7183. Near neighbor.

險[13] °hyien, 200, G.4458. An abyss, cliff, danger.

隩 au°, 625, G.117. A flat, a terrace.

隨 dzoe, 826, G.10396. To follow, accord with.

隧 dzoe°, 828, G.10412. A path to a tomb.

隰[14] dzih, 805, G.4126. Low marshy land.

隱 °iung, 1103, G.13276. Hidden, mysterious.

隳[15]見隓 hwe, 261, G.5159. To destroy, to raze.

隴[16] °long, 568, G.7501. A dike, a row.

171 隶

隶 de°, 846, G.10559. To reach, overtake.

隸[9] li°, c. di°, 524, G.7005. Attached to, belonging to.

172 隹

隹 tsoe, 100, G.2795. Birds.

隻[2] tsuh, c. tsak, 69, G.1869. A bird, one.

隺見確 chak, 219, G.3976. A bird flying high, truly.

I見鶴 ngauh. A crane, egret.

隼 °sung, 813, G.2850. A falcon.

难見難 nan, 614. Difficult, harass; Shanghai, — now.

| nan°. Calamity, trouble.

雀3 ts'iak, 997, G.1387. A sparrow.

雄4 yong, 214, G.4699. A male, brave.

雇 koo°, 435, G.6252. To hire, hired, workman.

| 見鳸 °koo. A hawfinch.

集 dzih, 985, G.906. To assemble.

雅 °ia, 1067, G.12807. Elegant, polished, real.

| ia. A crow.

雁 yan°, c. ngan°, 1089, G.13137. A wild goose.

雉5 °dz, 60, G.1870. Pheasant, embrasure, to rule.

雎 tsui, 1009, G.2981. A gull.

雌 t's, 1033, G.12397. Female, inferior.

雍 iong, yong, 1145, G.12676. To assist, affable.

雕8 同鵰 tiau, 885, G.11054. To carve, engrave, a sea eagle.

雖9 soe, 826, G.10131. Although, if.

雛10 dzoo, 93, G.2647. A young chicken.

雞 kyi, 334, G.811. A hen, fowl.

雙 saung, 787, G.10118. A pair, a couple.

雜 dzeh, zeh, 939, G.11454. Mixed, miscellaneous.

雝 iong, 1145, G.13479. The singing of birds, a pool.

離11 li, 517, G.6906. To leave, retire from.

難 nan, 614, G.8135. Difficult, grievous.

| nan°. Distress, calamity.

173 雨

雨 °yui, 1124, G.13623. Rain.

| yui°. To rain.

雪3 sih, 820, G.4845. Snow.

雰4 fung, 129, G.3524. Misty, foggy.

雯 vung, 1041, G.12639. Coloring in the clouds.

雲 yuin, 1142, G.13812. Clouds.

雷5 le, 510, G.6824. Thunder.

零 ling, 545, G.7216. Fragments, remainder, to fall.

雹 bok，bauh，708，G.8704.
Hail.

電 dien°，896，G.11201.
Lightning，electricity.

需[6] sui，818，G.4727.
To require，needful.

震[7] tsung°，18，G.642.
To shake，excite.

霉 me，584，G.7712.
Damp weather，mouldy.

霄 siau，794，G.4305.
Vapor，halo.

霆 ding，907，G.11295.
Thunder.

霏[8] fi，136，G.3476.
Driving snow and rain.

霓 nyi，273，G. 5434. The rainbow，colored clouds.

霍 hauh，257，G.3979.
Speed，celerity，cholera.

霖 ling，540，G.7164. Three days' rain，rainy season.

霎 sah，732，G.9648.
Fine rain，a wink，instant.

霞[9] ya，182，G.4201.
Red sky.

霜 saung，787，G.10120.
Frost，mist.

霧[11] voo°，1062，G.12791.
Fog.

霪 yung，1101，G.13245.
A long rain.

霰[12] sien°，802，G.4521.
Snow and sleet falling.

靇 long.
God of thunder.

露[13] loo°，557，G.7362.
Dew，to expose，disclose.

霸 po°，645，G.8533.
To usurp.

霹 p'ih，694，G.9027.
A loud noise，a clap.

霾[14] me，573，G.7605.
Sand storm，foggy sky.

霽 tsi°，964，G.826. Rain ceasing and blue sky appearing.

靄[16] e°，1，G.31.
A cloudy but bright sky.

靂 lih，537，G.6933.
A clap of thunder.

靈 ling，543，G.7222. Spirit，ingenious，efficacious.

靆 de°，846，G.10561.
Cloudy.

靉[17] e°，1，G.21.
Dark clouds.

174 青

青 ts'ing，995，G.2184.
Green，color of nature.

靖[5] °dzing，°zing，994，G.2131.
Still，quiet，at rest.

靛[8] dien°，897，G.11199.
Indigo.

靜 °dzing，°zing，994，G.2179.
Quiet，peaceful.

靝[10] 見天 t'ien，897，G.11245.
The sky，heaven.

Nature, providence.

175 非

非 fi, 136, G.3459.
Wrong, a negative.

啡3 c. fi, 649, G.8578.
The noise of vomiting.

靠7 k'au°, 327, G.5964.
To depend on, to trust.

靡11 mi, 591, G. 7823. Laid out, poured out, extravagant, not.

176 面

面 mien°, 595, G.7886.
The face, surface, front.

靦7 °t'ien, 900, G.11242.
To feel ashamed, to blush.

靨14 ih, 1081, G.13000.
A dimpled cheek.

177 革

革 kuh, c. kak, 428, G.6073.
Raw leather, to deprive of.

靭3 zung°, c. nyung°, 289, G.5605. Soft and tough.

靴4 hyoo, 229, G.4837.
A book.

靳 °jung, 400, G.2023.
To restrain, put to shame.

靶 po°, 645, G.8524. Target, reins held in the hand.

鞅5 °iang, 1073, G.12869.
A halter, to tie.

鞋6 ye, c. 'a, 187, G.4377.
Shoes.

鞏 °kong, 463, G.6565.
To bind securely, firm.

鞍 oen, 621, G.47.
A saddle.

鞘7 siau, 794, G.1424.
A whit.

| siau°.
A sheath, scabbard.

鞝8 °tsang, c. °tsaung, 24, G.420.
Sole-leather, a patch.

鞠 kyok, 457, G.2967.
To investigate, judicial.

鞤9 paung, 657, G.8658.
The leather in shoe heels.

鞭 pien, 687, G.9190.
A whip.

鞦 ts'ieu, 1001, G.2307. Traces, crupper, breast-strap.

鞵10 同**鞋** ye, c. 'a, 179, G.4071. A shoe.

鞹11 kw'auh, 493, G.6128.
Soft cured leather.

韡12 同**靴** hyoo, 229, G.4838.
Chinese boots.

韁13 kyang, 363, G.1227.
Bridle, reins.

韃 同**撻** t'ah, 841, G.10477.
Mongols.

韆15 ts'ien, 981, G.1712.
A swing.

韈 mah, 1037, G.12435.
Stockings.

⿰革龍[16] long, 568, G.7502. A halter.

178 韋

韋 we, 1048, G.12527. Leather.

韌[3] zung°, c. nyung°, 289, G.5606. Soft but tough, catgut.

韒[7] 同 鞘 siau°, 794, G.4306. Sheath, scabbard.

韓[8] ‘oen, 163, G.3827. Ancient feudal state.

韙[9] °we, 1052, G.12545. Right, proper.

韜[10] t‘au, 869, G.10819. A quiver.

韞 °’wung, 1144, G.13830. To guard, conceal.

179 韭

韭 °kyeu, 414, G.2279. Leeks, scallions.

韮[4] 同 韭 °kyeu, 414, G.2280. Leeks, scallions.

180 音

音 iung, 1100, G.13209. Sound, noise.

韵[4] 見 韻 iuin°, yuin°, 1143, G. 13823. Rhyming tone, chord.

韶[5] zau, 746, G.9778. Musical instrument.

韻[10] iuin°, yuin°, 1143, G.13843. Rhyme.

響[13] °hyang, 189, G.4263. Noise, echo, make a noise.

181 頁

頁 yih, 194, G.1529. Head, chief, page.

頃[2] °chung, 422, G.2195. Instant, moment, just now.

頂 °ting, 904, G.11265. The top, most.

頇[3] hen, 162, G.3794. A large face.

項 °‘aung, 191, G.3864. A sort, funds, a deposit.

順 zung°, 784, G. 10143. To follow, obedient, accord with.

須 sui, su, 818, G.4716. To expect, ought, required.

頒 pan, 651, G.8601. To disperse, publish.

頊 hyok, 825, G.4720. Confiding, walk erect.

頌 dzong°, 832, G.10448. Praise.

頓 tung°, 928, G. 12221. To bow the head, tune, time.

頑 wan, 1038, G.12456. Stupid, passive.

預 yui°, 1128, G.13675. Prepared.

領[5] °ling, 545, G.7219. A collar, to lead, guide.

頗 °p'oo, 705, G.9411. Very, rather, to lean, toward.

頦[6] °'e, 160, G.3762. The chin.

頡 yih, 194, G.1472. To fly, soar, to diminish.

頤 yi, 276, G.5421. The chin, jowl, to feed.

頞 oeh, 629, G. 8480. Roots of the nose, a saddle.

顖見囟 sing°, 808, G.4635. The calvaria, sinciput.

頫同俯 °foo, 889, G. 3733. High officers, to have audience.

頚[7] °zung, 21, G.11710. Ugly deformed.

頷 °'en, 164, G.3824. Hold in the mouth, the chops.

頰 kyah, c. kyih, 356, G.1138. The jaws.

頸 °kyung, 406, G.2126. The neck.

頼見賴 le°, c. la°, 500, G.6699. To depend on, lean on.

頻 bing, 697, G.9249. Imminent, continually, urgent.

頭 deu, 876, G.11441. Head, chief.

頹 de, 925, G.12191. The jowl, under the chin.

頴見穎 °iung, 1108, G.13337. An ancient district.

顆[8] °k'oo, 425, G.6096. A kernel, beads, pearls.

顇同瘁 dzoe°, 1018, G.11932. Wearied, sad.

顓[9] tsen, 117, G.2714. Sedate, obscure, dull.

額 nguh, c. ngak, 628, G.3322. Forehead, limited number.

顋 se, 722, G.9549. The jaws.

題 di, 883, G.11009. Theme, subject.

顏 yien, yan, c. ngan, 1083, G.13110. Countenance, color, paints.

顔見顏 yien, yan, c. ngan. Color, countenance, face.

類[10] le°, 512, G.6853. A class.

顙 °saung, 725, G.9571. The front.

顛 tien, 894, G.11193. To upset.

願 nyoen°, 1137, G.13708. A vow, desire, willing.

顕[11]見顯 °hyien, 199, G.4524. To reveal, appear.

顢 men, 575, G.7625. A full face.

顧[12] koo°, 435, G.6254. To care for, to look to.

顦[12] 同憔 dziau, 972, G.1406. Distressed in mind.

顫[13] tsen°, 45, G.288. Trembling, shaking.

顯[14] °hyien, 199, G.4523. Evidence, manifest, display.

顰[15] 見嚬 bing, 697, G.9253. To knit the brows, grin.

顱[16] loo, 556, G.7417. The forehead, the skull.

顴[18] joen, 452, G.3191. Cheek-bones.

182 風

風 fong 155, G.3554. Wind.

颭[5] °tsen, 44, G.273. Moved by the wind.

颯 seh, 722, G.6960. A sudden blast of wind.

颳[6] kwah, 470, G.6296. To sweep(as a whirlwind).

颼 sau, 745, G.9597. A drying wind.

颴 zien, 821, G.4786. A revolving wind.

颶[8] jui°, 440, G.3024. A furious cyclone.

颼[9] 同飀 seu, 755, G.10241. Cold blast.

颺 yang°, 1071, G.12884. To escape.

飀[10] 同颼 seu, 755, G.10235. Cold blast.

颻 yau, 1076, G.12924. A whirling wind.

飄[11] p'iau, 683, G.9133. A spiral gust.

飆[12] piau, 682, G.9101. A strong violent wind.

183 飛

飛 fi, 136, G.3483. To fly.

184 食

食 zuh, 766, G.9971. Food, to eat.

丨 z°. Food, to feed.

飢[2] kyi, 334, G.840. Scanty, dearth, hungry.

飡 見餐 ts'oen, 946, G.11558. To swallow, to eat.

飦[3] 同饘 tsen, 43, G.320. Congee, gruel.

飥 t'auh, 915, G.11369. A bun, a cake.

飭[4] ts'uh, 73, G.1942. To direct.

飯 van°, 127, G.3422. Boiled rice.

丨 °van. To eat.

飪 zung°, 288, G.5614. Fully seasoned and cooked.

飧 sung, 829, G.10437.
An evening meal, supper.

飩 °dung, 929, G.12238.
A meat cake or ball.

飲 °iung, 1102, G.13269.
Drink, to drink.

丨 iung°.
Soup, gravy.

飫 iui°, 1128, G.13690.
To eat much, glutinous.

飴[5] yi, 275, G.5411.
Sweet cakes, delicacies.

飽 °pau, 664, G.8705.
To eat to the full.

飾 suh, c. seh, 767, G.9907.
To adorn, ornaments.

飼 z°, 838, G.10257.
To feed.

餉[6] hyang°, 190, G.4285.
Taxes, rations of troops.

餃 kyau°, 372, G.1314.
A minced pie.

餅見餠 °ping, 699, G.9288.
Cakes, biscuits.

餌 °r, 720, G.3343.
To eat, cakes, dumplings.

丨 nyi°.
To bait, temptation.

餂 °t'ien, 899, G.11219.
To lick, taste.

養 °yang, 1072, G.12856.
Bring forth.

丨 yang°.
To nourish, rear.

餒[7] °neu, 618, G.8179. Hungry, famished, putrid fish.

餓 ngoo°, 627, G.3317.
Hungry, starved.

餙見飾 suh, c. seh, 767, G.9908. To adorn, ornaments.

餐 ts'oen, 946, G.11570. An evening meal, the sacrament.

餘 yui, 1121, G.13615.
Surplus, excess.

餚[8] yau, 192, G.4333.
Meats, food, a feast.

餡 yan°, c. 'an°, 202, G.4529.
The inside of cakes, secret.

餛 wung, 269, G.5241.
Pudding.

館 °kwen, 475, G.6353.
Inn, hotel, hall.

餳 dzing, 809, G.4614.
Sugar cakes, pastry.

餠 °ping, G.9288.
Cakes.

餞 tsien°, 979, G.1588.
A farewell dinner.

餧同喂 'we°, c. iui°, 1054, G.8180. To feed, to give.

餲[9] i°, oeh, 2, G.29.
Cooked rice, soured.

餱 'eu, 174, G.4019.
Dry provisions.

餬 'oo, 222, G.4942. Fill the mouth, porridge, paste.

餪 °noen, 643, G.8401.
A present of food.

餳 daung, 809, G.4615.
Cakes made with sugar.

餮 t'ih, 893, G.11159.
Glutinous.

餼 10 hyi°, 181, G.4152. A banquet, food, provision.

餻 kau, 325, G.5942.
A bait.

⿰飠臭 °hyeu, 418, G.2339.
Spoiled food.

餽 同 饋 gwe°, 488, G.6500.
To offer in sacrifice.

餿 seu, 755, G.10236.
Spoiled(said of rice).

饁 yih, 1081, G.13020. Provisions for field workmen.

⿰飠⿱日羽 t'ah.
Bread, cake.

饉 11 jung°, 400, G.2054.
Dearth.

饅 men, 575, G.7639.
Bread.

饈 sieu, 811, G.4660.
To feed with savory food.

饌 12 °dzan, 118, G.2719.
Food.

饐 i°, 282, G.5350.
Sour spoiled food.

| ih.
To choke.

饒 zau, c. nyau, 292, G.5585.
Plenty to eat, abundant.

饑 同 飢 kyi, 334, G.795.
A famine.

饋 gwe°, 488, G.6514.
Viands.

饍 zen°, 752, G.9717.
Prepared savory food.

⿰飠登 tung°, 864, G.10872. Food offered to gods, to hiccough.

饗 13 °hyang, 189, G.4264.
A banquet.

饕 t'au, 868, G.10837.
Glutinous, covetous.

饔 iong, 1145, G.13476.
First meal, breakfast.

饜 14 ien°, 1089, G.13038. Eaten to repletion, satisfied.

饝 16 moo, 602, G.7975.
Steamed bread.

饟 17 同 餉 hyang°, 190, G.4273. To prepare food and take it to field laborers.

饞 18 dzan, zan, 14, G.334.
Greedy, to love eating.

185 首

首 °seu, 756, G.10014.
The head, chief, first.

馗 2 gwe, c. jui, 488, G.6506.
The cheek bones.

馘 8 kweh, 493, G. 6608. To cut off the heads of enemies as evidence of victory.

186 香

香 hyang，188，G.4256.
Fragrant，incense.

馚[4] 同 馩 vung，fung，130，G.3525. A perfume.

馥[9] fok，151，G.3719.
Fragrance.

馨[11] hyung，206，G.4616.
Sweet smells，fragrant.

馩[12] vung，fung，130，G.3546.
A perfume.

187 馬

馬 °mo，571，G.7576.
A horse.

馮[2] vong，158，G.3586.
A surname.

| bing. To rely on，evidence，to ride，to mount.

馭 同 御 nyui°，1127，G.13686. To curve，drive，oversee.

馳[3] dz，64，G.1985.
To spread，to travel widely.

馴 dzing，813，G.4882.
Mild，docile，tame.

馱 doo，911，G.11338.
To carry on the back.

驴[4] 同 驢 lui，c. li，558，G.7537.
An ass.

駁 同 駮 pok，708，G. 9393. To argue，contradict，to annul.

駄 見 馱 doo，911，G. 11339.
To carry on the back.

駐[5] tsu°，89，G.2540.
To dwell temporarily.

駙 voo°，148，G.3679.
Near，rapid，to approach.

駕 kya°，c. ka°，353，G.1154.
To ride，go in a vessel.

駒 kyui，438，G.2953.
A foal，a colt.

駉 kyong，461，G.6585.
A pack-horse.

駑 noo，641，G.8397.
A broken-down steed.

駛 s°，760，G.9895.
To hasten.

駟 s°，836，G.10293.
A team of four horses.

駘 de，848，G.10591.
A jaded horse.

駝 doo，911，G.11359.
A camel.

駭[6] °hye，c. °hyen，°hyien，187，G.4380. Terrified，startled.

駱 lauh，553，G.7326.
A camel.

駢 見 骿 bien，690，G. 9231.
Come simultaneously.

駮 pok，708，G.9394. To dispute，criticise，splice，continue.

駬 °r，720，G.3344.
A famous steed.

駰 iung, 1099, G.13222. Cream colored horse.

隲[7] 見騭 tsuh, 68, G.1856. To promote, to fix.

騁 °ts'ung, 80, G.781. A horse running.

騂 sing, 809, G.4598. Chestnut color, fat, strong.

駸 ts'ing, 991, G.2086. A fleet horse.

駿 tsing°, 1019, G.3289. Dignified.

騏[8] ji, 343, G.1041. A dappled horse, a chess board.

騎 ji, 345, G.802. To ride horse-back.

| je°. A cavalry horse.

騄 lok, 564, G.7385. A famous steed.

騌 見鬃 tsong, 1022, G.11984. Mane of an animal.

骿 bien. To unite.

騐 見驗 nyien°, nyan°, 1091, G.13134. To verify, fulfill.

颿[9] van, 126, G.3430. Racing swiftly, boat sail.

騙 p'ien°, 691, G.9225. To swindle.

鬉 tsong, 1022, G.12005. Mane of an animal.

騭[10] tsuh, c. tseh, 68, G.1857. To fix, promote.

騫 chien, 389, G.1692. A girth, to fail, disgraced.

騮 lieu, 548, G.7267. A bay horse with black mane and tail.

騷 sau, 726, G.9581. Agitated, annoy, sad.

騸 sen°, 753, G.9675. To geld a horse or ass.

騰 dung, 864, G.10892. To ascend, to mount up.

騶 tseu, 961, G.11812. A groom, a fabulous beast.

驅[11] chui, 443, G.3091. To expel, to urge.

騾 loo, 551, G.7290. A mule.

驀 muh, c. mak, 583, G.7617. To leap on a horse's back, suddenly.

驁 ngau, ngau°, 624, G.99. A vicious horse.

驃 p'iau°, 684, G.9134. A fleet and brave horse.

驂 ts'en, 947, G.11556. A third horse.

驄 ts'ong, 1025, G.12037. A dappled black.

驍[12] kyau, 191, G.4316. Gentle, strong, to pitch, throw.

驊 wo, 240, G.5010. A fine chestnut steed.

驕 kyau, 368, G.1342.
Proud, arrogant.

驚 13 kyung, 403, G.2148.
To alarm, warm, startle.

驘同騾 loo, 551, G.7305.
A mule.

驗 nyien°, nyan°, 1091, G.13133.
To inspect.

驛 yuh, 1094, G.5496.
A post, stage.

驟 14 dzeu°, 962, G.11801.
Rapidly, abruptly.

驢 16 lui, c. li, 558, G.7418.
A donkey.

驥 17 kyi°, 338, G.939.
A perfect noble steed.

驤 siang, 791, G.4274.
A horse, frisky.

驩 18 hwen, 244, G.5055.
A gentle horse.

188 骨

骨 kweh, 454, G.6234.
A bone.

骯 4 °aung, c. °ang, 168, G.81.
Dirty.

骰 deu, 876, G.9658.
A dice.

骱 c. ga°.
A joint.

骷 5 k'oo, 436, G.6260.
A skeleton.

骸 6 ye, 306, G.4381.
The bones of the body.

骻 k'wo°, 468, G.6325.
The pelvis.

骾 7 °kung, c. °kang, 322, G.5999.
Fish-bones, blunt spoken.

骽同腿 °t'e, 926, G.12197.
The thigh, ham.

髁 8 k'oo°, k'oo, 425, G.6098.
The pelvis, a hip bone.

髈 10 °p'aung, 657, G.8667.
The humerus.

髏 11 leu, 513, G.7356.
A skull.

髓 13 °soe, c. °sung, si°, 827, G.10398. Marrow.

體 °t'i, 884, G.11025.
The body.

髑 dok, 922, G.12075.
The skull.

髒 °tsaung, °tsang, 949, G.11581.
Dirty.

髗 16 loo, 556, G.7419.
The skull.

189 高

高 kau, 324, G.5927.
High, elevated.

190 髟

髟 piau, 681, G.9111.
The hair.

髡 3 k'wung, 495, G.6552.
To shave the head.

髣 4 °faung, 135, G.3453.
Similar, seeming.

髲5 c. bi°.
A wig.

髮 fah, 121, G.3375.
The hair.

髴 feh, 154, G.3665. Disheveled hair, nearly, like.

髯 zen, 285, G.5561.
The beard.

髫 diau, 889, G.11092. Tuft of hair on a child's head.

髭 ts, c. tsoo, 1029, G.12336.
The mustache.

髻6 kyi°, kyih, 338, G.917. Tuft of Chinese woman's hair.

髼7 bong, 661, G.8898.
Disheveled hair.

鬂 見 鬢 ping°, 696, G. 9248. Hair on the temples, tresses.

鬈8 joen, 452, G.3169.
Frizzled or curly hair.

鬆 song, 830, G.10454.
Loose, lax, to let go.

鬃 tsong, 1022, G.11985.
A mane.

鬍9 'oo, 223, G.4943.
Beard on the cheeks.

鬐10 ji, 346, G.1100.
Dorsal fins of a fish.

鬚12 sui, c. soo, 818, G.4717. Beard, whiskers of animals, a tassel.

鬟13 gwan, 246, G.5050.
A female slave.

鬢 ping°, 696, G. 9245. To dress the hair on the top of the head.

髩14 見 鬢 ping°, 696, G.9245.
See above.

191 鬥

鬥 teu°, 874, G.11421.
To fight.

鬦4 見 鬬 teu°, 874, G.11433.
To fight.

鬧5 nau°, 617, G.8171.
A noise.

鬨6 hong°, 238, G.5257.
A quarrel, noise.

鬩8 hyih, 203, G.4160.
Domestic quarrel.

鬮10 見 鬮 kyeu, 412, G.2295.
A lot, ticket.

鬪 見 鬬 teu°, 874, G.11420.
To fight.

鬬14 teu°, 874, G.11422.
To fight.

鬮17 kyeu, 412, G.2296.
A lottery.

192 鬯

鬯 ts'ang°, 29, G.463.
Sacrificial spirits.

鬱19 ioeh, 1139, G.13535. Anxious, grieved, despondent.

193 鬲

鬲 lih, 539, G.6062.
A vase, caldron.

丨 kuh.
To sunder, separate.

鬻12 yok, 1140, G.530.
To sell, barter.

194 鬼

鬼 °kwe, c. °kyui, 482, G.6430.
A spirit.

魂4 wung, 269, G.5244.
A soul, spirit, the manes.

魁 k'we, 486, G.6499.
Eminent.

魅5 me°, 586, G.7738.
The demon of the wood.

魃 beh, 647, G.8530.
The drought demon.

魄 p'uh, c. p'ak, 711, G.9420.
Animal spirit, form.

魈7 siau, 794, G. 4307. The thicket or malaria demon.

魎8 °liang, 526, G.7014.
A demon of mountains.

魋 de, 926, G.12187.
A supernatural animal.

魍 °vaung, 1045, G.12518.
A water spirit.

魏 we°, 1055, G.12567.
Elevated.

魑11 t's, 63, G.1974.
A hobgoblin.

魔 moo, 602, G. 7973. The devil, a malignant spirit.

醜14 °ts'eu, 52, G.2496.
To discard, reject.

魘 °ien, 1088, G.12829. Nightmare, horrid, dreams.

195 魚

魚 yui, c. ng, 1119, G.13510.
A fish.

魴4 vaung, 134, G.3454.
A fresh water fish.

魯 °loo, 556, G.7388. Stupid, name of a kingdom.

魨 dung, 929, G.12239.
A scaleless fish.

魷 yeu, 1110, G.13417.
Cuttle fish.

鮒5 voo°, 148, G.3680.
Fish resembling perch.

鮎 'nyien, 634, G.8299.
Mud-fish, bull-head.

鮑 °bau, c. °pau, 665, G.8706.
Dried oysters or fish.

鮀 doo, 912, G.11360.
Snake fish, bull-head.

鮆 °tsi, 967, G.1131.
Thin fish with silvery belly.

鮰6 we, 262, G.5174.
A salmon fish.

鮫 kyau, 368, G.1315.
A large shark.

鮝見鯗 °siang, 792, G.4280.
Dried fish, perch,

herring.

鮮 sien, 800, G.4467.
Fresh, new.

丨 °sien.
Few, scarce.

鮦 dong, 934, G.12286.
A kind of perch.

鯁 7 °kung, c. °kang, 322, G.6000.
Fish bones, blunt spoken.

鯀 °kwung, 494, G.6534. A fish, name of Yu's father.

鯉 °li, 519, G.6883.
The carp.

鯊 so, 730, G.9631.
A shark.

鮹 siau, 794, G.4308.
A pike.

鯨 8 jung, 408, G.1296.
A whale, enormous.

鯗 °siang, 792, G.4281. Dried salt fish, perch or bass.

鯧 ts'ang, 950, G.11602.
The pomfret.

鯔 ts, 1030, G.12377.
A marine fish.

鰕 9 ya, hya, c. hoen, 182, G.4203. Shrimp, lobster.

鰉 同 鱑 waung, 251, G.5123.
Sturgeon.

鯿 pien, 687, G.9184.
A carp.

鰓 se, 722, G.9551.
The gills of a fish.

鯹 sing, 809, G.4610.
Putrid fish, fish smell.

鰈 t'ah, 891, G.11128.
The flounder, or sole.

鰂 同 鱡 zuh, 957, G.11658.
The cuttle-fish.

鯽 tsih, 984, G.883.
Common carp.

鰌 ts'ieu, 1001, G.2343.
Fresh water eel.

鰍 同 鰌 ts'ieu, 1001, G.2308.
See above.

鰥 10 kwan, 473, G.6371.
A huge fish, unmarried.

鰢 °mo, 572, G.7588.
Prawns.

鰣 z, 760, G.9926.
The shad.

鰹 11 kyien, 380, G.1624.
A mullet, fish.

鰱 lien, 533, G.7119.
The bream.

鰻 men, 575, G.7641.
Salt water eel.

鰵 °ming, 598, G.7935.
Fish resembling the perch.

鰲 見 鼇 ngau, 624, G.100.
A perch-like fish.

鰾 p'iau, 684, G.9099.
Fish's bladder.

鰷 diau, 889, G.11098.
Small white fish, dace.

鱅 yong, 1147, G.13467.
A dace.

鰳 luh.
A fish.

鱑[12] waung，251，G.5133.
A sturgeon.

鱖 kwe°，485，G.955.
A striped perch.

鱗 ling，541，G.7185.
The scales of a fish.

鱉同鼈 pih，685，G.9152.
A turtle.

鱔 °zen，753，G.9718.
Small fresh water eel.

鱓 °zen，753，G.9705.
An eel.

鱘 zing，807，G.4889.
The sturgeon.

鱟[13] heu°，176，G.4026.
Horse-shoe，rainbow.

鱡同鰂 zuh，957，G.11673.
The cuttle fish.

鱨[14] dzang，740，G.422.
A large fish.

鱭 °zi，967，G.1080.
The mullet.

鱸[16] loo，555，G.7420.
A perch.

鱷 ngauh，628，G.3328.
A crocodile，alligator.

鱺[19] li，517，G.6920.
Fresh water eel.

196 鳥

鳥 °'nyau，632，G.8246.
A bird.

鳧[2] voo，144，G.3725.
A wild duck.

鳩 kyeu，412，G.2267.
A pigeon，turtle dove.

鳳[3] vong°，159，G.3560.
The phoenix，the bride.

鳴 ming，598，G.7960.
The cry of birds.

鳲 s，758，G.9901.
Turtle dove.

鳶 ioen，1133，G.13710.
The kite，a paper kite.

鴆[4]同酖 dzung°，18，G.632. A falcon，poison，deadly.

鴇 °pau，664，G.8723. A bird allied to the goose，a bustard.

鴉 ia，c. au. 1066，G.12808.
The crow.

鴈同雁 yan°，c. ngan°，1089，G.13139. A wild goose.

鴟[5] t's，63，G.1980.
An owl.

鴞 hyau，192，G.4327.
A white owl.

鴣 koo，432，G.6203.
A partridge.

鴒 ling，545，G.7217.
The wagtail.

鴕 doo，911，G.11361.
The ostrich.

鴨 iah，c. ah，1068，G.12826.
A duck.

鴦 yang, iang, 1070, G.12871.
Mandarin female duck.

鴛 ioen, 1132, G.13719.
Mandarin drake.

鴻6 ‘ong, 236, G.5269.
A wild swan, vast.

鴽 zu, 297, G.5674.
A quail.

鵁 kyau, 367, G.1316.
The egret.

鴿 keh, 428, G.6060.
A dove, pigeon.

鵝7 ngoo, 627, G.3318.
A goose.

鵞 同 **鵝** ngoo.
A goose.

鵠 ngauh, 455, G.4980.
Snow goose.

丨 kauh, kok.
Venerable, a target.

鵑 kyoen, 450, G.3138.
The cuckoo.

鵓 beh, 718, G.9364.
A wood pigeon.

鵜 di, 882, G.10999.
A pelican, pheasant.

鵡 °voo, 1061, G.12747.
A parrot.

鵾8 k‘wung, 494, G.6526.
Heath-cock.

鵪 en, 621, G.52.
The quail.

鵬 bung, c. bang, 661, G.8885.
A large bird.

鶉 dzung, 783, G.2866.
A quail.

鵰 tiau, 885, G.11055.
Sea-eagle, bird of prey.

鶄 tsing, 993, G.2139.
Bird resembling the ibis.

鵲 ts‘iak, 998, G.1388.
The pie, jackdaw, jay.

鶂 nyih, 1092, G.13197.
A heron.

鶘9 ‘oo, 223, G.4944.
A pelican.

鶩 mok, voo°, 607, G.8085.
Wild ducks.

鶚 ngauh, 628, G.3325.
Fish-eagle.

鶴10 ngauh, 219, G.3888. Crane, stork, emblem of longevity.

鶻 kweh, 234, G.4998.
Migratory lark or pigeon.

鷄 同 **雞** kyi, 334, G.810.
A fowl, hen.

鶼 kyien, 382, G.1637. Strange bird resembling a duck.

鴣 koo, 423, G.6048.
A dove, pigeon.

鶺 tsih, 986, G.897.
A wagtail.

鷀 ts, dz, 1033, G.12409.
A cormorant.

鶿 同 **鷀** ts, dz.
Cormorant.

鷂 yau°, 1078, G.12926.
A falcon, a paper kite.

鷃 ien°, 1089, G.13127.
A quail, crow.

鷁 nyuh, 1092, G.5490.
Bird, figure-head on junks.

鶯 iung, 1105, G.13304.
A thrush.

鷓 11 tso°, 39, G.538.
The common partridge.

鷙 ts°, 61, G.1802. Birds of prey, violent, to seize.

鷹 mo, 571, G.7597.
Bird like the wild goose.

鷗 eu, 625, G.8499.
A gull.

鷟 zok, 774, G.11848.
A felicitous bird.

鷯 12 liau, 528, G.7061.
Small bird like the wren.

鷥 s, 835, G.10261.
The water egret.

鷦 tsiau, 970, G.1328.
Grass warbler, wren.

鷲 dzien°, 1000, G.2285.
The condor.

鷸 ioeh, 1140, G.13685.
A water bird.

鸇 13 tsen, 43, G.292.
The sparrow-hawk.

鷺 loo°, 558, G.7370.
The heron.

鷹 iung, 1106, G.13297.
Eagle, hawk.

鸑 14 ngauh, 1118, G.13368.
A felicitous bird.

鸕 16 loo, 555, G.7421.
The fishing cormorant.

鸚 17 iung, c. ang, 1105, G.13327.
Parrot.

鸛 18 kwen°, 476, G.5056.
Herons(all kinds).

鸞 19 loen, 570, G.6746. A fabulous bird, denotes a marriage.

197 鹵

鹵 °loo, 556, G.7423.
Salt.

鹹 9 yan, c. ʻan, 198, G.4504.
Saltish, bitter.

鹻 10 同鹼 °kyan, °kyien, c. °kan, 385, G.1638.
Impure carbonate of soda.

鹾 ts'oo, 1004, G.1935.
Briny, salt.

鹼 13 °kyan, °kyien, c. °kan, 385, G.1663. Impure carbonate of soda.

鹽 yien, 1086, G.13112.
Salt, saltish.

| yien°.
To salt.

198 鹿

鹿 lok, 562, G.7434.
A deer.

麂 2 °kyi, 337, G.971.
A large deer.

麀 ien, 1109, G.13392.
The female of the stag.

麄[4] 見 麤 ts'oo, 1008, G.11865.
Rough, rude, vulgar.

麈[5] °tsu, 88, G.2541.
Large beast like a deer.

麇 chuin, kyuin, 419, G.3296.
Hornless deer, to bind, seize.

麋[6] mi, 590, G. 7826. Large species of deer like the elk.

麒[8] ji, 344, G.1044. The unicorn, a fabulous animal.

麗 li°, 524, G.6911.
Beautiful, elegant.

麓 lok, 563, G.7442. The declivity or bottom of a hill.

麙[9] ngen, 199, G.4505.
An elk.

麛 mi, 590, G.7828. A fawn, new-born quadruped.

麝[10] ze°, c. zo°, 749, G.9794.
Musk.

麞[11] tsang, c. tsaung, 23, G.407.
Animal like a deer.

麟[12] ling, 541, G.7186.
Stag, splendor.

麤[22] 同 粗 ts'oo, 1008, G.11866.
Rough, rude, vulgar.

199 麥

麥 muh, c. mak, 583, G.7602.
Wheat.

麩[4] foo, 142, G.3623.
Bran.

麪 mien°, 595, G.7895.
Flour.

麯[6] chok, 458, G.3066.
Yeast.

麰 men, 587, G.8048.
Barley.

麴[8] chok, 458, G.3110. Leaven, the mother on vinegar.

麵[9] 見 麪 mien°, 595, G.7892.
Flour.

200 麻

麻 mo, 571, G.7591.
Hemp.

麼[3] moo, mo.
Small, interrogation.

麽 見 麼 moo, mo, 602, G.7599.
See above.

麾[4] hwe, 261, G.5161.
To signalize, single.

201 黃

黃 waung, 252, G.5124.
Yellow.

黊[10] waung, 252, G.5135.
The yolk of an egg.

黌[13] wung, 'ong, 236, G.5262.
A college or gymnasium.

202 黍

黍 °su, 776, G.10070.
Millet, pencilled wheat.

黎[3] li, 515, G.6942. Brown, black. The Chinese.

黏[5] nyien, 634, G.8300. Paste, sticky.

黐[11] t's, 63, G.1975. Glutinous, sticky.

203 黑

黑 huh, 218, G.3899. Black, dark.

黔[4] jien, 390, G.1701. Black.

默 muh, 605, G.8021. Dark, secret, silent.

黙見默 muh. See above.

黜[5] ts'eh, 98, G.2622. Degrade, dismiss from office.

黛 de°, 845, G.10553. Painted eye-brows.

點 °tien, 895, G.11170. To punctuate, a dot, spot, to count.

点見點 °tien. See above.

黝 °ieu, 1114, G.13397. A color almost black, ashy.

黠[6] kyah, kyih, 186, G.4225. Deep black, crafty, artful.

黥[8] jung, 408, G.2201. To brand the face.

黧 li, 515, G.6941. Blackish yellow, dun color.

黨 °taung, 858, G.10731. A gang, band, clique.

黯[9] °en, 1087, G.13131. Dark, very black.

黷[15] dok, 922, G.12068. Dirty, moldy, black color.

204 黹

黹 °ts, 58, G.1891. Embroidery.

黻[5] feh, 155, G.3702. Blue and black embroidery.

黼[7] °foo, 146, G.3630. Embroidery.

205 黽

黽 °mung, 598, G.7793. A toad, energy.

丨 °ming. To exert, strive.

黿[4] nyoen, 1135, G.13751. A great sea-turtle.

鼂[5] dzau, 37, G.526. A marine animal.

鼃[6]同蛙 'wo, 1036, G.12427. A green striped frog.

鼇[11] ngau, 624, G.101. A sea monster, turtle.

鼈同鱉 pih, 685, G.9154. A turtle.

鼉[12] doo, 912, G.11397. A water lizard.

206 鼎

鼎 °ting, 904, G.11268. A tripod, emblem of Imperial power.

鼑見鼎 °ting, 904, G.11269. A tripod.

鼐 2 ne°, °ne, 613, G.8117. Censer with three legs.

鼒 3 ts, 1029, G.12355. A round lid or cover of a tripod.

207 鼓

鼓 °koo, 434, G.6241. A drum, to arouse.

鼔 °koo, 434, G.6243. A drum.

鼕 5 dong, tong, 935, G.12208. The rattle of a drum.

鼗 6 dan, c. daung, 870, G.10812. Drum tied with strings.

鼛 8 kau, 325, G.5948. A large drum twelve feet long.

208 鼠

鼠 °su, c. °s, °t's, °ts'u, 776, G.10072. A rat.

鼫 5 zak, 770, G.9968. Grayish yellow long tailed marmot.

鼯 7 ngoo, 1060, G.12712. The flying squirrel.

209 鼻

鼻 bi°, c. bih, 677, G.8919. The nose.

鼽 1 chau°, 375, G.1430. A turned up nose.

鼿 2 chau°. A turned up nose.

鼾 3 'oen°, 162, G.3795. To snore.

齁 5 heu, 174, G.4004. To snore, breathe hard.

鼻夷 7 同涕 t'i°, 884, G.11000. Tears, mucus.

齅 10 hyeu°, c. chong°, 211, G.4686. To smell.

齆 ong°, 1016, G.12679. Stoppage of nose, nasal tone.

齈 16 ti°, c. t'i°, 880, G.10949. Sneeze, running at the nose.

210 齊

齊 dzi, zi, 966, G.236. Even, together.

丨 ts. The vent or slit at the side of a Chinese coat.

齋 3 tse, c. tsa, 10, G.234. To respect, abstain from.

齎 7 tsi, 964, G.835. To offer, supply.

齏 tsi, 964. To compound, blend.

211 齒

齒 °t's, 65, G.1989. Teeth, age.

齕^{3} chih, 'eh, 220, G.3988.
To bite, gnaw.

齗^{4} nyung, 1101, G.13256.
The gums of the teeth.

齙 po, c. bo°.
Projecting teeth.

齣^{5} ts'eh, 459, G.2626.
Act of a play.

齡 ling, 545, G.7218.
Teeth, age.

齠 diau, 889, G.11093.
To shed the teeth, childish.

齟 °tsui, 1010, G.2982.
Irregular, discordant.

齦^{6} k'ung, 318, G.5985.
To gnaw, bite.

齩同咬 °yau, c. °ngau, 1077, G. 12940. To bite, gnaw.

齧 nyih, 1080, G.8295.
To gnaw, crunch.

齪^{7} ts'auh, 85, G.2941. Dirty, to grate the teeth, vile.

齬 °nyui, 1127, G.13627. Row of irregular teeth, discordant.

齶^{9}同腭 ngauh, c. hauh, 628, G.8464. Roof of the mouth.

齷 auh, 1057, G.12693.
Small minded, vile, dirty.

齾^{20} ngak, 1069, G.13002.
A nick, flaw.

212 龍

龍 long, 567, G.7479.
The dragon.

龐^{3} baung, 659, G.8692. Palatial house, filled, crammed.

龕^{6} k'en, 314, G.5866.
A shrine.

龔 kong, c. kyong, 462, G.6579. To give, present, reverential.

213 龜

龜 kwe, c. kyui, 481, G.6421.
The tortoise, terrapin.

龜見龜 kwe, c. kyui.
The tortoise.

龞^{12}同鼈 pih.
The turtle.

214 龠

龠 yak, 1117, G.13358.
A flute.

龡^{4}同吹 ts'oe, c. t's, 101, G. 2826. To blow, puff.

龢^{5}同和 'oo, 254, G. 3773.
Harmony, concord.

[illegible]^{8}同唱 ts'aung°, 28, G.430.
To sing, to call out.

龤^{9}同諧 ye, 187, G.4399. To harmonize, agree.

龥 yui°, yak, 1117, G.13364.
To pray, implore.

图书在版编目(CIP)数据

汉英上海方言字典 / (美) 戴维斯 (Davis D. H), (美) 薛思培 (John Alfred Silsby)著; 钱乃荣编. 上海 : 上海译文出版社, 2025. 3. -- ISBN 978-7-5327-9797-4

Ⅰ. H173-61

中国国家版本馆 CIP 数据核字第 2025863R1P 号

汉英上海方言字典

[美] 戴维斯 [美] 薛思培 著 钱乃荣 编

责任编辑/徐玲 装帧设计/胡枫

上海译文出版社有限公司出版、发行

网址: www.yiwen.com.cn

201101 上海市闵行区号景路 159 弄 B 座

江阴市机关印刷服务有限公司印刷

开本 890×1240 1/32 印张 9 插页 5 字数 244,000

2025 年 3 月第 1 版 2025 年 3 月第 1 次印刷

ISBN 978-7-5327-9797-4

定价: 158.00 元